The Novel and the World's Dilemma

The Novel and the World's Dilemma

EDWIN BERRY BURGUM

NEW YORK: RUSSELL & RUSSELL

1963

REISSUED, 1963, BY RUSSELL & RUSSELL, INC.
BY ARRANGEMENT WITH THE AUTHOR
L. C. CATALOG CARD NO: 63—8358

PRINTED IN THE UNITED STATES OF AMERICA

For Mildred and Naomi

Contents

The Novel and the World's Dilemma

1

Social Forces and the Art of Fiction

THE significance of fiction in the modern world can hardly be overestimated. It is not only the single literary form to compete for popularity with the film and the radio; it is the only one in which, by consensus of critical opinion, a great deal of distinguished work is being produced. The number of good novelists today is certainly larger than that of good dramatists or poets. The publication of a novel by Thomas Mann or John Steinbeck arouses the same sort of response as was awakened at the Restoration by a new comedy of Dryden or Congreve or in the Victorian period by a new volume of Tennyson's poems. It is an important cultural event. Poetry, which had been for over twenty-five centuries the most significant literary form, is of negligible public interest today. The present century may be in error in rejecting so august a tradition, but the facts are clear. Fiction has obviously superseded poetry as the literary form of greatest prestige.

Since the novel seems to be the type of literature which meets the needs of the modern world as conspicuously as poetry does not, the reasons for this break with precedent are worth investigating. Although they are undoubtedly complex, one of them may be found in the relation between basic social change and the difference between poetry and prose fiction as artistic forms.

Romantic criticism, anticipating, in Peacock's notorious essay, the rise of fiction and the decline of poetry, gave a hint of the reason in the writings of Coleridge. The essence of poetry for Coleridge was its blend of the positive and the negative, the pleasant and the unpleasant, the particular and the general. In short, its merit was its capacity to convey more than one meaning at a time. It provided compression of meanings through metaphorical expression. Recent criticism, better than any previous research into the nature of poetry, has clarified this definition. I. A. Richard's *Principles of Literary Criticism,* William Empson's *Seven Types of Ambiguity,* and C. M. Bowra's *The Heritage of Symbolism* are three indispensable works of twentieth-century criticism which explain how poetry, through its use of the metaphor (or what Empson prefers to call the 'ambiguity'), manages to distill into a brief expression a whole range of meanings, appealing to both intellect and emotion. By a reasonable extension of this definition, fiction is a form which does not compress in this way; and therefore either surrenders less of the same sort of meaning or is quantitatively more bulky in achieving a similar end.

But although such critical works as these show *how* poetry attains its aim to say much in little, none of them (with the exception of implications in Bowra) inquire *when,* under what circumstances, such a use of the metaphor is possible. This basic investigation is neglected very largely because of the compartmentalization of research today which leads the specialist to assume rather than to investigate the relationship of his field to others. Criticism, in the best instances, has broken through this unfortunate limitation in exploratory forays into the psychological origins of expression and the psychological conditions of communication, but it has almost wilfully neglected the sociological referents which lie still further away, behind the psychological. If we are to have a useful and valid criticism, it is necessary to get a complete picture of the literary experience. And if one does, it becomes clear that compression of meanings can take place only when certain aspects of them can be taken for granted.

Compression can be achieved only when some elements of the metaphor or 'ambiguity' are assumptions held in common to start with by both the poet and his audience. Otherwise it becomes impossible (unless communication is disregarded by the poet) and must be replaced by explanation, which is a long-winded performance. In the language of Coleridge, synthesis must give way to analysis. Under such circumstances poetry either, striving to retain its own nature, becomes unintelligible or turns into prose in which metaphorical expression is permissible but not essential.

The compression of the metaphor is thus dependent upon a certain compression in the society, the best definition of which so far to appear in print is that of David Daiches in his *Poetry and the Modern World.* In his introduction he makes a brief but suggestive statement that poetry cannot exist without a common basis for it in the prior existence of what he calls 'public truth' in the objective world. His phrase seems to me misleading to the extent to which the word 'truth' implies the conscious verbalization of what are taken for common principles of conduct. What we often declare to be 'public truth,' as Freud and his followers have long since pointed out (and all Proust stands to testify), is a hypocritical rationalization which conceals and contradicts the real springs of our conduct. A man says, for instance, that he is fighting to 'save the world for democracy,' and he would seem to be stating a truth of general acceptance which motivates his activity. But when you analyze his conduct, interpret his words in the light of his deeds, it turns out in our society that his statement has any one of three divergent meanings. It means either that he desires to preserve our 'system of free enterprise,' or that he desires to replace it by a system guaranteeing 'freedom from want' to every citizen. But the third interpretation is the more common one: that he wishes both 'free enterprise' and 'freedom from want,' but is completely at sea about how to bring the two conceptions into a functioning relationship. Or again, a man says that he believes in the home when, judged by his conduct, he is either attempting to impose the Victorian conception of a home upon his wife and children; or is seeking some modification of its structure in the light of modern psychology and the conditions of modern life; or, what again is probably most common, when, owing to conflicting demands and conceptions, he is quite cynical or confused, and is unable to act consistently without anxiety. Clearly the word 'home' today, with our frequent divorces and our conflicting opinions about the relationship of parents and children, about infidelity, about jobs for mothers, is no longer a 'public truth.' Far from being capable of metaphorical use, its use instead can only start a debate. And one would go far today to find any term of emotive content literary to begin with, which illustrates what Empson intends by an 'ambiguity,' that is, a rich suggestive statement capable of a variety of interpretations on a common basis of essential meaning and emotive reaction.

But even when there is a society in possession of 'public truth,' the use of the term remains open to objection. It continues to stress the rational as opposed to the emotive aspects of conduct. And, though there need not be (and ideally should never be) any contradiction between the two, since poetry is fundamentally a structure of human emotions and activities rather than a structure of ideas, any definition of the conditions under which it is possible should stress its fundamental elements. The basis for poetry, therefore, is the existence in the individuals of a society of some common pattern of psychological reaction which has been set up by a certain consistency in the childhood environment. Truisms, abstract principles, slogans, the verbal statement of 'super-ego influences' are at best inadequate descriptions of this pattern. Essential as they are as part of the picture, they are only one element of the style and form of our activity. They become a valid clue to that style and form only when they are no longer mere philosophical statements, but have themselves become metaphorical, enriched by emotive overtones. The term 'public truth' is thus paradoxical, since effective 'public truths' (in the past; for one cannot speak of the future) have seldom been verbalized at all. They are the assumptions we have taken for granted. We have usually become aware of them only when they have been challenged, and they have been most commonly challenged only when they have been in process of decay. But, whatever the degree of conscious or unconscious, of emotive or rational elements, the important thing is that they are habitual and held in common. They are both the springs and the form of our conduct. All our freedom to differ, which looms so large in our daily practice of living, is within the restriction of this common 'not-difference' we so completely accept as part of our established mores that we do not ordinarily feel any restriction upon our freedom at all. All the various 'ambiguities' which lend subtlety to poetic expression, likewise, are dependent upon a similar basis of common stimulus and response the definiteness and consistency of which is not ambiguous. Only in a society which, beneath the eternal disorder of the surface, is dynamically functioning towards goals of accepted value is to be found this basic psychological integration of the personality which is requisite for the flourishing of poetry.

Now, I think it is clear that we are no longer living in a period which can be thus defined. What Arnold said of his age is even more true today. We are caught between two worlds, one dying, the other seeking to be born. In the conflict between the two, the common basis for poetry has disappeared. One passes from one group to another in our society and finds different languages spoken. Meanings that are taken for granted in one circle would be incomprehensible in another (as I have sought to show in my essay on Richard Wright). But most commonly the western man tends to be ambivalent, erratic, swayed by conflicting intentions, incapable of consistency, whether of thought or feeling or action. Faced by alternatives, we find choice impossible; and the Gordian knot is cut either by pressures upon us we cannot resist or by the hysteria of the moment which the next moment reverses. It is not, in the ordinary case, that we have chosen between communism and capitalism, between belief in God and skepticism, confidence in science and fear of the atomic bomb. Every belief we think we hold is riddled by doubt. It is difficult today to find a single area in which the very postulates of human conduct are not infinitely debatable to the accompaniment of the most violent oscillations of mood. Compression of meanings under such circumstances (if one may judge by the nature of the poetry that has been published in the twentieth century) becomes a Herculean task. Poetry, when it is not trifling, becomes almost purely personal statement, as the author of any seriousness seeks vainly to reach through his poetry that basic psychological integration he should have had to aid him to begin with. Sometimes the isolation of the poet is so extreme that his writing becomes autistic, incomprehensible to anyone but himself, as is certainly true of Gertrude Stein's middle period. But the very reasons which make the writing of poetry difficult become an opportunity for the writer of fiction. In prose those clarifications of meaning can take place which are necessary to explain what can no longer be assumed, at the same time that whatever metaphorical expression continues possible can be retained in communicable form.

But it is not merely the loss of common patterns of psychological response with their accompanying community of aims and methods which paves the way for the ascendency of the novel. One aspect of the modern personality (as Peacock and Macaulay were surely correct in pointing out) is not particularly interested in metaphorical expression. The influence of science (which seeks to explain away the metaphor) guaranteed the emergence of fiction, and as long as this influence continues, prose fiction will remain an important literary form. With the development of psychology in particular, we have become so curious about the motivation of our conduct that the intellectual fascination of its exposure provides us with the most agreeable of emotive overtones. Presumably, should our interest turn from the psychology behind the action to the action itself, only another type of detailed presentation in prose would follow. Though the emphasis would have changed to the outer fact, to history, away from the inner facts of the psychology of the individual, the novel would still remain the medium in which the complicated causes of our human activity could best be clarified. Even should we recover basic integration with its accompaniment of 'public truth,' as it is to be hoped we some time shall, novels would continue to flourish side by side with the revival of poetry, as a complementary type of literary expression.

Modern fiction, then, reflects both constructive and disintegrating phases of contemporary society. One of the chief sources of pleasure in reading fiction is its satisfaction of our desire to know more about ourselves as we function together in society. But, at the same time, in the process of surrendering this valid information, the modern novel suffers in its own way from our loss of basic integration. That disintegration of personality which always accompanies social disintegration will be not only registered in the content of novels, but quite as frankly exposed in their form. The same conflict of social forces which makes the composition of poetry virtually impossible will put difficulties in the way of prose constructions also. Such a conclusion is obligated both by the nature of the novels in question and by the definition of art, of which the novel is an instance. Unlike a work of science or philosophy, a work of art is not a structure of ideas determined by some rational method of abstraction from experience. It is rather a reproduction of experience itself, as a pattern of sensory impressions, the meanings of which are not so much stated as inferred. It cannot, like science, isolate aspects of our basic integration. Dependent directly upon that integration, it can only disclose its quality, its presence or its absence, in life itself. Though the novel is closer to non-artistic forms of expression such as philosophy, and uses them more frankly than the other arts, as long as it remains an art at all and does not turn into sociological or psychiatric comment, it must to a certain extent share the embarrassment every art faces in an era of the disappearance of common principles of action.

Form, therefore, in every art, is the adaptation to a particular medium of the 'form' inherent in the social life of man. When a dynamic functioning of some basic integration is lacking in society, the form the artist achieves becomes a *tour de force,* whether it be a poem, an abstract painting, or an introspective novel. It becomes a parody of that flexible, dynamic, comparatively simple form which has been characteristic of the great art of history. Such an art does not face the observer with conundrums, but is some sort of aid to him for the mastery of living. But when the artist is driven (as though in obedience to a law of the creative process) to impose a form upon what he finds formless, the conception of form becomes a paradox. Seeking to contradict in his form the truth he reveals in his content, the artist can attain no more than a caricature of life through ingenious but mechanical arrangement of parts. The writer of fiction who recognizes nothing but decadence in society cannot escape contamination, and its presence will be perceived in his heroic labors of Sisyphus to escape his destiny. There will be plenty of essentially random activity, but no action, that is to say, activity with a direction and a resolution. There will be the structure of a lay-out in advertising but no plot; the veritable bones and muscles of men, but no man. Or, if plot is achieved and men remain lifelike, the novel will show (as in Proust), through some elaborate technique that seems intended as much to delay as to expose the process, the falling into pieces, as though from some insidious fatal disease, of the individual and his society. Or (as in Kafka) it will show him already in pieces, pursuing contradictory goals at the same time, oscillating between aggression and retreat, a mounting tension finally giving away to what is more like exhaustion than even the paltry resolution of despair.

In other words, the only method such novelists can find to aid them in submitting what they find formless into some sort of form is the conscious adoption of a specific philosophy. Often their perception of the disintegration of the objective world leads them to philosophies which accept such a state of affairs as man's inherent destiny. They abolish the paradox of form and reach a sort of consistency by choosing those philosophies which are least systematic. In other words, they are driven to those philosophies which are literary rather than logical in their method, which tend to deliquesce into mysticism or depend upon intuition. Thus Kafka goes to Kierkegaard, whose existentialism is founded on the despondent paradox that the individual is completely isolated in a universe in which he is somehow inextricably involved. And Proust borrows from Bergson his rejection of historical process and the reality of the objective world. But the philosophy of widest acceptance has been the Freudian, which has offered a more definite method in its theory of the stream of consciousness. This theory posits the existence of certain unconscious instinctual drives which ultimately determine conduct. By breaking the tie of the individual to his environment, it appears to free him from dependence upon the external disorder. But unfortunately its recourse to the internal facts only reveals an equivalent disorder there so that it does not promote any easier integration than other methods. This tendency reaches its extreme in *Finnegans Wake,* for which Joyce uses the most mystical of the revisionists of Freud (Jung, whose theory of the race unconscious in the individual permits him to present life as endless, purposeless, repetition under the impetus of completely unconscious stimuli), so that the individual disappears into the race of man and even Kafka can give his characters a greater integration of individual personality.

Only when the philosophy chosen meets two tests does it promote the writing of a novel that is comparatively easy to read, and whose characters act as wholes rather than as bundles of conflicting traits. It must be a philosophy of more or less general acceptance by the public, and it must (as such philosophies generally do) stress the importance of the conduct of the individual in society, whether it is essentially on a materialistic or an 'idealistic' basis. It is no accident, therefore, that Thomas Mann is more intelligible than Joyce. For he uses a philosophy which is in the agreed-upon tradition of western culture and still survives in an afterglow of conviction among us. His acceptance of the cyclic theory of war and peace, representing the alternation of dominance of the good and the evil in society in such a way as not to deprive man of his free will, but to make his functioning in society an empirical test of the validity of his principles: his acceptance of this type of philosophy guarantees to his novels a sort of form that remains intelligible to the reading public. But whether this intelligible philosophy is one still effective in living situations, whether it is really the ideological representation of any psychological integration still in existence, whether it is any longer actually dependent upon the test of practice, may be doubted; since the more frankly and clearly he accepts it, the more indifferent he becomes to the idiosyncrasy of the particular situation in time, the more vague and abstract becomes his characterization, the more repetitious his narrative, and the more pontifical his tone. It seems likely that his philosophy, thus tested, represents a dying 'public truth' that leads to a more and more ineffectual activity but is nevertheless still half-believed: so that its half-belief sets up a contradiction between the conscious side of man and the real disorder in his psychological reactions.

These impositions of philosophy upon fiction in our day, furthermore, though they afford an ideological form, are unable to provide a parallel clarity of characterization. A sort of clarity there is, to be sure, in the personality as well as in the form; but it is, like the form, the deduction from analysis, rather than from contact with whole and functioning personalities. Here doubtless no escape from the thesis of disintegration is possible. But the decadence of personality in real life is not so extreme as in many of these novels, whose methods often rely to such an extent upon the subjective and the unconscious as almost altogether to omit presentation of the immediate surface of experience; which, however inconsistent or unimportant, nevertheless remains part of even the disintegrating personality. The novelists like Joyce and Kafka who fail to take into account these obvious everyday relations of the surface (which are the first manifestations of personality one strikes in actual situations) are themselves pushing the delineation of decadence to an extreme, because of a perverse or melancholy demand to share in it themselves. Proust, despite the immense amount of analysis in his work, escapes this criticism because he accepts the surface as part of the personality.

Novelists who reject the surface make difficult reading because they fail to achieve this dynamic characterization of the whole personality in all its aspects. But although this may be taken as a criticism of their artistry, of their method of presentation, it is not a criticism of the meanings presented. From this point of view they have every right to simplify the picture and stress the essentials. Kafka, and Joyce in *Finnegans Wake,* offer, therefore, because of these very artistic defects, the more impressive picture of the disintegration of personality. They show men and women lacking dynamic form in their daily lives, falling apart, torn perpetually by internal conflicts, unable either to govern themselves or to know themselves or to know and relate to other persons. Will and reason and awareness of what one is doing and its probable consequences within the individual are dependent upon a parallel purposive integration in society. And so these people either, like the characters of Virginia Woolf, grope for friendships they cannot make because their demands for friendship are exorbitant and unrealistic or they are incapable of making any overt demands at all; or, on the contrary, like Mr. Earwicker, they live in perpetual aggressive automatic hostility towards other persons. In every instance the treatment of personality in these novelists betrays the impossibility of normal interpersonal relationships as modern psychiatry would define them.

If I have stressed the philosophy or the striving for social meanings in the contemporary novel, it has been that the evidence of the novels themselves is inescapable. Only the critic who is obsessed by the concept of pure form could ignore the apparent concern of modern fiction with the social background. In more normal times of social integration, it is true, novelists did eschew the conscious aid of philosophy and limit themselves to the direct presentation of human experience. But these are not normal times, and it is only the lesser novelists today who write novels in the old way. Such writers have given up the quest for integration in advance and are content to present the disorder of the surface. They are more readable, their characters appear more lifelike, but these traditional qualities of fiction are attained only by the sacrifice of richness of meaning. A certain amount of the driftwood of thought floats through the pages of such fiction, and may for the discerning reader become their confession of the futility of thinking. Sometimes, as in Saroyan, the melancholy recognition of this futility alternates with an equally futile reach for optimism in some feeble grasp of democratic belief. These records of contemporary life may be clarifications of the contemporary state of affairs, refreshingly easy to read. But they are scarcely capable of encouraging any tendency towards integration in the reader. Their overall picture is too despondent. They palsy thought by the very faintness of their optimism, and encourage us to be reconciled to drifting like the characters at the end of *Antic Hay*.

Only, I think, in a small group of novelists emerging in the 'thirties can one find anything like the achievement of a dynamic comprehensible form in fiction. The rise of fascism and the shock of the economic collapse of the late 'twenties throughout the western world led to a search for a better understanding of democratic principles and a great deal of co-operative activity in their application. A valid base of 'public truth' appeared emergent, bringing with it tendencies towards the psychological integration of the individual, to facilitate the attainment of literary form. But to recognize the presence of fascism in the world was to recognize disintegration also. These new writers do not contradict the observations of the Joyces and the Prousts. They differ from their predecessors in finding decadence only a part of the picture. Accepting Arnold's statement, they sense also the dawning of a new world. Defining democracy with some precision as guaranteeing 'freedom from want' to the masses of mankind, as guaranteeing to each individual the satisfaction of fulfilling his potentialities, their attention as novelists was naturally directed to the common man. And seeing the need greatest there, and there the greatest recognition of the need, the focus of their interest shifted from despair at the muddling of the middle class to hope and trust in the superior sanity and resoluteness of the common man. In the common man they saw the recovery from decadence in the restoration of 'public truth' and psychological integration. Here in life, philosophical and psychological form seemed to be coming closer together, and through their mutual interaction to become more sharply defined, reducing the contradiction between the conscious and the unconscious motives in conduct.

Finding in life the rudiments of a new form, such novelists take it over and clarify it in the structure of their fiction. And through this clarification, presumably they set up a reciprocal reaction in society; so that, if there were enough of them, by making their readers validly aware of their own selves, they would promote the still further integration of personality on the level of living. Through their discovery of an authentic public truth in our day, they are able to restore to the novel in a measure its traditional capacity to communicate a significant content without too great a strain upon the reader's attention. Doubtless in a society in which decadence still predominates, the tendencies of a comparatively small segment cannot dominate the whole. And the novelist whose past training as an artist and whose past experience as a man has taken place in an atmosphere of decadence must retain vestiges of his past. His insight into the new social possibilities is bound to outstrip any corresponding change in his personal integration. Thus André Malraux, who has gone as far as anybody in the new direction, retains traces of decadence in his fascination with the violent act and in his preoccupation with the conception of death. This psychological dichotomy in him between his concern with the philosophy of death and his acceptance of an optimistic sociology is a subjective parallel to the spectacle of conflict between hope and despair, democracy and fascism, proletarian and bourgeois in the objective world. But Americans have not yet caught even as full a view of the new potentialities as Malraux. Only Steinbeck in *The Grapes of Wrath* has afforded it adequate representation, and he only in this single novel. In his other books he reverts to various aspects of the contemporary decadence.

The perception that there are tendencies in society making for a recovery from decadence not only gives readability to the novels which reflect it, but also produces a new type of literary form. To depict within the same novel both decadence and recovery from it is to present an opposition of ideational and psychological attitudes. It is to contrast the despair accompanying disintegration with the hope that revives with the restoration of purpose in living. Under such circumstances events evoke both a short- and a long-distance view. Acts are parts of a process of development in which the new vies with the dying, but in which the dying is often victorious for the time being. Individual situations reach immediate resolutions, but those reached may be of temporary significance. The particular battle is lost, but the war is won. The particular book has an action which must conclude, but life flows on. There are not only the trees but the woods, and there is a relation between the growth or decay of the single trees and the expansion or contraction of the whole forest. Whereas the decadent novel sees only contradictions, the new point of view recognizes that every contradiction contains a relationship. One likes and dislikes one's parents or children, and the likes and dislikes, though constantly shifting, through this very process are found at some time to have taken a direction. Not only are these statements true for the grand plan of the plot of the novel; they are also characteristic of every detail that goes into it; but in any specific instance, they may be more apparent in the details than in the grand plan. In other words, such a view does not reduce life to a stereotype, but it does do away with static conceptions of character and action. The difference between the dynamic and the static conceptions forms the contrast between two novels, fortunately written on the same theme: Malraux's *Man's Hope* and Hemingway's *For Whom the Bell Tolls.* In Hemingway's novel of the war in Spain there tends to be a static contradiction between the inner or spiritual quality of an act and its outer or practical consequences. To sacrifice one's self for a cause in which one believes is a subjective good, whether the act has beneficial consequences or not. But in Malraux's novel, the spiritual and the material are in a dynamic relationship even when they are contradictory, because individuals are no longer thought of as isolated. Their inner integration is dependent upon the nature of external ties. When a character in *Man's Hope* dies, he knows that what he stands for has not also died, because he has experienced its presence in the hearts of his friends (despite their being individually different from himself). He has left behind him, through his dying, a greater determination for victory the next time, whenever that may come.

A valid relatedness between the individual and his group or his country or indeed mankind means that any single resolution of conflict bears within it the promise of a further development. Of everything that is concluded, there remains a part that is not yet concluded, but in process of further change. Such a structure I have elsewhere called the form of 'tragi-comedy.' Life is no longer seen as mere drift of incident, as it used to be in 'comic' writing (the form of which at no time has criticism been successful in defining). Nor is life seen as the complete contradiction of drift in the conception of eternal law which lies behind our ancient conception of tragedy. The tragic conclusion continues to exist; men are indubitably killed, certain principles of conduct determine particular events with an immediate finality. But at the same time, through the death of the individual, other men seem enabled to live the more abundantly in certain instances. And the circumstances which have determined the immediate debacle may themselves give way to others later that produce a victory. Thus a novel written about fascism during the period of its flourishing would validly state its ascendency, but with such conditions and qualifications, such a clarification of the nature of its opponents, that the reader could predict its ultimate defeat. And to suggest such a conclusion would not expose any wishful thinking on the part of the author. It would express the traditional identification of the artist with the best in human aspirations, become somewhat less vague in a period of human history when the causation of social movements is better known. The modern author, writing about Spain, could become aware of those forces in our lives, then existent but not successful, which history has already proved were to be successful in the long run.

Such a conception of literary form is flexible and complicated enough to satisfy those fastidious readers, trained in the fiction of decadence, who are afraid of being bored by too much simplicity. To be clear and readable is to be shallow only when it is an escape from recognition of decadence, when it is itself a form of decadence. But the new form can hardly be said to have yet revealed its potentialities. Its continued use and development will depend upon the nature of social change. In proportion as decadence continues to characterize society, the preponderance of difficult novels with their involved introspective techniques is likely to continue. But as society recovers from decadence, we shall have its record in the development of new forms such as the one I have described, and the restoration to our fiction of men and women made resolute by a plausible trust in their common destiny.

2

Into the Night: Marcel Proust's Account of the Collapse of French Civilization

Proust's theory of the discontinuity of conscious experience has usurped attention in the study of his work. A second and compensatory theory has received little stress beyond the comments of a few critics such as Ramon Fernandez. This is Proust's belief that literary expression remedies the deficiency of ordinary experience by revealing the underlying continuity which otherwise escapes detection. Unfortunately, the only continuity of which Proust became aware was the relentless acceleration of cultural decay in his own era. This plunge into decadence, he felt, was generally unrecognized, remained concealed by a shallow optimistic belief in some sort of progress or by an equally shallow contentment with the immediate pleasure. But his own bitter disillusionment of recognition veiled itself in irony, since he sought to believe that he had escaped contamination by the mere fact of discovering and recording its existence. I shall comment upon the impossibility of such an escape, but I am mainly occupied with Proust's description of decadence as the mortal disease of contemporary society.

Proust is for the most part concerned with exhaustive analysis of specific situations. His method is a far cry from the conscious symbolism of such a writer as Thomas Mann. But what in life seems only a specific act with its own complex causation may in the light of later events be taken as representative of a whole series of similar acts. For the most part, Proust is symbolic only in this fashion. But occasionally, and especially with regard to the major lines of conflict which form the plot of his novel, the representative element of the specific reference becomes conscious and therefore genuinely symbolic. The titles to the separate volumes, like all good titles, are symbolic summaries of their contents. Two of these titles, Proust himself has admitted, establish the major lines of his plot. *Swann's Way* and the *Guermantes' Way* do not merely summarize certain events of childhood recollection. They express also two different but related social attitudes which environment imposed upon the boy and which he sought to utilize later for the guidance of his maturity.

Swann's way, one recalls, was the walk usually chosen. In a climate of frequent showers, it had the advantage of being short and offering the friendly necessary shelter of any number of doorways or church porches. But even in childhood, there was a difference between Proust and the older members of his family. For at one point the walk led past the estate of their wealthy friends, the Swanns. The rest of the family would never take advantage of the chance to saunter through its pleasant shade, because they disapproved of Charles Swann's marriage. But the young Proust took the greater delight in this portion of the walk because he already idolized Charles Swann and his family. If Swann's way was becoming not entirely safe for his conservative relatives, the Guermantes' (or Méséglise) way was generally avoided for somewhat different reasons. Since it was longer and led into the open country, it called for especially fine weather. It afforded no shelter in case of rain. And yet if they would take the chance and walk far enough, it rewarded them with a glimpse of the famous estate, if not of the actual château, of the Guermantes, so remote from their familiar concerns, so aloof from their personal contact, but nevertheless, like the castle in Kafka's novel, indirectly dominant now, as it had been for centuries, over the life and imagination of the town. Swann's way was the possible, the practical; along it one rested within the security of one's class, although the Swann estate itself was beginning to offer embarrassment to the older generation. When the family took the Guermantes' way, however, a passage of imagination was required of all of them, a hazardous venture into the ideal that surely determined the ordinary, but just as surely inhabited an unknown region beyond it, glamorous and unattainable.

For the structure of Proust's novel, these two walks are as important as the incident of the madeleine and tea is for his conception of the structure of the human personality. And in a parallel way, the aspect of discontinuity is present in both. If memory is involuntary and the individual life ordinarily a sequence of separate fragmentary impressions, similarly the classes, the major social groups into which society is divided, are, in Proust's conception, fairly absolute barriers, rarely broken through. One of the many sources of his irony is the fact that the novelist is among those who are able to break through and discover the true situation within. Generally, he says, we erect untrue fantasies about matters beyond the experience of the circles to which we belong, and the nature of our fantasy will be largely determined by the limitations of the group experience. Thus Swann, who knows the facts, is continually amused that the height of his mistress's, Odette's, ambition is to be seen alighting from her own carriage at the opera. She thinks, in bourgeois fashion, that this is *le dernier cri* in aristocratic conduct. But Swann, who has mingled with the old aristocracy, knows how they despise these aspirations of the *nouveaux riches* who are incapable of more snobbish, less exhibitionistic satisfactions. Proust comes to share Swann's superior perspective, since he too has been able to surmount the usual class restrictions. But he is well aware that he once shared them, and the story of his boyhood at Combray is the record of his period of illusion.

It becomes important, therefore, to examine those partly illusory conceptions of society which his Combray relatives took wholly for truths. They are the particular and immediate meanings of the two walks I have described. Put bluntly, they comprise that belief in aristocratic domination subscribed to by the old middle class as it existed generally before the French Revolution, and as it continues to exist even today in the more conservative backwater regions of France: the bourgeoisie of the old provincial town, still unindustrialized, still dominated by some local family of title. Proust's grandmother illustrates the extreme expression of this attitude in the face of democratic and degenerating tendencies within the aristocracy itself. She carries her old bourgeois acceptance of the social hierarchy to such a pitch that when a nobleman who has too lightly carried his trust salutes her graciously on the street, she snubs him so that he will remember in future his superior position in society. The Guermantes' way still represents the proper governing ideal of society which the old middle class deferentially adopted without understanding, save as it had set up, by influence from above, a definite code of middle-class mores. Swann's way, by contrast, as the Prousts take it, is quite frankly and simply this old bourgeois mode of life, thus established in subordination to the aristocracy.

Later, in *The Sweet Cheat Gone,* Proust completes his symbolism by stating that he discovered, after some years of life in Paris, one could reach the objective of the Guermantes' walk via Swann's way, if only one continued long enough and took the right turning. As he escapes provincial limitations, the first lesson the young Proust learns is that this rigid distinction of classes is breaking down. A bourgeois person now, if he has the talent and the income, will take the pleasant walk through the Swann estate and continue, as Charles Swann himself had done, along Swann's way until the château of the Guermantes has been reached. His relatives, lacking the initiative to leave the old confines of their class, had assumed that the Swanns, however rich, were still essentially at one with themselves. How incomprehensible, Proust exclaims, would it have been to grandmother that Charles Swann, in Paris, had been able to rise above the social stratum of his birth and become an intimate of these same Guermantes, so remote in Combray, a member of the Jockey Club (the name or social significance of which they had never even heard), and an authority upon painters they did not know had ever existed. Obviously the older certainties are breaking down. The hierarchy of class distinctions is crumbling. Every theoretical problem the novel raises follows from Proust's discovery that his grandmother's attitudes are out of date. But if Proust became more bitterly cynical, it was that he became less certain they had been wrong.

Experience for Proust only made the paradox the more depressing. It can hardly be described in the familiar terms of personal development from childhood illusions, through the zestful actualities of adolescence, into the worldly acceptances of maturity. It did not provide a passage from the comforts of illusion into the certainties of truth and reality, however apparent the imperfections. For Proust, the illusion retained at least the kernel of the truth. It remained a psychological belief which could not be dissipated despite the fact that he could never either validate or adequately define it. When he had been a boy, the aristocratic ideal had not only been shrouded in the normal inexperience of childhood, but it had suffered the further embarrassment of then existing only through its partial representation in the old bourgeoisie. But when, with maturity, he had enjoyed the privilege of meeting it first hand because of the interest the Guermantes took in him, he discovered that by this time they had lost contact with it themselves. The ideal became an abstraction which Proust, as representative of these new bourgeois aspirations, could not penetrate, because it had become an illusion to those who were supposed to embody it. He had expected to find it substantiated by his mature experience of the world. But the unfolding of the real circumstances of life compelled instead an unbearable increase in morbid pessimism as his recognition grew of the increasing gulf between the actual and the ideal. A man otherwise conditioned might have conceived it possible to look for the embodiment of the ideal elsewhere, in some other section of society. But for Proust it must be an aristocratic ideal or none at all.

When such limitations existed, if life was to continue, some stop had to be put to this accumulating recognition of the nature of actuality. Proust must somehow save both himself and society. After reading Bergson, it became easy for him to save society. Since, for most men, life is a discontinuous succession of immediate impressions, they are not troubled by his problem because they remain unconscious of its existence. As for himself, it turned out, there was both a consolation and an escape. The discrepancy between the ideal and the actual, he concluded, had always existed. From his reading of Saint-Simon, from his comparison of the letters of Mme de Sévigné and the diaries of the brothers Goncourt, it seemed plausible that the aristocratic ideal had been just as illusory at the time when history assumed it to have been at the peak of its embodiment as he now saw so clearly it was in his own period. Fortunately a satisfactory means of bringing the ideal and the actual together had always existed too. In the cause of his difficulty itself lay the cure. For if his novelist's insight had forced upon him a disillusionment from which most men are free, it had also afforded him a superior form of freedom. To translate life into literature, he now believed, was to use the one method by which the ideal might be brought into a valid relation with the actual. In the world of fiction, which alone was 'real,' the ideal ceased to be illusory and the actual could be taken as such; even though the bringing of them together meant the revelation that there is a pattern to life which grotesquely contradicts the ideal. Proust adopted a particular variation of the esthetic of art for art's sake which was dominant at the time, and which is best known to English readers through Somerset Maugham's *Of Human Bondage.*

I have been content to present in this brief way Proust's theory of fiction because it seems to me that, although dictated by his personal needs, it is not essential to an interpretation of the action of his novel. His action is still grounded in the objective facts. Few of the great decadents of modern fiction, Gide and Thomas Mann no more than Proust, have been able to shake off the influence of the naturalistic tradition. From Flaubert to the present day, our better novelists have been in general agreement in regard to the facts; they have found them very depressing; they have often found them too depressing to be endured. They have sought to escape despair, not by denying the validity of the evidence, after the fashion of second-rate authors, but by rationalizing away its significance. Their individuality is to be found in the sort of rationalization differences in temperament have dictated. Proust's theorizing was especially involved because the range and quantity of material turned up by his experience left him in an extremity of pessimism. His factual discoveries were so contradictory to his aristocratic prejudices that, since he could not recognize the limitations of his point of view, he was forced to deny any real relation between the actual and the ideal on the level of life itself. He had no alternative except to translate the possibility of coherent relationship onto the level of fiction, or commit suicide. But those who have not been conditioned by Combray need not face the same ugly dilemma. They will be able to restore Proust's remarkably coherent dialectic picture of the decay of the French upper classes to the objective world, where the very fineness of its circumstantial evidence will convince them it really belongs.

I wish to deal, then, only with those aspects of the novel which are symbolized in the two different conflicting ways of life we have already described. But to a simple account of the action, it is desirable to add some consideration of Proust's changing emotional reactions to the progress of his plot. These changes, I believe, are more important than his elaborate philosophical statements to explain the real changes in his attitude towards the objective world. The argument from style is often more convincing than an author's rationalization of his intention. As far as Combray is concerned, I have already given it. The elegiac tone of Proust's childhood recollections registers his regret at outgrowing a period when, however illusory his perception of the aristocratic ideal, it was still a psychological belief of his inexperience. With adolescence the style ceases to be elegiac and becomes almost hopeful, with spontaneous acceptance of experience as keen, direct, exploratory sensation, not inconsistent with the aristocratic ideal and possibly in due time substantiating it. Fundamentally, I will grant, the change in style is only a response to the nature of adolescence itself. One thinks of early adventures at Balbec, of all that is implied of alert and charming sensitivity in the phrase, 'A l'ombre des jeunes filles en fleur.' Surely the elegiac has now faded and no more than a hint of the cynicism to come hesitates in the background. A similar style, with only a slightly greater infusion of the cynical, I find in the story of Swann in love. Doubtless it is for biographical reasons that Proust identifies himself more closely with Swann than with any other character in the novel, sympathizes with him, indeed, as a young man may with some older man he admires and would imitate. Probably this is the correct causation. But I am rather concerned with what may well have been for Proust himself a largely accidental association, but which retains its validity notwithstanding. It is the fact that to sympathize with Swann is, in sociological terms, to take hopefully the possibility that the haute-bourgeoisie may achieve the aristocratic ideal.

Swann typifies that stage in social history when the middle class, no longer 'knowing its place' in eighteenth-century terms, was seeking to take over the aristocratic tradition, just as it had bought and restored the physical property of the château. It expected to revitalize the old ideal through its adequate wealth, its splendid vigor, its alert intelligence, its demand to add to the more vulgar bourgeois accomplishments the fulfilment of the age-old precept concerning the well-rounded, the cultivated man. As we know, the attempt was a failure. Swann frittered away his magnificent possibilities. It must be said that the aristocracy corrupted him, rather than that he, Swann, gave new life to its traditional values. He did nothing with his scholarly knowledge and good taste in painting, not even finishing his one brochure. He did nothing with his superb wit beyond using it to gain entry into the Guermantes' circle; nothing with his extraordinary charm but dissipate it in countless affairs with all sorts of women; nothing with his acceptance by the most aristocratic circles in France but throw it away by marrying a courtesan 'who was not his style.' And yet the demoralizing irony with which Proust would have dissected every petty instance of this failure, if he had been anyone else but Swann, is quite lacking. Proust prefers to emphasize what was vital, wholesome, promising. His criticism of Swann is like Swann's criticism of himself; it has the melancholy of an after-thought, of a might-have-been. The symbolic significance of Swann is without question the fortuitous accompaniment to other interests Proust has in him, as a Jew, as a man who is not to any degree homosexual. But his social signification all the same is there, to represent the failure of what at one time seemed possible, of what once Henry James had expected, the achievement of a bourgeois leisure class that should bring once more together the wealth and the title, the new vigor and the old culture. In Swann, Proust is, so to speak, playing fair with the haute-bourgeoisie, giving them their chance to show their mettle and to carry out the expectation they held at one period of their development, to extend their control over the material world to include the spiritual world as well.

But if Swann achieves success, though in a charming, superficial way, only to toss it aside through internal weakness, the success that the Verdurins do not throw away at a later stage in the social degeneration has become, to Proust's mind, an altogether empty mockery. During the greater part of the novel, Proust contrasts the salon of Mme Verdurin with that of the

Guermantes, in order to differentiate the conceptions of culture within the aristocracy and the haute-bourgeoisie. The Guermantes' salon gains its distinction solely through legend promoted by its inaccessibility. Almost everyone who is not a close relative of the thinnest blood is excluded. And so it goes unrecognized that the Duc is an ignoramus; and the brutal snobbism of the Duchesse, by the time it reaches lower quarters, has been distorted into wit. The Verdurin salon, by contrast, attracts some of the most notable men in France, scientists, painters, novelists, musicians; only, to qualify the comprehensiveness of the symbolism somewhat, no men of practical affairs, politicians or financiers. M. Verdurin, it must be admitted, is an extreme example of the detachment from its material base of finance capitalism. Any vulgar attention his affairs may demand is kept out of the consciousness of his higher interests as represented by his wife's salon. But of these more sublime concerns the salon is a cross-section of the best in almost every important cultural field. Yet these great men, as Proust views them, are as dull and empty as their hosts, once they have left their special fields for the unfamiliar realm of social intercourse. They haunt the Verdurin's famous Thursdays because they like good food, because they have their own lower-middle-class pretensions to aristocracy, and because their hostess insists upon their duty to the 'little clan.' This relation of host to guest is a parody of that between the central administrative aspect of business and the incommunicability of specialization. The social ideal of a culture shared and understood in common has been supplanted by the mere physical juxtaposition of specialists whose common ground is not on the side of their values but, in so far as it exists at all, is on the side of their weaknesses and undeveloped possibilities. Mme Verdurin's esthetic aspirations grotesquely personify the pretense of those who seek to acquire culture as they would a share of stock, and care no more about the real cultural values represented than the real human values that have produced the stock so long as they can enjoy the fact of domination. Unable to penetrate the aristocracy which still commands a higher price, Mme Verdurin has been forced to fall back on the lower commercial cost of science and fine art, and make the best of what to her is a bad bargain. But after the World War has immensely increased her wealth, and after the fortunate death of her husband, she finds the price of aristocracy lowered in the new social confusion, and she is able to marry into the heart of the Guermantes family. When a success that has long been culturally meaningless is by way of becoming meaningless on the shallow terms of mere exclusiveness, Mme Verdurin achieves the summit. The social and financial disaster of the war has crumbled those distinctions which, even though fictitious, had kept some sort of hierarchical order in society. Now everybody, so to speak, is marrying into the aristocracy, advancing himself, so that even the final shell of meaning has vanished from the word. Odette, the one-time prostitute, after Swann's death has captured a nobleman, although he is of minor dimensions. Her daughter Gilberte does better by marrying Saint-Loup, who by this period has become homosexual. What the bourgeoisie has now grasped in its upward progress is the final descent and decomposition of the aristocracy in both body and soul.

But to the novelist, the seeds of decay had long since been recognizable, and had furnished him the sardonic irony of contrast between two related orders of illusion and actuality. The illusion of the aristocracy has been that it continues to occupy the dominant social position; that to rule a salon is more important than ruling a nation. The illusion of the haute-bourgeoisie has been the folly of believing that aristocracy exists. The main source of humor in the long series of novels comes from the bewildering rush of evidence that neither of these opinions is sound. Perhaps the most intriguing testimony is the existence, side by side, of two aristocracies, that created by Napoleon and the more ancient, each insisting upon its prerogatives, neither of which is recognized by the law of the Third Republic nor by the practical machinery of French politics and business.

Of all that relates to aristocratic pretension, the best and the worst, the Baron de Charlus becomes the representative. He would have his social position so taken for granted that he has chosen to use one of the humblest of his many Guermantes titles. But he is the one aristocrat presented by Proust who might vie with Swann in capabilities. He has attended lectures at the Sorbonne and been able to follow their drift. He is of course a connoisseur of fine art; and he is as well informed in politics and international affairs as his violent prejudices will permit. But he makes even less use of his capacities than Swann. (Indeed, his importance for my purpose is partly the extent to which his aristocratic birth limits certain fundamental parallels with the bourgeois Swann.) He is so remote from reality that he insists on declaring the ruling family of Belgium impostors, since the title, Duc de Brabant, properly belongs in the Guermantes family; and fancies he is of some practical importance because a remote cousin has not yet tottered from the Austrian throne. To do him justice, he has had no time to develop his real talents, because his entire effort is required to hold together the meaningless fabrics of his many titles. But as snobbism inevitably becomes the public necessity of a superfluous nobility, a contradiction develops in the private life. Homosexuality, like a disease, seizes snobbism insidiously at its tenderest point, and spreads to cripple and devour it. Proust's attitude towards homosexuality is conflicting only because he too, as one adopted into the aristocracy, feels a secret attraction for what his reason tells him tends to become a loss of all value in personal relationships in our time and especially of the pretension of aristocratic superiority. And so the Baron de Charlus, who has for years compelled obeisance to the spirit of snobbism, conceiving of himself both as the personification of heraldry and the college of heralds together, is more and more insidiously assailed by the most vulgar and perverse desires. For a time it was easy to lead the double life: to retire from the public snubbing of a duchess of Napoleonic extraction and surrender clandestinely to the assault of some tailor or uncouth musician or unknown workman from the streets. Finally his need to be brutally overpowered, to have his snobbism demolished in the most humiliating fashion, so gets the better of him that he can no longer maintain his authority as arbiter of distinctions of noble rank. He has been seen too often on the streets in the company of men who clearly are of more cloudy pedigree than a Napoleonic duchess. As though to drive home the importance of this particular symbolic meaning, Proust's book turns up homosexuality almost everywhere, in most appalling and unexpected places in women as well as men, the old and the young, the middle class by contagion, and the proletariat, good-naturedly, for an income. The more we penetrate the hypocrisy of appearances, the fewer normal relations survive. Homosexuality symbolizes the negation of value in the return to social chaos.

Such, then, defined in terms of the Baron de Charlus, is the height of distinction to which Mme Verdurin has climbed when she marries the Prince de Guermantes after the First World War. It is the Verdurins and not the Swanns who represent the final triumph of the moneyed class in France. The novel for our purposes comes to an end, and as Proust certainly thought, French civilization mirrors its own extinction, in that last reception given by a Guermantes. Proust scarcely emphasizes now that it is the former Mme Verdurin who presides. Returning to society after many years of absence, with old memories strong upon him, he thinks at first that everyone is wearing masks at a ball. But it proves to be a more ghastly one than Poe had earlier described. Here it is no plague, no infection assailing them from without, that has caught at the vitals of the well-dressed men and women whom he cannot seem to recognize. The representations of senility and death, which Proust took for masks recklessly advertising what their wearers do not recognize to be their true psychological state, he soon discovers to be physically valid.

The twisted muscles which are reducing to burlesque a face he once knew to be beautiful are not fastened onto a cardboard surface, but on second examination can be seen in a movement no less real for being involuntary. In other instances, the mask of cosmetics that had formerly established a duplicity has now been discarded as no longer effectual. 'The disappearance of the pink in his lips and cheeks,' says Proust of Legrandin, 'which I had never suspected to be an artifice, gave his skin a grey hue and his long-drawn and mournful features the sculptured and lapidary precision of an Egyptian God. A God! More like one who had come back from the dead.' In this single sentence, Proust has compressed the entire history of his aristocratic idealism—at first impression, in youth, a divine illusion, but now, with the passage of time and the acquirement of experience, he sees with a shock, 'a pale and tenuous phantom' of reality. Whether this reality ever existed is beside the point. It does not exist now. Death wins the final battle. But it is more than the inevitable death of those who grow old. When the entire room is thus populated, it has become the death of a class. And when one has been told that these people are a heterogeneous mixture of bourgeoisie and aristocracy, it has become, to Proust's imagination, the death of a culture.

As usual, the Baron de Charlus is the extreme symbol. In him the mind has decayed even more than the body, until he resembles an actor in the part of Lear. Proust describes him also as he saw him on the street during his decline: his hair now white against the rosy complexion of a healthy baby; his body responding without the power of resistance to the jolts of his carriage; the vacant eyes and the palsied head of this once choleric snob now turning aimlessly and bowing in a parody of exaggerated and democratic courtesy to whoever might be passing by. The passage of class distinctions that once had seemed to promise an education towards the truth is now observed to mean the dissolution of all distinctions, the loss of all values, in a chaos of democracy, personified by Charlus' now universal but completely meaningless benevolence. Proust had never sensed the possibility of any other choice than between Swann's or the Guermantes' way. And now both these have met in the embrace of a common degeneration.

For a novelist of his sensitivity, he was astonishingly untouched by the accelerating upsurge of popular democracy in France during the twentieth century, with its tremendous self-confident authority and its new philosophy of popular welfare. His life ironically illustrates his own precept of class limitations, since any sympathy with the ideals of popular government and the use of science to the common good was entirely beyond his comprehension. He associates democracy, rather, with the senile loss of values. If he had taken it seriously, he would have feared it. To one of a more generous perspective, everything Proust discusses so seriously beneath his gay humor is valid, but does not comprise either the whole or the essential story. Unfortunately for his personal happiness, Proust could see only the distressing half of the picture; since his ideals had proved illusory, every ideal must be illusory save that of writing novels.

I doubt, however, that the writing of his novel was as satisfactory an escape as his theory stated. For the time being and especially for the distant years, the exposure of the universal hypocrisy and decay he had discovered, and the gradual process, indeed, of his discovering it, may have been positively amusing. And it must have been perennially a distraction from the ugliness of the facts to run down their remotest, most ingenious motivation. But if his novel was a substitute for living, to end it was to sentence oneself to death. The repetitions, the hesitations, the sheer inability to clarify or even to complete the words of sentences as he approached 'the present' of those final pages, are not so much evidence of the progress of physical disease in him as of his fear to reach a conclusion that would leave life without further meaning. His disease, rather, was a safeguard against such a calamity. I think we have a right to say that he feared, as a man, the emptiness of life once his novel had been finished, more than, as an esthete, he disliked the imperfections of form a premature death would leave uncorrected. Whatever the edicts of his philosophy concerning the nature of reality, his conception of fiction was so closely bound to the actual circumstances of life, arranged into a coherent comprehensive pattern, as to leave no possibility of a second novel. The flaw in his theory of escapism is that it permits only one pattern to evolve, only one novel to be written, the one that he finds to be faithful to the facts. Otherwise, as Maugham has suggested, he might have arranged the facts in any number of amusing designs. But we may profit by his limitation. For it permits us to accept *Remembrance of Things Past* as a convincing objective history of the degeneration of the aristocratic ideal in France before the rise of fascism and the Second World War.

3

Compensations to Despair in the *Remembrance of Things Past*

TIME REGAINED, after Proust's long remembrance of things past, that consummation of a lifetime of incessant observation, with its picture of palsied old men and women mocking the gestures of their prime, induces a depression of the greatest intensity. Nor is it lessened by the evidence in the hiatuses of his narrative of Proust's own dying, those passages, fragmentary and incoherent because he had not regained the time to revise them. The sympathetic reader sees his own depression also darkened by another factor. Having noted the tendency to repeat earlier generalizations with a surplus of familiar illustrations from *The Captive* on, and aware that these form no fugal motif in his design but merely betray his overzealousness and lack of time to revise, one reaches the hiatuses as the climax, not of the plot, but of this personal breakdown that had long been preparing. And he knows how Proust would have been disturbed, had he lived, with his belief that only art is real, by these evident flaws in his artistic structure. It would have been the last irony possible to his observation, this ultimate victory of the actual over the creative talent, the dissipating of the last illusion, that concerning the nature of art itself.

Yet, when at some remove from the finish of the great work, one recalls Proust by an act of involuntary memory, such as he trusted without reserve, it is never in a mood of gloom. One remembers Proust always with a kind of gaiety. The reasons for this paradox are not obscure. The philosophy is forgotten in the pleasure of its proof. To Proust himself, piling up the evidence for so morbid a conclusion was postponing the necessity of facing it as proved. The dissection of each inconsistency or self-deception or pretense, as it presented itself was, from the perspective of the philosophical system, to live, as it were, on a surface of one's own in the very act of exposing the surfaces of others. For there was no reason why Proust should have been so vastly amused by these minutiae of human conduct except for the nature of his own temperament. Another writer, a Swift or a Huxley, would have performed the act of analysis to the accompaniment of a dirge instead of a rondo. But Proust's interest was as much in the fiction of the surface as in the truth below, and balancing the one against the other, being neither victimized by the surface nor disgusted by its falsehood, he enjoyed, for its own sake, as he wrote, the exposure of the discrepancy between the two. Indeed that part of his philosophy which dealt with theory of art, as distinct from the theory of living, supported this inclination of his temperament. If men live in illusion, which experience gradually dispels when it is broad and rich, but which it is the particular function of the creative artist to fully understand, the artist and the reader who follows him can hardly find in the superiority of their perceptions a cause for sadness. They are special people, capable of penetrating the delusions which hold their fellow mortals in spell. And so Proust's apparently unending analysis of these delusions maintains reader and author alike in a continual euphoria: their minds exhilarated by the belief that they have made contact with the truth, while their egos take pride in the impression of mastery this rare acumen affords. Doubtless this same reader (as Proust would have pointed out if he had got him into his work) is under the spell of his own set of illusions from his particular world of experience; just as I have had the temerity to suggest that Proust's basic philosophy is an illusion of his own limited experience.

Meanwhile we are in Proust's hands; and there are few authors who accept their readers more open-heartedly as their confidants than Proust. Shy in his actual relationships, Proust is most frankly himself, without reserve or caution, when he has merely the anonymity of an absent reader to face. His absorption in his work and his confidence in his own power to perform it dispel his fears of a hostile reception, and those fears are few since he has arranged his dying so that he is, for the most part, speaking to the greater tolerance of posterity. Brilliant in his daily contacts, but too often curbed by the need for discretion, not needing to fear so much the retaliation of posterity, he can be brilliant without reserve and assume his reader to be his ideal friend. So he talks to us as intimately as he would to Saint-Loup, only more frankly. In fact the only limit he sets to frankness is the concealment of his own indulgence in homosexuality. To have been frank here would have introduced an inconsistency into his philosophy as well as offended the dominant mores of the French, which, in this respect, he theoretically accepted. By making himself a part of the decadence he criticized, it would have deprived him of the optimism of the surface (just as doubtless the gloom of his conclusion reflected this darker deeper side of his own personality). Otherwise he is without discretion in his revelations to us. Rarely has there been in literature a more complete democracy between reader and author, a more generous assumption of equality of understanding in the reader on an author's part. His piling up of detail and illustration is, in fact, to a certain extent, his tact in translating an assumption of equality into a context that facilitates its becoming real. In those days of grudging admission of the reader's existence on the part of so many authors, Proust offered, with his characteristic generosity, every subtlety of interpretation he had himself enjoyed, confident that it would be equally understood and appreciated.

Even Proust's method is evidence of this confidence in his reader, this decision to trust, this spontaneous desire to share. But his attitude was not merely a personal one. He was conscious of the social tradition of French letters. He felt himself, as his pages surely show, to be part of a culture where literature is a topic of general conversation, however badly handled. And if he is aware of this aristocratic inheritance from the old neo-classical tradition of his grandmother, Proust, unlike the aristocrats in literature of his own period, did not withhold from sharing because the age had become democratic.

So, once within the circle of his readers, which is anyone who cares to read him, one faces none of the snobbery or detachment to be detected in those literary methods so difficult that only a highly selected audience may be conceived to survive the ordeal. There is none of the laborious pretense of informality and objectivity, to conceal the author's pulling the strings of the action behind the curtain, as is found in the stream-of-consciousness method. And none, certainly, of the more disagreeable pretentiousness of Henry James, whose characters seem wilfully to withhold information, both out of a supercilious sense of propriety, of its being nobody else's business to know what they really mean and feel, but also, alas, out of a conspiracy with the author to put difficulties in the way of surrendering meanings that turn out hardly worth the suspense into which we have been so firmly thrust. When Proust is hard to understand, most of the time we can only blame ourselves. He has been doing his best, and, save in those rare instances where he has been over-clever, if we do not understand, it is because the subject is beyond our experience.

For Proust's method requires no key from some special body of knowledge to unlock it. We do not need to know Bergson, though he was the philosopher most influential upon Proust's thinking. Nor do we need to know Freud; for Proust's method was more flexible. Indirect influences from many theories prevalent in his day are there, and doubtless account for the differences between him and the Goncourts and those still less systematic diarists, the Mme de Sévignés, the coiners of aphorisms of the eighteenth century. But here is the tradition that gave Proust his method. It is no more than the observations of a man of breeding upon the life he has experienced, only become more intricate and systematic because a man of breeding now lives in a more complex world, both intellectually and emotionally. He has a wider range of knowledge and more acute sensory perceptions. But the method itself is simple and ancient. Having observed a person for many years in many contexts and acquired a great amount of detailed information about him, Proust becomes aware of the inconsistencies of the surface and the pattern of personality behind them. He is thus able as an amateur of psychology and philosophy to isolate the vital motives from those other manifestations which are either the tools of these motives or some form of protection of them. But this is basically no more than the application of common sense, and it is to the common sense of the reader that Proust appeals. We forget that Freud, in certain basic parts of his theory, only rediscovered the commonplaces, which had been the common property of sophisticated persons from remote antiquity and had only been lost sight of as a result of the stunting of experience under Puritanism and bourgeois provincialism, and of that more extensive stunting of man's awareness of himself which followed. What chiefly marks Proust as a modern, and distinguishes him from his confreres of the previous century, is his greater interest in what lies under the surface. They could more safely than any modern fix their attention upon the surface, as their social codes of conformity bade them do; they could take the underground more or less for granted, because they indulged it as a matter of course in their lives, because their very codes assumed their own discreet violation. But that strange loss of knowledge in the area where it most directly counted for human happiness, in the area of personal relationships, at the very time when other types of knowledge were expanding as never before, is the stigma of the bourgeois period. By a natural recoil, this loss of knowledge provided that even the partial recovery of its breadth should not only become the 'science' of Freud (itself half the error of the man of limited experience), but should stress above all the unconscious motives of human conduct. Proust, as a man of his own period, like every other modern novelist, therefore, took a greater interest in the hidden world beneath than did the literary tradition which also influenced him. It became his hunting ground for the absurdities of human behavior.

If one takes a simple example of his method, it seems to have no originality at all, it is so close to the common sense of our era. For instance, Proust observes Mme Verdurin at one of her musicales holding her head back with her eyes closed as though in a state of ecstasy over the music. He immediately proceeds with what look like *obiter dicta* instead of analysis. She actually finds listening to music an effort, he says, because she has no real interest in it, so that this gesture serves a double purpose: at the same time that it appears the utmost reach of exalted sensibility, it is actually a long practised means of getting relaxation from the strain of attention. In a later volume, when Mme Verdurin is much older, there is a similar observation:

Under the influence of the countless neuralgias which the music of Bach, Wagner, Vinteuil, Debussy had given her, Mme Verdurin's brow had assumed enormous proportions, like limbs that are finally crippled by rheumatism. Her temples, suggestive of a pair of beautiful, pain-stricken, milk-white spheres, in which harmony rolled endlessly, flung back upon either side her silvered tresses, and proclaimed, on the Mistress's behalf, without any need for her to say a word; 'I know what is in store for me tonight'; her features no longer took the trouble to formulate successively aesthetic impressions of undue violence, for they had themselves become their permanent expression on a countenance ravaged and superb. This attitude of resignation to the ever impending sufferings inflicted by Beauty, and of the courage that was required to make her dress for dinner when she had barely recovered from the effects of the last sonata, had the result that Mme. Verdurin, even when listening to the most heartrending music, preserved a disdainfully impassive countenance, and actually withdrew into retirement to swallow her two spoonfuls of aspirin.*

Now it will be noted that the proof of Proust's assertion here lies not in either description of Mme Verdurin's external appearance, but in the relation between the two. The latter statement depends upon the former; and its proof is only its consonance with the accumulation of detail that has been gathering from many scattered references, of which I have isolated only two. The theory behind his method he defines obliquely in personal terms in *The Sweet Cheat Gone* (p. 126): '. . . the truth of our sentiments, the truth of our destiny, how often without knowing it, without meaning it, we have expressed them in words in which we ourselves doubtless thought that we were lying, but the prophetic value of which has been established by subsequent events.' And a little later he refers to '. . . the truth of our natures, the essential laws of which escape us and require time before they reveal themselves. . .' Thus, generally in Proust's work, it is having come to know so much about a person that lends plausibility to any single reflection upon his nature, and not the application of some scientific or pseudo-scientific theory of human behavior.

Under the bidding of his very delight in the complexity of the personality, Proust shies away from any rigid interpretation of it. He enjoys pointing out the manifold explanations possible for any single act, never forgetting that the choice of the right one for the particular situation must depend upon the knowledge of many particular factors, and that all these instances are going to appear somewhere in his work. But he does not freeze his method into pedantry. He feels free to put forth generalizations and interpretations quite on his own authority in his early volumes, when, according to his theory, their proof must await our further acquaintance with the persons concerned later on.

* Proust, Marcel, *Cities of the Plain*, New York, 1934, vol. III, pt. 1, p. 72. By permission of Random House, Inc.

He passes freely from generalization to analysis of the specific, trusting to this eventual accumulation of relationships, and his confidence in his own acumen. What he likes best, perhaps, is the making of nice discriminations, of which a typical example is his account of the meaning of the variations in shaking hands among the Guermantes and their more conventional cousins, the Courvoisiers, which stretches over some fifteen hundred words of *The Guermantes Way* (II: 187-91).

But this description is not merely an accurate distinction of idiosyncrasies; it is a devastating exposure of individual weakness or pretension, a new order of the comic spirit. Its method is to choose a descriptive image of great delicacy, which is emphasized by the distortion of magnification. As though one had put a drop under the microscope and then suddenly brought it into focus, the act of discrimination carries an emotional shock which would be violent if the object were of more formidable proportions in the first place. Even when the comparison itself is commonplace, the surprise immediately follows of Proust's not having used it in a commonplace way. The commonplace turns out to be not in him, but in the one he is describing when he says that certain of the Guermantes accompany their greeting with a 'gaze, generally blue, always of the coldness of a steel blade which he seemed ready to plunge into the deepest recesses of your heart.' But this trite simile is at once followed by the justification: 'Which was as a matter of fact what the Guermantes imagined themselves to be doing, each of them regarding himself as a psychologist of the highest order.'

The subject here justified a simple, direct explanation. But generally, in Proust (as in the description of Mme Verdurin I quoted), any single situation turns out to be tremendously complex; and he reproduces the feeling of its complexity by using a whole stream of distorted images, so that the effect is subtle as well as sharp, not ordinarily like the simple flash of a blade, but rather like the smooth turning of a cut gem in the proper light. And among the images employed to isolate the quality of a situation are references from the arts and history. These are very seldom found as direct quotations from poetry in the pompous, careless manner of the classical literary tradition. A quotation is more often alluded to than given; just as the historical reference is crisply suggested: both because Proust will not distract attention from his own text, and because he pays his reader the compliment of assuming that suggestion will be enough. Furthermore he uses such an order of references for a different reason also than their mere effectiveness as illustration. He uses them to show history repeating itself, to leap across time and space, and through the several arts; and to reveal kinships of style in diverse human activities, whether they be the brush strokes of a painter, the street cries of an illiterate vendor, or the intonations of speech of a diplomat. Here, again, his interest in art makes Proust more rather than less democratic. It takes him away from the depressing effect of his aristocratic conception of society into what, by appearing universal, is certainly equalitarian, without distinction of time or class or sophistication.

This order of his sensitivity doubtless reaches its climax in the famous passage in *The Captive* in which he compares street cries to orchestral music forming an 'Overture to a Public Holiday.' Its statement of the beauty of popular pursuits (when not corrupted by bourgeois interference) and its thesis of the kinship of folk and fine art (like the clustering of homes and shops around a medieval cathedral) is well known in musical theory and an evidence of one aspect of the aristocratic tradition in him; but it is the one aspect containing a conception of fraternity which had disappeared from the decadent aristocracy of his own day, and would have to be looked for now in some other quarter. In this passage there is no distortion or wit; for Proust, who generally finds people to possess fewer admirable qualities than weaknesses, is not obligated similarly to spend his attention upon art that calls for satire. Here, not having to reject what he fears or dislikes, he can give himself freely to what he appreciates; and though his appreciation is not often the taste of today, but more precious and romantic, sometimes verging (for all his mechanisms for disguising it) upon the sentimental, it always turns up an original facet that has escaped us, and is most valuable where the interest is literary. As perhaps indicated by his extraordinary sensitiveness in the area of the neglected senses of taste and smell, Proust is at his best not when he is describing the record in other arts of the sense impressions of others, but when he is utilizing his own sense impressions of the same order in his own art of literature. His appreciation of a sunset by Elstir is not so good as his own painting of sunsets in words, when he has brought the impression from nature within the embrace of his particular subjectivity, whether as a type or of the moment. This disciple of Ruskin is the great master of the so-called pathetic fallacy, and his basic theory of art is a contradiction of the Englishman's from whom he drew his method, but not his philosophy, and applied it to the architecture of men instead of buildings.

A similar sobriety of comment, free from the criticism of distortion, is also found in his description of people in those rare cases when he can sympathize with them because he finds them admirable or they appeal to his affections. The number of such persons is small, but enough to show the range of Proust's emotional responses, and absolve him from the charge of being solely a social satirist. The picture of the young girls of Albertine's circle at Balbec is not entirely cynical, as the poetry of the title he gave their volume proves. 'A l'ombre des jeunes filles en fleur' is an unforgettable description of the charm of adolescence. But the Proustian touch is there too in the notion of the tranquilizing effect of the spectacle upon him. Generally the 'shade' of Proust's sympathy is a little darker; for at this point his philosophy becomes directly involved. What we love and admire is always a shadow just out of reach, whether it be an ideal way of life or a personal contact. When the personal contact is with a lover, when Proust possesses Albertine, the effect is not one of melancholy but of emptiness, and Proust distracts himself by listening to the street cries without any implication of irony. The irony here passes to the reader, if he is not simply exasperated by a theory of sex so defiant of common experience and traditional attitudes. (Indeed, since Proust's philosophy is finely articulated, the fantastic, abnormal quality of its application in the area of erotic stimulation, where one has either sadistic indulgence or this ineptitude of possession, seems to lay bare the falsity of the whole structure.) But where the love is from the beginning, and by its very nature, confined to the ideal by the impossibility of physical possession, as it must be with a grandmother; when there can never be the disillusionment of possession, when possession must always be on the removed level of the spiritual, then there is the deepening of the poignancy when even the possibility of illusion is removed by death. Proust's grief at news of Albertine's death is an emotional paradox; death has halted the sado-masochistic chase. It has temporarily reawakened the illusion of love which had seemed dead. It has evoked not sorrow but guilt. But since the relationship with the grandmother had been on a different plane, the grief for her death will for Proust be without alloy. And after her death she will seem to become completely and perfectly the illusion of the ideal. She will seem to have returned among 'les jeunes filles en fleur.'

Her face, he says, in death had grown young again. [From it] had vanished the wrinkles, the contractions, the swellings, the strains, the hollows which in the long course of years had been carved on it by suffering. As at the far-off time when her parents had chosen for her a bridegroom, she had the features delicately traced by purity and submission, the cheeks glowing with a chaste expectation, with a vision of happiness, with an innocent gaiety even, which the years had gradually destroyed. Life in withdrawing from her had taken with it the disillusionment of life. A smile seemed to be hovering on my grandmother's lips. On that funeral couch, death, like a sculpture of the middle ages, had laid her in the form of a young maiden.*

Beautiful as this passage is, it shows how, when Proust is most deeply moved, emotion and philosophy come into closest contact in him. For wrinkles are not always the record of suffering. They may be chiefly records of growth and mastery in the process of living which, though it has its tragic moments and its sad defeats, nevertheless is predominantly a spectacle of courage. But Proust's perceptions were not altogether limited by the deficiencies of his own temperament. What affords the portrait of Charles Swann a quality not found in any other character (save with reservations in Françoise), is that, despite his ultimate failure in living, he never lost somewhat of the courage which takes life as clay to be molded and does not merely submit to it as a destructive influence. In Proust's portrait of Swann, survives the possibility still of escape from decadence. His unfortunate marriage was in part an attempt to relive his life, to replace the frivolities of polite society by the virtues of domesticity, and above all by the indulgence of paternal love. It is a certain old bourgeois stability of character in him that Proust, remembering his childhood at Combray, continued to admire. Even though the fulfilment of its potentialities was at every point denied by external circumstances, his inner spirit retained its core of integrity. And upon Charles Swann, therefore, as an ideal that was not altogether illusory, Proust lavished neither the wit of his scorn nor the melancholy of his affection, but rather a respect for his manhood which was beyond both jealousy and imitation.

* Proust, Marcel, *The Guermantes Way*, New York, 1934, vol. II, pt. 2, p. 48. By permission of Random House, Inc.

4

The Sense of the Present in Thomas Mann

IN popular opinion, Thomas Mann is the greatest of modern novelists. Like an established deity of letters, he towers above his age, comprehending and not rejecting it. His feet seem as surely planted upon the solid ground of experience as his gaze has remained tranquil and dominant above it. Other novelists may have fled from so resolute a stance in so disorderly an era, and preferred to hiss at the world from their private corners. Mann has stayed at the center of the disturbance, sure of his insight, and able to detach himself by the irony of his comment from whatever he can neither approve nor ignore. An extraordinary consciousness of what he is doing and determination to control his material distinguish him from the typical novelists of our time whose writing often appears the dictation of neurotic impulse. The fruit of his determination has been an array of novels, of unusual variety of flavor and theme, in a period when many novelists of quality have exhausted themselves over the details of some single gigantic and abstruse act of creation.

Mann, it is true, has come ultimately to this latter attempt. His recent concern with the Joseph legend marks his belated acceptance of the type of novel for which Proust and Joyce have been notable, in which a systematic philosophy emerges from the intricate weaving of an immense amount of detailed observation. But, unlike these other novelists, Mann's synthesis is the empirical conclusion of a lifework of separate novels, each of which has been stimulated by some special problem. It would therefore seem to have a more objective basis than that of the other writers. It would seem to have been reached, like a scientific statement, as a result of the solution of these different special problems. Upon examination, the final attitude appears to have been made possible by the use of some dialectic method, which has disclosed relationships among what otherwise must have remained quite separate studies.

Mann's novels may be divided into two groups. In the one group are the objective or sociological works, with elaborate plots and many characters; in the other, though retaining the objective method, he limits his attention to a simple situation and a single problem, which is often the esthetic or the personal aspect of the larger social theme of the longer works. But the longer novels themselves divide according to the periods of social history they specifically cover, and change their tone and structure with change in tone and structure of objective events. Such range of variation is unusual in a novelist, and would seem at first sight to make any synthesis impossible. The philosophical interest of the Joseph stories is that Mann has in them utilized the only feasible solution by adopting a kind of dialectic resolution of opposites.

The final gesture of the Joseph stories, however, cannot be properly understood unless the earlier novels have been first examined. Though, taken together, these early works form a series of contradictions, each one of them, taken by itself, is comparatively free from inner contradictions. Each is rigidly designed to secure a particular accumulative uniformity. In his early years, Mann writes under the general influence of that esthetic formalism which abhors the inconsistent as much as the irrelevant. To secure uniformity of tone, harmony of detail, simple consistency of theme is his aim during the greater part of his life. It is as though, like a prudent youth, he was unwilling to introduce complications he might not be able to control; as though, like the social reformer, he sought to clear up some specific area of esthetic inquiry before proceeding to another. And yet take even this earliest group of novels together, and they are seen to represent a resolution of conflicts in social attitudes that is quite unique in the history of fiction. Mann's early orientation becomes perceptible, not in any single early novel, but in the relationship among three, *His Royal Highness, Buddenbrooks,* and *Tonio Kröger.*

In what is logically the first of these novels, *His Royal Highness,* Mann gives the *coup de grâce* to the old feudal Germany. This Germany of small principalities, rigid in class distinctions, pretentious in culture, as archaic intellectually as economically, survives in the novel only through the paradox of a personal embrace of the new order that is killing it. The prince falls in love with the naively wilful personality of an American heiress who impulsively breaks down the aristocratic principle her capitalistic fortune is intended to buttress. That the theme, though valid enough, belonged to the past, Mann stated by the *opéra comique* style he adopted. He could afford to be gracious to the dying foe, and he was not sufficiently able to identify himself with the old feudal culture to elaborate any possibility it might afford of the tragic theme. Inferentially, nevertheless, the book is a devastating attack upon the whole school of international novelists in America. Henry James, who did take the aristocratic principle seriously, could only reach the note of pathos when he sought one of tragedy. Mann's firm bourgeois perspective forced him to view the decline of the aristocracy from the outside, and, the predominant direction of history being on his side, he could not fail to translate James's pathos into the whimsical burlesque, which was all it deserved if one thought in terms of history at all. Obviously such a theme, by the very insight Mann brought to it, could offer little of intrinsic worth. The wonder is that Mann should have chosen it in the first place. The belated tug of the past in Germany doubtless brought it to his attention, and by the process of composition he rid himself of any vestiges of sentimental attachment. His sense of history, evoking a specific consciousness of what he was doing, by determining this attitude toward his theme, also enabled him to escape the cumbersome seriousness of the German tradition in satire. Recognizing that he was dealing with what the progress of history must regard as fantasy, he was able to achieve something approximating grace of style, although the key remained subdued and the tempo less callously sprightly than a disciple of Voltaire would have brought to the theme.

In *Buddenbrooks,* by contrast, where Mann turns to a bourgeois theme, his personal relationship to the new material is defined, as one might expect after reading *His Royal Highness,* by a style of objective realism from which every trace of fantasy has been removed. If the tone of *His Royal Highness* was that of the quaint but benevolent distortion of late twilight in summer, that of *Buddenbrooks* is full afternoon in autumn when the bright clear air gives no more than a hint of winter to come and the particularity of a few dying leaves is lost in the rich general sense of fruition. When cool objective statement gives way, it is to humor and not to irony, and only intermittently as the sun's warmth strikes the back in crisp health-bringing weather. The humor only intensifies Mann's identification with his theme, as we reveal the security of our love for someone by loving also what we recognize to be the merely human blemishes upon his personality. To be sure, the tone becomes troubled before the end because this is the story of the decline of a family. There is the foretaste of storm, but not of winter, because *Buddenbrooks* is not intended to narrate the decline of a social system.

This freedom from satire or any kind of essential criticism permits us to conclude that *Buddenbrooks* gives the true conviction of Mann, at least at the time that it was written, and records his belief in the old bourgeois way of life. The unruffled composure of style, only a little less matter of fact than Defoe, fosters the reception of the novel as a valid social history by its very reluctance to wear its love upon the sleeve. If the style thus defines the certainty of Mann's belief, the substance of the novel leaves no doubt as to the content of it. It concerns three generations of a family of wealthy merchants, like Mann's, in a German town, such as Lübeck, beginning in 1838 and coming down toward the end of the century, the period of his own boyhood and maturing. In terms of economic history this is the period that begins with the flourishing of free trade and the open market in Germany, and ends with the rise of consolidation and state aid. But the novel does not intentionally reflect this change from competition to monopoly. It assumes to the full the validity of the attitudes of the earlier period when the precepts of Adam Smith were being actually followed. It assumes, in other words, that competition is the law of trade. Any changes the novel mentions are not presumed to be fundamental changes in the economic structure, but only manifestations of the unending discovery of new mechanisms to keep competition alive by tossing the ball of prosperity to that firm which gets hold of the new idea. We may be able to see that the failure of the Buddenbrooks' firm to join the customs' union was its failure to recognize the first historic step toward consolidation. But Mann treats the customs' union in the old bourgeois manner, as only a new tool to force profits, on a par with a better system of bookkeeping or the discovery of a new product to sell, and not for what it really was, a change in the nature of the system. If, therefore, Mann truly records an historic situation, he records it through its own eyes, and gives it a consistency within itself which turns out to be misleading if examined from the larger perspective of later history.

Within this fixed framework, the novel presents the only distinguished, thoroughly faithful, thoroughly sympathetic picture of a society that once existed, with its happy assurance that an eternal competition guaranteed an everexpanding prosperity.

It is a picture that once was typical, but now survives, with increased tensions and completely on the defensive, only in the minority of small businessmen not yet crushed by finance capital. *Buddenbrooks* is probably the best of that surprisingly small group of literary works which take this old bourgeois world seriously. For the bourgeois period is unique in literary history for having bred chiefly critics and satirists of itself, in sharp contrast to the tendency of literature traditionally to defend the world it writes about. It is noteworthy that Mann was capable of this rare accomplishment. At this period in his career he was able completely to identify himself with the dominant social system. That the 'weaknesses' of the system are displayed need not cause hesitation. Every system has its weaknesses and makes allowance for them. In *Buddenbrooks,* just as the head of the family lays up capital against a period of depression or a bad investment, so he accepts vicissitudes in family life as a law of nature. The family takes in its stride, though of course not with rejoicing, the daughter who makes a bad marriage from which she has to be bailed out from time to time; and it counts the son who has no head for business on a par with a poor investment to be covered from other sources. These weaknesses only keep men alert. The system was stable, so men reasoned, precisely because no single part of it could be. Prosperity, in Napoleon's phrase, followed the talent, and for the individual the only stabilizing element was the possibility of training him to be shrewd and aggressive by use of the family.

Naturally, therefore, when the family produced an individual esthetically inclined, this old bourgeois system found digestion difficult. For this was an attack upon its essential narrow-mindedness. An occasional case of sheer depravity, a plain and frank roué, might be handled. Culture was more insidious. If not taken seriously, if treated like a commodity, it might be harmless enough, like a good dinner. It was safe to collect cultural objects, indeed to clutter one's rooms with them. The harm began when one passed from absent-minded comfort in their mere quantity to trying to understand their values in their own right. Unfortunately from the family point of view, art had a way ultimately of arrogating attention from business. It was still the period when the adage, three generations from shirtsleeves to shirtsleeves, was not absurd if loosely interpreted. Competition was kept healthy by the fact that no ascendancy was assured and by the belief that the command of wealth was a greater handicap to success than the need to command it. Art was a demoralizing distraction from these demands, especially since, unlike drinking or gaming, it could not be proved fundamentally bad and clearly put in its place.

Such was the code of living in the middle class during the greater part of the nineteenth century, of which the story of the decline of the Buddenbrooks is a candid illustration. The first generation makes the money by tending strictly to business. Necessity for hard work diminishes with the second generation, and this Buddenbrooks marries a wife for her beauty rather than for her frugality and common sense. The new interest in having a *salon* and being concerned with public affairs not only distracts attention from business, which is no longer talked through three square meals a day, but produces a son in the third generation who is not satisfied with a fringe of artists about him, but is no better than an artist himself, incapable of managing, to say nothing of increasing, the family business. This theme concerns the most important dilemma of the old bourgeois family; for it cannot be called a tragedy, since the particular decline of the Buddenbrooks does not land them in poverty or disrepute, but only paves the way for the emergence of a new family of another name whose lack of ascendancy has kept fresh in them the old Buddenbrooks virtues.

But the easiest way to isolate the esthetic merit of *Buddenbrooks* (whatever one may think of its mores) is to contrast it with *The Forsyte Saga.* Galsworthy refuses to take sides. With his charitable liberalism, he states the case for art as well, and tries to resolve the dilemma while remaining fair to both parties.

Mann confines himself to putting the case for business, and by thus limiting his attempt, he avoids the esthetic blunder of finding himself unable to resolve his plot. To put it bluntly, there could be no case for art, recognizable by an artist, in the old bourgeois society, and Mann in this novel does not pretend that there can be. When the entrepreneur became the *rentier,* as competition gave way to the less strenuous exertion of clipping dividends, the change in the system allowed at least a temporary adjustment, of which the strange history of art in the twentieth century is in large part the consequence. Now Galsworthy's novel deals chiefly with this later period, and one would think that a more adequate handling, if not a resolution, of the dilemma might have been possible. Instead, he repeated its statement in a voice that grew more and more faint until death intervened. The reason for his failure lay in his retention of the old bourgeois code of morals when the new bourgeoisie was, for the time being, flourishing under the equivocal use of some form of art for art's sake, which severed art completely from relationship to morals. Galsworthy's interest in Soames Forsyte shows that he recognized this to be not the right solution. When the businessman was no longer willing to remain the specialist, the dilemma had only been transferred to the subjective sphere where it became personally distressing. Yet enough of Old Jolyon survived in both Soames and his creator for them to believe that it could be solved without compromise of either art or bourgeois mores; when, as Proust proved so admirably through the Verdurins, the only possible resolution is the mutual degeneration of both. Galsworthy's solution should have been Proust's; instead, he attempted the one that Mann avoided.

What Galsworthy sought to do, Mann, however, realized had to be tried. But the needs of his personality, quite as much as his superior esthetic sensitivity, dictated a more satisfactory approach. It was as though Mann had said to himself: I must be fair to my family before I reject their aspirations for me, and became an artist. By writing *Buddenbrooks* essentially as his family would have written it, he became free to declare himself an artist and seek to justify his profession in another novel. His personal difficulty permitted him to handle the theme, no longer as a plot involving the objective relationships of individuals, but as the biography of a critical stage in an artist's development. Under such circumstances a philosophical conclusion that may be untenable may nevertheless be esthetically satisfactory if it is true to character. In *Tonio Kröger* Mann, by utilizing the suitable esthetic vehicle, at least achieved an explicit statement of Galsworthy's attempted solution. For the nature of Mann's defense of art shows that he was even less willing than the English writer to compromise the old bourgeois mores. When the general tendency among artists of every sort was either toward the esoteric, which denied the existence of the problem, or toward Galsworthy's befuddling of the issue, Mann retains the old Puritan ideal (for it does not matter that he was technically a Catholic) quite as much as any clergyman or literary humanist. As an artist speaking of business, he confines his objection to the limited conception of the good life among men of affairs. But when he turns to art, he no longer accepts the attitude so sympathetically presented in *Buddenbrooks.* Art is no longer regarded as *ipso facto* degenerative. Art and business he now holds to be two complementary aspects of a duality, whose relationship must no longer be neglected. If the values of both are thus admitted on both sides, he believes they will both be purged of their present inadequacies. If art is frivolous or self-indulgent, if business breeds the crude and rigid man, an art that is rooted in the reality of everyday life as the bourgeois lives it, but does not submit to his superficial interests, will succeed in ennobling both. The dilemma, according to this private statement of Mann's, is temporary and not at all a consequence of the inherent character of the bourgeois mores, which he seems to believe capable of transforming the profit motive into a superficial interest. 'For surely,' he says in his own italics, 'it is my *bourgeois* conscience that makes me see in the artist life, in all irregularity and all genius, something profoundly suspect, profoundly disreputable; that fills me with this lovelorn *faiblesse* for the simple and good, the comfortably normal, the average unendowed respectable human being. . . . If anything is capable of making a poet out of a literary man, it is my *bourgeois* love of the *human*, the living and usual.' The artist ceases to be decadent, to be an ordinary artist, when be becomes aware of the neglected ethical basis of the ordinary bourgeois qualities within himself. It is true that Mann's hero makes these assertions in a mood of self-pity, as though beseeching his readers to protect him against his weaker side corrupted by the prevalent trend in art. But verbally, at least, his conviction is explicit.

As far as Tonio represents Mann, the pessimism gained the immediate ascendancy. The tide proved overwhelming, and *The Magic Mountain* is the monument to the defeat of Tonio's ideal. Indeed, as Mann took this second, later, and more comprehensive view of the social scene, it seemed to him that Tonio had come too late; the old bourgeois ideal seemed to have disappeared from the objective world, degenerated into a sinister anarchy. *The Magic Mountain* is the negation of *Buddenbrooks.* What had earlier been taken as a particular failure set within the social frame of glorious robust success, is now observed to be the symptom of at least the temporary decay of the system itself. In the same way, the hero of the later novel is the young Buddenbrooks of the third generation generalized; that is, no longer drifting toward art, but possessing the same qualities of personality. If young Buddenbrooks was Mann pretty much as he had been, Hans Castorp is the same Mann as he would have been deprived of his artist's insight. Hence the transformation of style from the judiciously sympathetic, back to the ironic of *His Royal Highness,* only now the seriousness of its use deepens. There must be a check upon the levity with which Mann patronizes that nonartistic three-quarters of himself which walks the streets. In fact an ironic style today is generally a device of rhetoric by means of which an author separates himself from a world in which he is indubitably, though not at all gloriously, involved but which he will not be held responsible for making. Whether it veer toward the bitterness of Hardy's pessimism or toward frivolity in Meredith's comic spirit, our ironic style has the same psychological origin. It is the conscious creative aspect of the personality registering through recognition of defect its superiority to the world it lives in. Frequently, and notably in Mann, this world also includes the noncreative aspects of the author's own personality, and there is therefore often a latent self-depreciation involved. There, Mann might say of Castorp, but for the grace of being a writer, go I. Sometimes the irony is also deceptive since it sets up only the appearance of superiority; as when a writer, though the reader can discover no coherent conclusions of any sort from his writing, seems to have reached them solely because he has so devastatingly bared the inconsistencies of other people. Mann never stoops to this low use of irony, nor requires this desperation of personal defense. But he sometimes, as is shockingly illustrated in his essay on spiritualism, tries to elevate this type of confusion into a tentative broadmindedness, an honest agnosticism which is doubtless only temporary. Though philosophically regrettable, such a use of irony is esthetically profitable since it forces narrative enrichment by presenting all sides of the picture, while leaving the author in the safe position (should the future play him a nasty trick) of not having taken the wrong side. But irony, as Mann uses it, is also a device for escaping the melancholy induced by a conscientious observation of the facts. The significance of the style of *The Magic Mountain* is that it is typical of the intellectual of the 'twenties.

Mann's indecisions make the narrative fairly glitter as ideas are spun to show their facets. One cannot decide whether he considers psychoanalysis fraudulent or truly therapeutic; for the evidence for both interpretations is insidiously presented. In regard to the practice of medicine which is surely on a scientific basis, one cannot be quite certain whether the profit motive does not paralyze its good intention. The age, it is true, enjoyed such ambivalencies since there seemed no way of resolving them; and Mann co-operates ironically with the pretense that discussion is directed to this end. At the same time, since the difficulties are real and other first-rate novelists are with obvious persistence striving to clear them up philosophically, Mann's ironic style in *The Magic Mountain* tends to break under the strain of being forced to be at once serious and frivolous about them. His talent will not permit him to compete with Proust as a philosopher in fiction. His style becomes ponderous under the attempt, and discloses the strain the intricate process is putting upon his faculties. The simplification of reaching some general conclusion was necessary, and he sought to try for a decision on the age-old problem of the nature of evil. (As for his discussion of time, I put that aside since, in comparison with Proust's really magnificent, though not always satisfactory insights, his is only the common-sense observation that time sometimes seems longer or shorter than it really is by the clock.) But the problem of evil, baffling enough to the Puritan conscience, had become even more vexing since Baudelaire had said that evil is good and Nietzsche had dismissed it as a concept not applying to the superman. Here again Mann's discussion boiled down to a simple statement which only records the unavailing pull of the social degeneration upon the core of Puritanism within him. He now sees that we may learn through suffering. Evil may become the mechanism for deeper understanding of its opposite, the good. What remains a little doubtful is how far it should be indulged by the individual to extend his perceptions beyond the commonplace (which is not extolled in Hans Castrop as it had been in Tonio Kröger) and thus facilitate a more distinguished ultimate perception of the good.

The problem, however, becomes academic when one turns from these speculations in *The Magic Mountain* to the plot itself. For the plot (in distinction to these philosophical passages) reaches indubitable conclusions in its representation of European society before the First World War. In the realm of actuality evil dominates the modern world. It is temporarily irresistible and scarcely needs to be cultivated. If plots are of significance, all the theorizing, one must conclude, is unimportant in the face of this fact. This is the conclusion that Mann finally reaches, but he cannot forego the pleasure of first discussing what a fact is. This, in philosophical terminology, means discussing the nature of reality, and Mann raises it in relation to the question whether Hans really has tuberculosis or merely thinks he has; whether he was tubercular before he came to the sanitarium or became so under the influence of its environment; whether, in short, the body materialistically influences the consciousness or an imaginary As-If can affect our physical condition. It is characteristic that after all the insinuation, Mann's final answer is essentially that of old-fashioned humanistic Protestantism. The problem is dismissed as pragmatically not worth discussing since Hans (however he got that way) is sick enough of something, whether mentally or physically, to incapacitate his normal functioning, which the necessity of going to war automatically restores to him. Inferentially, one concludes from the action of the book, Mann does not really care about the speculations over which he has spent so many teasing pages. It is the objective activity, what Hans does or does not do, measured in old bourgeois terms, that counts. By this test, the book concludes, society is in a state of degeneration, and the education of experience (all this glitter of ideas to which we have been treated) implies a loss of standards.

So one reads with his own irony the remarks of those critics of Mann who consider him our great philosophical novelist. A certain professor, for instance, has extravagantly declared that *The Magic Mountain* is a 'pedagogical, autobiographical, psychological, mystical, above all a symbolic novel.' He proceeds to state that the only *ism* not represented is the economic or sociological. But the truth would seem to be that all these other *isms* are ambiguous and often irrelevant in the novel; only concealing a practical interest which is to Mann's credit, I believe, but to express which quite frankly in the 'twenties might have made comparisons with Proust and other stellar figures less spontaneous. Of all the *isms* in the novel, that which is developed most coherently is the sociological, which Professor Weygand says is not there at all.

Mann's absorption in the practical-historical, though elevated by a mystical superstition about numbers, is shown by his putting the start of *The Magic Mountain* as definitely seven years before the outbreak of the First World War as *Buddenbrooks* began in 1838. It is a history, therefore, of the breakdown, after the rise of monopoly capitalism, of a system that *Buddenbrooks* showed had once been stable. By making one further change in the character of his hero Mann defines the change; Hans has trained neither for art nor entrepreneurship, but to become a specialist in engineering, a cog in the new business machine. Needing a vacation, he goes to visit an ill cousin taking the cure at a tubercular sanitarium in Switzerland. The relation between the sanitarium and the world below is of symbolic importance; most of the inmates lose touch with it completely and fester in their segregated private world. Either they have enough money or do not worry about its sources. They are Veblen's leisure class. The fact that they are of various nationalities, though it adds piquant detail, only emphasizes the dispersion of the malady. In contrast to the world below, which is that of practical affairs, they are the vanguard of decadence; they represent in the present what the rest of the world is coming to. It is noteworthy that persons of any surviving strength of character unwillingly submit to the domination of the mountain. Though they know that they are diseased, they refuse to revel in their malady; they refuse to follow a regimen that is supposedly curative but is actually an orgy of licentiousness of speech and action, of frivolity and callousness, of narcissism become exhibitionistic, worthy of a Soho drawing room or a *café* on Montmartre. Hans, the weak, average bourgeois of the new decadence, falls prey to this atmosphere. Although it awakens his dormant interests in culture and knowledge, at the same time it gives him a culture and knowledge that eventually prove not worth having. Hans's cousin, whose rank as officer in the army makes him symbolize the old aristocracy, rejects the sanitarium, returns impulsively to the practical world, where he dies almost like a hero since he has felt the necessity to act. The intellectuals, Settembrini and Naphta, hover about the flame but will get no closer than the inn on the mountainside, whither Hans comes to hear them talk. The great Java plantation owner, Mynheer Peeperkorn, comes to the inn occasionally to be near his mistress, whose occasional visits he is willing to indulge.

In the relations among these characters is indubitably to be found a basically authentic materialistic history of society under monopoly capitalism. The philosophers, knowing something is wrong with society, have their cures typical of the dominant panaceas of the period. Naphta, whom Mann presents with callous objectivity, is a Jew who has become a Jesuit, and would reintroduce what he calls medieval communism. His scheme is systematic and logically foolproof. Settembrini, Mann treats with a trace of disdain, but more sympathetically, since he represents the weaknesses in Mann's own liberal position. Mann shows him paradoxically defeating his avowed purposes. The grandson of a Mazzini patriot, he is wasting his time and distracting the energies of his associates by compiling not some textbook of hopeful action, but a compendious history of human suffering, which he pretends will pave the way for later progress. Actually he is so selfish and indifferent that he does not even attend the congress of the international society of which he is secretary and which is a parody of the Second International. These two men may be said figuratively to hover in mid-air, escaping the world of the practical. But their rationalizations prevent them from admitting that they are sick enough to enter the sanitarium which draws them like a magnet. Finally, after pages of discussion, to which Hans listens with open mouth, they get so angry with each other that they fight a duel. Settembrini refuses to fire at Naphta; whereupon the Jesuit, infuriated that his adversary has not even tried to kill him, kills himself. Obviously he has not really believed in his perfect system at all. But Settembrini's psychology is equally interesting. Though he claims that his abstention from firing is a magnificent gesture of humanitarian impulse, it actually represents his inability to take any kind of action. All his pretensions curiously manage to keep him alive and somehow fed in an atmosphere of instability which he really enjoys and which is quite in keeping with his restless pragmatic pleasure in juggling ideas so that his opponent at least is driven to suicide. But he conceals from his consciousness this use of the Socratic method by constantly mouthing all the empty abstractions of the old liberal movement.

As though to drive his meaning home, Mann does not stop here. These men have won Hans's puzzled admiration. For him they are significant, and the world should stop to listen. When Mynheer Peeperkorn appears on the scene, an opposite reaction takes place. The two philosophers have been talking as volubly and heatedly as usual. Peeperkorn, who must dominate every environment he enters, shuts them up, as though with a single savage command, and takes the center of the stage. Wealthy as this international capitalist is, he knows he is dying; his kidneys have given way under Rabelaisian self-indulgence. But in place of heeding any doctor, he only spends his excessive profits the more recklessly, and, we are told, later dies in a kind of suicide of magnificent drunken brawling. It can hardly be doubted that Mann is here personifying not only the future of finance capitalism but its relationship in the present to free speech and the high life of the mind. Beneath the superficial geniality, the willingness to play the host, Peeperkorn is a wilful man who must do what he pleases with his power. The possibility that Hans might have become interested in his mistress, the dissolute Frau Clavdia of the green eyes, never occurs to him. Hans, in the feverishly erotic atmosphere of the sanitarium, has fallen into a desperate verbalization of love with this woman, who resembles a youth he once knew, though he puts his sensuality into French and doubtless would never have acquired the courage for a sustained affair. Nevertheless, when Peeperkorn returns, all his interest vanishes as though Peeperkorn had commanded. He has been saved for the time being from the growing tyranny of his baser nature by submitting automatically to an equally abject tyranny imposed from without. Writing during the years of the Weimar Republic, Mann is not only depicting the degeneration of the German character which deepened after the First World War; he is also, in an uncanny way, foreshadowing the birth of fascism. The anarchy is awaiting the dictator's command.

The symbolic interpretation of *The Magic Mountain* that is least open to the charge of ambiguity is, then, its accumulation of evidence of social decadence. Characterization and action unite to this clear interpretation. Always ambiguous where abstract ideas are concerned, Mann shares the degeneration sufficiently not to recognize its full extent. His sympathy for Settembrini and his acceptance of almost any mental stimulus as good, is proof. But he can never free himself from scientific respect for the facts of observation, whatever his theoretical indulgence for the insidious philosophy of As-If. As though to close any doubt one might have about the validity of this interpretation of *The Magic Mountain,* Mann, as usual, furnishes the pendant work in which the problems of the longer novel are presented in terms of his own esthetic attitudes. Perhaps the very fact that *Death in Venice* is the peak of his accomplishment as a writer, written with a disingenuous simplicity that facilitates the transfer of its psychological subtlety, shows the congeniality and importance of its theme for Mann. For *Death in Venice* depicts the sort of writer who was beginning to abound, and who Mann himself might have become if certain Puritan elements in his character had not enabled him to write *Tonio*

Kröger. He can therefore write with indulgent pathos of what he recognizes must be condemned: so indulgently that he sets up a mood of delicate hesitation between the contradictory impulses to resist and to submit. But here again, if one separates the verbal meaning of the action from the emotional response, there is no confusion. It is again a story of the impossibility of separating life from art. The superficial writer, who has always pursued the beauty of abstract design in his work, finds himself inviting death in the end. On the beach at Venice, he falls in love with the abstract beauty of a homosexual youth. Unable to bring himself to speak to the boy, he is equally unable to take his eyes from him. When a pestilence drives virtually everybody away save the youth, who seems held by the same spell, despite warnings, the writer stays also and falls victim to the plague. If he had not been a believer in art for art's sake, he would not have been deceived as to the nature of his interest in the boy; he would have followed the advice of common sense and escaped the plague. But the plague offered him a further view of the Grecian urn at the risk of death. And he was willing to die because he could not stop indulging in imagination what he had neither the courage nor quite the folly to indulge in reality.

The real problem for the most consciously intellectualistic writer of our time was thus to look for a valid escape which did not deny the incontrovertible facts of social degeneration. The intervention of the war gave him a new set of facts upon which he could build. If art had not yet exercised its leavening authority, the very process of life itself could now be relied upon to do so. The war, however horrible on the surface, could be interpreted as regeneration. He had only to avail himself of the most popular prevalent theory of history. The belief that history proceeds in cycles could easily be brought into harmony with his bourgeois habit of arranging ideas and events into separate categories. The cyclic theory gave him the necessary law of contradiction to bring his social categories into relationship. If the sanitarium of *The Magic Mountain* represented a new low in human depravity, it could not last. The good must arise, like the phoenix, out of its own burning ruins. And so he appended to his diabolically depressing account of actuality a prophecy (in a more ecstatic style than he ever elsewhere allowed himself, so desperate was the situation): that the First World War must prove a purification of mankind by death and suffering. It would burn away the old sin in man, and educate him into obedience to his higher nature once more. Whether this creditable result would come automatically did not need to be raised in *The Magic Mountain.* But the unexpected return and deepening of the same depravity during the Republic and the ultimate emergence of fascism as the sort of false purgation that seemed to come of itself, forced Mann to examine his theory anew.

Mann gave his answer in two works, as usual, one short and one long, one a negative and one a positive approach. In *Mario and the Magician* he stated with unmistakable symbolism that the people, hypnotized by fear of their dictators, would find the leader who would break the spell by killing the dictator. It is worth noting that the leader in the story is the waiter from Mann's hotel; for this is the only instance in Mann's writings where he has paid any attention to the working class, and one should treat this symbol perhaps a little gently as the accident of this particular narrative. All of Mann's tracts against fascism have otherwise assumed that the intellectuals of the bourgeoisie would effect the cure. The positive prototype of the true leader who later emerged from his pen was that representative of the eternal entrepreneur, Joseph of the Old Testament.

In the sequence of Joseph stories, Mann has repeatedly stated its underlying philosophy, of which this passage is only a single example:

> We are justified in drawing a parallel between his sin against Potiphar's wife and his earlier sin against his brothers. Once more he had

gone too far, in his craving to make people 'sit up'; once more the working of his charm . . . had been allowed to get beyond control, to degenerate into an actual danger. In his first life these workings had taken the negative form of hate; this time the immoderately positive and equally destructive form of passion. He had in his blindness given fuel to the flames of both; in the second case, misled by his own response to a woman's uncontrollable passion, he who stood in such need of instruction himself had tried to play the pedagogue. His conduct cried out for retribution, there is no doubt of that; but we cannot help smiling to see how the punishment which so justly overtook him was directed to the furtherance of a good fortune much greater and more brilliant than that which had been destroyed . . . [God makes] misfortune a fruitful soil whence renewed good fortune should spring.*

Here, I take it, Mann is stating a universal philosophy. The career of Joseph is symbolically that of Mann himself. But it is more than this. It symbolizes the fate of all who suffer and are exiled, not merely Jews, but all anti-fascists who have been forced into exile from their native lands, like young Joseph. The blame is not put either on Joseph's cruel brothers or upon Potiphar's unscrupulous wife. If there is any general meaning here, we should not so much blame Hitler as ourselves, and in either case, no blame at all should be attached to the particular organization of society, system of economy, of which for many of us Hitler himself is only the tool. Instead, Mann prefers to have recourse to the old Hebraic and Greek ethic that makes *hubris* the most dangerous of sins and the humility that follows suffering a salutary process of rebuilding the ethical life upon a sounder basis. If applied to modern politics, this theory is a dangerous form of appeasement. But in the broader sense, by neglecting the importance of the practical forms of political and economic organization (since Joseph falls twice, once under the old tribal form of society among the Jews and later under

* Mann, Thomas, *Joseph in Egypt,* trans. by H. T. Lowe-Porter, New York, 1938, vol. II, pp. 624-5. By permission of Alfred A. Knopf.

the different system of the Egyptians), Mann is accepting a philosophy of pure idealism.

What happens to the life of the individual also happens to the collective life of men. Nations will always require the therapy of suffering, whether in the specific form of war or not, and through it will be restored to dignity and prosperity. The humiliation of individual exile parallels the temporary loss of national integrity; and both, as the negative aspects of the cyclic oscillation of history, will periodically recur. If fascism and other forms of social degeneration result from the human tendency to indulge base material interests under the domination of either national or individual pride, this indulgence sets up its opposite. The men of stronger moral character are called to their senses and begin consciously to work for the ascendancy of man's better nature once more; and their exile will end in a victorious return. Despite his unusual fidelity to sociological change, Mann philosophically sees all this as subordinate to and governed by the spiritual nature of man himself. Change is important only as a clue to whether in the inner spiritual nature of man good or evil is getting the ascendancy. Of course, the good will win, generally speaking, but it will win only when the need for its winning has been brought by sad external events into men's consciousness and has focussed their energies once more upon the recovery of the ideal. The need for the good, like the desire for wealth (which was taken for a good) in *Buddenbrooks,* awakens the energy to attain it. The Joseph stories only spin thin the idealistic philosophy of the concluding chapter of *The Magic Mountain.*

Such a philosophy is dialectic, to be sure, but it is not the dynamic progressive dialectic of either Marx or Hegel. It is specifically the static dialectic of the Manichaenism in the Protestant or the Augustinian tradition of the Renaissance humanism. Early Protestantism, emphasizing the practical value of its new moral code, neglected these abstract implications. When modern society was observed to be headlong in its plunge into decadence, the re-examination of fundamentals became essential. Protestantism revived its latent dualism, and put it on a new philosophical basis of Romantic intuitionalism which excused its ideational ambiguity. A thousand voices are now raised, declaring that fascism is the force of evil let loose in the world and that anti-fascism is the rallying of the dormant forces for good which must in the nature of things win. These voices come from the preacher and the educator; they turn the New Humanism in literary criticism from its authoritarian direction into more democratic channels. They are of commendable and indispensable aid. But it remains to be seen what risks of ultimate defeat lurk in their indifference to material mechanisms and their careless rejection of the ideal of human progress.

But if the esthetic test has any validity, this dualistic idealism is an unsatisfactory substitute for that use of history as an evolving process of events which was the conspicuous but involuntary concern of Mann in his earlier novels. Readers, both philosophically naive and trained alike, find the Joseph stories dull, and this dullness is a consequence of Mann's rejection of his earlier method. It is certainly not the result of any loss of fastidiousness as a craftsman on Mann's part. He has been keenly aware of the difficulty of writing historical fiction. He has sought to escape the failure of much historical fiction in which human nature disappears in incident and description of setting. Not only has he studied the history, the religion, the anthropology, the various cultural interests of both Hebrews and Egyptians; he has rigidly limited himself to reproducing only so much of this detail as will not overwhelm his characters and make them the puppets of this information. Even in dealing with his characters, he has been equally careful to proportion the relation of subjective and objective, the amount of inner mood and outward action. He has escaped all the faults of the Scott tradition.

The opposite risk, however, he has invited by his shift of emphasis from his earlier method. Then he succeeded in isolating the idiosyncratic features of the period of his novel. Now, when he passes into a remote past most difficult to make come alive, he prefers the opposite course of stressing the eternal sameness of human nature and human struggles. This is to violate the particularity which must distinguish the novel as a literary form from the poem. The great historical novels, *War and Peace, Salammbô,* Sholem Asch's *Nazarene,* Sholokhov's *And Quiet Flows the Don,* all recognize that the past can be fictively revived only when delineation of human differences make it seem historical, while those aspects of human nature closest to certain contemporary traits are emphasized to make it seem validly alive. Thus *Salammbô* is both historical and alive because it stresses the undisciplined emotions of the Carthaginians and their subject peoples at a time when Frenchmen had escaped the discipline of classicism, the primitive superstitions at a time when decadence was stimulating interest in the perverse and diabolical, the callousness of the ancient world toward suffering and the welfare of the masses when the modern world had become sensitive to the good of the greatest number. Thus Asch, in his picture of Jerusalem at the time of Christ, emphasizes the vested interests, the class rivalries, in which the modern reader is interested while he shows the particularities of difference in their operation. Indeed, to do otherwise and write fiction is impossible. Despite his attempt to stress only the enduring traits of man in his portrait of Joseph, Mann has introduced unawares his own particularity of interpretation. This is, in contrast to both Flaubert and Asch, to ignore altogether the existence of the masses of men. In this respect Mann is 'historical' with a vengeance, but it is to be hoped that Joseph's sole interest in his own welfare, or at best, that of his family, is not a universal trait of human nature. But Mann is not content to generalize the personality of Joseph in this fashion. He rubs his generalizations home through interpolated passages of mystical philosophizing. These sections of the book read like paragraphs from some Protestant *Imitatio Hominis,* whose repetition holds up the narrative, and whose vagueness succeeds in giving a sense of unreality to the most specific situations. The dullness of the book is the effect of its philosophy upon the characterization of its hero.

This shift in Mann's recent work has given it an air of pretentiousness. He now stands above his age somewhat as Dryden did above his; and yet both writers were concerned with immediate and political affairs. If they have been taken for leaders in their eras, it is that, in spite of their most conscientious and honest effort, they succeeded only in becoming representative of typical and prevalent ambiguities. They failed because they sought to become the comprehensive expressions of periods of disunity, when to be comprehensive at all may well be impossible, and certainly must be, when outmoded attitudes alone are employed. In his earlier periods, Mann's pragmatic interest in the facts of a changing world led him close to a recognition of history as an irreversible process of development. But when the process seemed to have become one solely of degeneration, he felt himself forced to discard a vague notion of progress for a still more vaguely comprehensive one which Protestantism has never lost: the notion that our physical life reflects an eternal spiritual struggle for domination between good and evil. He has become indifferent to the world of actuality which once intrigued him as thematic material for a novelist as he fixes his attention upon the nostalgic hope that this everlasting spirit of the good, in time, will once more assert itself to restore the equilibrium of free trade in both goods and ideas. The pallid austere dignity he now wears testifies to the unreality of this interpretation of the disorders of modern life in what are essentially the terms of the old bourgeois beliefs of his grandfather.

Indeed the publication of *The Beloved Returns* almost abjectly turns the circle. In this novel, in which a woman vainly seeks to revive the thrill of Goethe's smile upon her as a girl, Mann has become spokesman for the sentimental feminine weakness for lavender and old lace, the belated romanticism of the *Buddenbrooks* period, with which the masculine dominance of *Bud-*

denbrooks has disdained to concern itself. But now the atmosphere of fantasy of *His Royal Highness* revives, though its gay irony has faded into a falsetto of garrulity; as the sharp shrewd insight of *Buddenbrooks* too has deliquesced into archaic platitudes of style and meaning. Leaving all modern attitudes and themes behind, Mann in this novel becomes a popular novelist whose wit the Victorian lady would have admired for its daring.

5

Franz Kafka and the Bankruptcy of Faith

WE speak sometimes of our own writers as the 'lost generation' of the 'twenties. But such terms are relative. American writers were by no means so lost at that time as their contemporaries in defeated Germany, and the importance of Kafka is that he was without question the most lost of them all. The fact that he was born of Jewish middle-class parents in Prague, when it was under Austrian domination, emphasized the alienation and insecurity which had become typical of the middle class generally. Culturally, moreover, Kafka was a German. He lived in Germany and wrote in the German language. And, though his writing was mostly done before the First World War, his attempt to escape a dominating father left him afraid of the responsibilities of freedom in a way symbolic of the later passage of German society from the tyranny of the Empire to the Weimar Republic.

His own deep-seated despondency, which had not yet routed traditional obsessions of blind faith and vague hope, lay bare the perplexities of mind and the vacillations of conduct generally typical of German life under the Weimar Republic. His own diseased personality symbolized the disease at the heart of German society. The progress of his personal deterioration paralleled the degeneration of the society that produced him. And his own life ended as abruptly and prematurely as that of the young republic, though he died of tuberculosis some years before Hitler set himself up as the brutal father-symbol of the German people. Whether the work of so disordered a talent will live at all or only for a select audience may be disputable. But its historic importance can hardly be denied. Kafka's novels cut through the distracting irrelevancies of superficial realism and afford a direct participation in the degeneration of personality of the petty bourgeoisie, which began under Bismarck and was completed under Hitler. They present this degeneration even more vividly to the foreign reader than *The Magic Mountain* does, because the picture is unaccompanied by any distraction of interpretation. As though unaware of the existence of the surface, they take us beneath it into the personality structure itself, remaining quite unconscious of its concealment in ordinary men beneath the conventions of social intercourse.

This interpretation of Kafka has received curious confirmation in the kind of praise lavished upon him by the small group of his admirers that existed in Germany and repeated by its even smaller American counterpart. They have extolled him not for the reasons which I have put forward here, but for those which would have appealed alike to his own attitudes and those of the Weimar Republic. They have given an almost hypnotic attention to his perverse and mystical religious faith. In that conflict which kept him morose and helpless, between a belief in God he could not renounce and a skepticism he could not deny, they have condoned the skepticism out of veneration for the faith. They have not seen that this dubious faith is psychological evidence of the dissolution of the reasoning process itself. Kafka was incapable of the common sense of everyday life, so obscure and contradictory had become the springs of personal conduct in him. Like Kierkegaard, his favorite philosopher, he represents the breakdown of mysticism itself, both as a discipline and a philosophy. In the light of the great religious mystics of history, to emphasize Kafka's religious mysticism can only mean to share his own incapacity for reasoned judgment.

Only Max Brod, the wisest among his admirers and the closest to him, has suggested the possibility of a non-mystical approach to his work. Brod has published—apparently out of sheer sense of duty to the facts, since he does not relate it to his own exposition of Kafka's mysticism—considerable evidence that his personality verged upon the psychopathic. We may anticipate that sooner or later psychiatrists will discover that his novels are as rewarding an object of investigation as those of Dostoievsky. The types of abnormal personality are not as varied as in the pre-revolutionary Russian writer. But the presentation of the particular type of which Kafka was himself an example is even more rich and detailed within its limits since his books became progressively more alien from normal attitudes as his short life ran its course. But a novel is presumably something more than the book of devotions for a degenerate mysticism or a case history in psychiatry. It is also a communication to some sort of general public. I shall therefore limit my interest in the theological and psychiatric aspects of Kafka's work to their bearing upon his novels as an expression of certain patterns of living in our own era and as the satisfaction of the esthetic needs of a limited contemporary audience.

Since Kafka's last stories are almost exclusively devoted to hallucinations, they may be used to clarify the orientation I am seeking. I take for this purpose the most extremely subjective of them all, 'The Burrow.' In this short story, which has a beginning but no end, the hero conceives that he is being pursued by what must be vaguely called enemies. But there is nothing vague about the defenses with which he surrounds himself. He first digs a tunnel into the earth in which he hides like a mole. He conceals the entrance with foliage, and for a time feels safe from pursuit. But it seems wise to make safety doubly sure by digging many branches to his tunnel. Thus he will be able to elude the enemy at numerous points by circling around behind him. Next, in case through some accident he should not be able to do so, he decides to make an exit at the other end. But no sooner has he completed this escape into the upper world than he realizes with dismay that he has also created another possible source of attack. Enemies may now enter at both ends and leave him caught at the middle. He becomes so frightened that he leaves his tunnel altogether. But above ground, even though he hides in the bushes, he feels unprotected on every side; he lacks the tangible comfort of both walls and darkness. So he returns, determined at least to protect his valuables (which remain as abstract as his enemies) by building a special vault for them. His labor is baffled by the sandy soil. But he manages to beat the wall firm by desperate blows of his head; and he is delighted to discover that the blood flowing from his wounds actually welds the sand into a cement. His satisfaction is immediately interrupted, however, by the faint sound of digging elsewhere. The disconcerting suspicion crosses his mind that his enemies may have turned his own plan against him, and started digging parallel tunnels so that they may break through almost anywhere at the strategic moment. Though he listens intently and in every part of his maze, he cannot define the direction of the sound. He tries to close his ears to see whether it is a figment of his imagination. But he is too excited to make a fair test. In a crisis when his enemies may fall upon him at any moment, he flings himself the more hysterically into action. His only hope is to make the maze more labyrinthine. When the story breaks off, his frenzied digging is no longer guided by a plan and is already beginning to be baffled by fatigue.

That Kafka's anxieties have passed the norm and approached the psychotic in 'The Burrow' is obvious. But there are curious proofs from the story that they have not yet reached the extreme and passed out of control. The first is a bit of symbolic action which shows that they are being kept in check by the sense of security he obtained from his disease. The image of blood from the hero's head, which firmly cements the walls of his storage place for his valuables, reveals Kafka's attitude toward his tuberculosis. Brod has quoted him as expressing relief that it obligated his breaking his engagement, which had dragged on for five years. This passage makes it clear that his later hemorrhages afforded a more active protection of his spiritual values in general. The weakness of physical prostration, by taking the burden from will and consciousness, expiated his sense of guilt, and at the same time, by diminishing his material values as a person, seemed to reduce the liability to attack from without. The progress of his bodily disease, in other words, retarded the progress of his mental disease. The second evidence is the communicability of the story as a whole. Kafka has used no eccentric imagery or artistic language, but the simplest everyday diction. A child could understand the story as readily as an adult. Perhaps its lack of overtone, its lack of the irony I have allowed to creep into my summary, is pathetic evidence of his surviving will to remain sane, of his direct reaching out to an audience he is willing to assume is receptive, is certainly not 'enemies.' Indeed, the suggestion in the story, weak though it is, that the sounds may be imaginary is a literal measure of the degree of sanity remaining; while the complete absence of humor testifies to the desperateness of his situation. But at the same time his capacity to write is not only an unconscious appeal for help; it is also a temporary source of security; it is the part of himself most adequately under control. And paradoxically, since his obsessions have become more simple as they grow more extreme, his stylistic expression of them can give him the satisfaction of becoming more simple too. The simple casualness of the style, its frank colloquial air, is somehow not inappropriate to the abnormality of the content. A complete psychiatric investigation of Kafka would certainly shed light on that *terra incognita,* the nature of the creative talent in more normal persons.

But my problem here is rather with his audience. Presumably Kafka would not have developed as a writer and have eventually written 'The Burrow' if he had not sensed a similar agony in the society around him. The presence of a Kafka cult proves that he was not mistaken. The existence of the story, as lucid as a parable from the Bible, must be taken as an alarming measure of the amount of similar anxiety in the Weimar Republic. If an investigation could be made, I think it would be discovered that a large percentage of Kafka's admirers (excluding of course many critics whose attitude must be in part one of professional interest) share his disorders of personality. In the problem of the relation of literature to its audience, therefore, I believe that Kafka is important evidence as to the meaning of 'esthetic distortion,' 'literary idealism,' the difference, in short, between life and art. In the broadest sense, psychologically, we are permitted to conclude that art brings into the open the latent tendencies of society, whatever they may be. From this point of view, the Kafka cult would not necessarily be composed of persons as abnormal as he, but rather of those who possess similar tendencies which different life experiences may be holding in check or which are in progress of formation and doubtless will be formed more rapidly as a consequence of their admiration. I cannot imagine any other readers accepting Kafka without qualification. These alone will respond to his appeal to aid him by entering the confraternity of the doomed. For the time being, for them as for him, the very lucidity of 'The Burrow' may be consoling. But in the end, content passes out of esthetic control, the story breaks off; art ultimately fails in its attempt to control life.

With more normal readers, the reaction, I think, must be more complex. We live in a period of unusual instability, and the average reader will not wish to add through his fiction to the amount of real anxiety circumstances are forcing upon him. He will reject 'The Burrow' as repulsive, and probably decide the rest of Kafka is also a waste of time. A certain few may find a sadistic enjoyment in a story which seems to present anxieties they are free from. I find my own recollection of the story alternating between a re-experiencing of its disturbing effect, and a protective recoil into humor; to take it as funny is to alienate one's self from contamination. The future will probably take it in similar fashion as a literary curiosity, though only a minority of readers will be interested at all. When we live in a society which permits us to accept its content without a sense of personal threat, it will appear too monotonous to sustain interest. Its concern with only one character, its unvaried repetition of the same motive, will cause its rejection for esthetic reasons. But from this point of view also, Kafka retains his importance for the esthetician, since this story illustrates the wide variation of reaction the same story may arouse in different readers.

One puts aside these later defects of personality in Kafka, and turns with relief to the esthetic defects of his earliest work. Here the shortcomings are of a sort to testify to the initial possibility of normalcy in him. As a youth, Kafka seems to have had his share of our wholesome human desire to meet the world on its own terms, to act and to survive, indeed, to bring, however grotesquely, order out of conflict. He was scarcely more eccentric than the average petty bourgeois youth, anxious to get ahead and dominate other people. As a writer also, he responded to the prevalent and, I believe, desirable practice of leaving whatever intellectual conclusion his novel was reaching to be implied symbolically from the action. But, although these are his aims in *Amerika,* he did not succeed in writing a gracious or even a comprehensible novel. *Amerika* consists of a series of episodes, each clear in itself, but culminating in a fragment the incomprehensibility of which emphatically registers his inability to solve his problem in terms of plot or symbolic meaning. Even though the ultimate failure so graphically presented in 'The Burrow' may be latent here, and the immediate failure is evidence of his apprenticeship in his craft, most of the blame at this time must be put, I believe, on the inadequacy of the social situation, of which Kafka was painfully conscious. The structural defects of the book are Kafka's record of the bankruptcy of what we sometimes call 'the American way.'

As though convinced of the validity of Spengler's thesis in *The Decline of the West* that the European situation was hopeless, Kafka sought to embrace Spengler's opinion that the future of European culture might lie in the United States. He goes in imagination to the country in which bourgeois attitudes have been least checked by aristocratic precedents, in which pragmatic philosophy has endeavored to relate the ideal to the actual without in the least sullying its purity. In contrast to all his later work, *Amerika* presupposes an acceptance of the validity of the objective world, with the concomitant belief that one's ideals must be written into actuality by sweat and blood. Its hero, Karl Rossman, is the only one among his writings to whom Kafka gave a name. The others are unnamed or generalized into 'K.' And he is the only one who is conscious of a certain security in his physical strength. Whatever timidity he possesses may have been due to Kafka's latent masochism, but it is also normal to the inexperience of the adolescent. And it is concealed by a conscious acceptance of aggression as normal in human relationships. In short, Karl accepts the philosophy and psychology of rugged individualism. But like our own political reactionaries, he fears the combined aggression of the working class, since he conceives of the individual worker as a selfish illiterate brute and his labor union as the organization of racketeering to devour society. At the same time, Karl is alarmed and disgusted to find that men of wealth live in a false security. He refuses to avail himself of their friendly offers to work, not merely because he has an adolescent desire to make his way by his own will, but because he cannot trust men who are so obtuse to their real dangers. The millionaire, whose palatial home outside New York he visits, sits chatting in his vast drawing room indifferent to the drafts that blow through it because workmen employed to build a new wing have struck, leaving walls as open to invasion as the entrance to what was later to be the burrow. This attitude may already be a neurotic one, but it has a valid objective basis if one is an industrialist who continues to believe in rugged individualism. In other words, it anticipates the psychology of fascism. It is interesting to note that Karl ceases to worry on another occasion. He has been alarmed at the riotous street meetings of a political candidate; but he calms down when informed that all these disorders mean nothing since the outcome has already been arranged by powerful interests behind the scenes. He does not inquire as to who or what they are; that they are powerful enough to dominate is sufficient for him.

Yet Kafka remains fundamentally an individualist. Stated in political terms, his dilemma was that he could not become a fascist. Not its cruelty, but its apparent denial of individualism prevented. In his concluding chapter, he sought a solution in which the actuality of free competition might lie at peace with the spiritual presence of co-operation. Ruthless competition clearly has bred an unsatisfactory anarchy. The problem was to find some machinery to bring the spiritual and the material together, without corrupting their essentially contradictory character: to provide that competition become spiritually co-operative, and that the ideal chasten the practical like a catalyst without bureaucratic loss of its own integrity. But when one examines the final story of the 'Nature Theater of Oklahoma' (as when one tries to give content to 'the American way'), no tangible program for action can be found. It is impossible to determine whether the mechanism is to be governmental activity or the emergence of some private organization. Whichever it is, the improvement is clearly to be made gradually; the new organization is presumably a model which either will be imitated elsewhere or will gradually and painlessly absorb the functions of other organizations into itself. The title of the new theater suggests that Kafka is giving the naturalistic basis of pragmatism a trial, that he is testing the spiritual possibilities latent in the world of actuality. But the most confident deduction one can make from this ambiguous and fragmentary allegory is that any such approach to the problem is likely to be hypocritical, whether consciously or not. To take the project in the best light, it is probably a well-intentioned hoax. Its instigators, whoever they are (for we never get to the real motivating power in Kafka), are impelled by the delusion that the material and the spiritual can be brought together. Certainly, when Karl and his friends, wearied by the hazards of competition in the East, go, like the latterday pioneers of the New Deal into the West where handbills (such as the Joads had naively accepted) promise employment to all with the initiative to come, they find nothing adequately prepared. To be sure, a dramatic spectacle is being acted at the entrance. But one has positively to fight his way beyond the captivating static beauty of this tableau into the amphitheater behind, where everything is still chaotic. Clerks take down Karl's name, though his qualifications seem uncertain. Not only does nobody know what sort of pageant will be enacted on the cluttered race course; the reader feels an uneasy suspicion that the whole venture, the very project of a theater, is being put into the terms not of life but of some fictive and therefore practically useless if not spiritually delusory allegory of life instead. He is tempted to conclude that to believe the material world can have a spiritual aspect, to imagine that competition can be in any way allied with co-operation is a fallacy. Nor does he know whether it is wisdom on the part of the many that had kept them indifferent to the handbills; or whether the few, like Karl, who have the initiative to venture, are not themselves under the enchantment of 'the American way.'

Now I take it that within the limited social outlook available to Kafka, all this is impressively sane comment. In *Amerika* Kafka's tendencies to abnormality have only freed him from the easy fallacious rationalizations which leave more normal individuals of prosperous bourgeois family in the realm of illusion. American readers will at first sight find Kafka's picture of American life amusingly inaccurate. He is as absurdly uninformed about the surface facts as he is incapable of the surface rationalizations. He knows America only as it is presented in our tabloid newspapers, in which the contradiction between the ideal and the actual glares from every column but is denied to exist on the editorial page. At one and the same time they present our country as the haven of the downtrodden, the land of opportunity, the hope of the future; and as the battlefield of anarchic individualism, of murder and racketeering, of Anglo-Saxon dominance, and the devil's right to the hindmost. The tabloids cut through the veil of distortion which the respectability of other papers draws over this living contradiction between our ideals of democracy and their too frequent violation in our practice. There is, of course, another side to the story, but one does not get it from this quarter, in these simon-pure reflections of petty bourgeois hysteria and inconsistency, the validity of which Kafka could recognize from his foreign land.

When he turned back to the European society he knew directly, however, Kafka became convinced that his observation in *Amerika* was superficial. Men might appear to live in a state of brutal personal competition. Go deeper into their actions, and they are found to be the puppets of a hidden authority. A different kind of Nature Theater, so to speak, is actually in operation. It is only men's trust in it that is delusive. They do not realize that they are helpless under the authority of the evil that controls the material world. So now it is not their competition but their apathy that impresses Kafka: their ignorance of their own dilemma, their indifference to the difficulties of their fellow men. Kafka anticipates the picture of the 'little man' that was to become established in German fiction as one of the types of the Weimar Republic, restless, impotent, insignificant. If he treats him without the usual contempt, but as a tragic figure, it is that he saw in the story of his helplessness the bankruptcy of his own optimism in *Amerika.*

In *The Trial,* the hero, 'K,' a clerk, trusted and expecting promotion for his fidelity, is served in his roominghouse with a warrant for an unnamed crime by two policemen. The officers themselves do not know nor care what the crime is, since their function is only to issue warrants for court appearance. K, thereupon, in his humility and desire to co-operate with the civil authority, drops his business, assumes the preoccupied air of the guilty man, and takes over the function of pushing his case through to a decision. His uncle secures the aid of an important lawyer who assures him, to his surprise, that all legal cases are actually settled out of court by influence or bribery. When neither works for him within a reasonable length of time, he invades the judicial offices where he makes a nuisance of himself since nobody has heard of his case. In due time he begins to grow desperate, not only because his quest remains futile, but because he begins to feel that some sinister authority has been ever-watchful and is becoming annoyed at his anxiety for the speedy triumph of justice. Perhaps this intangible authority may be outraged that so insignificant a man should inflame its own guilty conscience. So K, who has been hypnotized by trust, gradually becomes hypnotized by fear. Finally, two other policemen show up, take K to the edge of town, hand him a knife to slit his throat with, and when he demurs, thrust it home themselves.

The Trial has several layers of symbolic meaning, the most superficial of which I have just presented. It is an exposure of the evils of bureaucracy from the point of view of the common assumptions of democracy. Even though Kafka's experience of a decaying bureaucracy was that of the moribund Austrian Empire, it will apply equally well to the bureaucracy, struggling to be born, of the Weimar Republic. The reader takes it first of all as a trenchant satire upon the delays of justice, the red tape by which the average man may well feel himself strangled in the modern democratic state and its characteristic business corporations, and which the inefficiency of the Weimar Republic merely pushed to the extreme of a tragic burlesque. It emphasizes the sadistic self-importance of some petty officials, the callous indifference of others, until the average citizen appears to get either no attention or abuse for having expected it. But at the same time that the action clarifies this contradiction between our bureaucratic structure and our ideals of democratic equality and individualism, it does not permit us to assume that any evil capitalists are to blame. Though bureaucracy surely defeats the natural aspirations of the common man, there is no assurance that it does anybody good. The fault is in the system, in the fact that life must be organized at all on a practical level. It would perhaps be appealing to conclude that the policemen who finally kill K have been authorized to do so by Nietzsche's supermen. But made sadistic by the system, they may have been acting at their own impulse or in obedience to an authorized or unauthorized command anywhere along the line.

A second level of meaning is perceptible if we take the action as prophetic of the change in the German personality structure as a result of the functioning of bureaucracy under the Weimar Republic. The Republic, it must be remembered, arose after the collapse of an Empire which had functioned fairly efficiently within the surviving forms of feudalism. To defeat in the First World War, therefore, was added the insecurity caused by a graft in government less disguised and more reckless than under the Empire, accompanied by an unsettling confusion of novel ideas and policies. Faltering experiments in social reform and magniloquent pretense of progress alternated with the unexpected fall of the iron fist of police repression. But the little man with his feudal background humbly took the blame for his unhappiness upon himself, believing that only his insignificance prevented his recognizing the remote organizational wisdom that must exist at the top. Indeed, behind apparent inefficiency he felt the abject need for, and could sense the rising anger of, some new external authority that at whatever cost would remove the spiritual burden and the practical uselessness of the new freedom of the Weimar Republic. From this point of view, K's murder symbolizes the final ascendancy of fascism, with its delusive promise of a security beyond good and evil. Psychiatrically, K was waiting to be slain, going out of his way to get somebody else to remove the burden of seeking justice, and the guilt of ambition and the mirage of freedom which had grown so disturbing that the security of individual annihilation drew him like a magnet, only he must, with the pathetic submission of the Bismarck tradition, receive even death as an imposition from above. K's death is thus also this strange novelist's prophecy of the fictive life beyond either pride or humility of the Nazi automaton in which the human spirit has been slain. Here, I believe, the value of the novel for most readers is to be found. It affords us the most complete and subtle delineation of the petty bourgeois German temperament, in which feudal attitudes of obedience were translated into the needs of a belated capitalism under Bismarck; then were confused by the ineffectual democracy of the Weimar Republic; became suspicious of their own dawning self-reliance, and when this self-reliance seemed of no profit either to the individual or to society invited its slaughter and replacement by an even more excessive obedience and submission under Hitler than feudalism had imposed.

But it is a third level of meaning which gives Kafka's own intention in *The Trial.* He used the book to reject his toying with the possibilities of a naturalistic theology in *Amerika,* and to state his conviction that whatever is not spirit is evil. His hero's tragedy is that he repeats Kafka's error in *Amerika,* by seeking to root the spiritual in the material when he acts to promote justice. Governments and corporations, being materialistic, the powers of evil that control the practical world, are naturally aroused by the threat of virtue. Other ordinary citizens who accept the conditions of the material world, that it knows neither good nor evil, and act automatically without idealism or insight, are not molested. One best survives in proportion as he can live as the passive unconscious automaton of the powers of evil, in proportion indeed as he can remain completely in the realm of fantasy as far as our notions of democracy and progress are concerned. K made the mistake of acting in daily life upon principles which are real in the spiritual world but must remain a fantasy in the material. Thus he violated the nature of the material world, aroused the powers of evil that control it, and promoted its revenge in his own death. The theme was fortunately such as to permit *The Trial* to become the only one of Kafka's writings in satisfactory esthetic form. The finality of its conclusion, moreover, is of an order superior to that in other novels with a fatalistic philosophy such as Thomas Hardy's. For there is no emotional ambiguity. The horror and the relief of dying cancel into a state of tranquillity. The book has fulfilled its own laws of inevitability, and we are done with it.

But though *The Trial* adequately explains the source of Kafka's mysticism, it is concerned with only the negative aspect of it and does not illuminate its essentially paradoxical nature. His observation of life had become so cynical that no other escape was possible than the rejection altogether of the importance of the material world. Yet he was so involved in that world that he must reject it both verbally and emotionally in its own terms. His mysticism had the same flavor, as well as the same origin, as Tertullian's despair at the corruption of the Roman Empire. He too was forced to believe what the evidence of his senses had convinced him was absurd. Indeed, his paradox was the more glaring. In the fourth century Tertullian's axiom was less 'absurd' because his era, though disillusioned, had inherited a disposition partial to a mystical view of the world, to which his dogma gave the assent of a man by temper skeptical. But Kafka, living in an industrialized world which had not secured order and happiness at the price of its loss of faith, was overtaken by a bitterness so harsh that he could not let it rise into consciousness. He was forced to bury it beneath the level of emotive expression, to reduce it to a matter of no importance, to grope for belief in spite of its being absurd. He was, in short, compelled to embrace a mysticism which, unlike previous types, subdued the body, neither in the oriental fashion by inducing hysteria, nor in the western fashion by chaining it to will under the authority of abstract logic. His must be a mysticism which justified the paralysis of will and the shrinking back from sensation, by setting up a complete dichotomy between the spiritual and the material life. Against his background of scientific rationalism, to believe the absurd might be eccentric and psychopathic. But for the time being it seemed to make the facts of his experience endurable.

But the absurdity of the paradox has now to be directly faced. Experience was forcing Kafka further into his labyrinth. If *The Trial* had to be written because the optimism lurking in the conclusion of *Amerika* had proved unfounded, *The Castle* had to be written because life was scarcely possible if one accepted only the approach of *The Trial.* Personal salvation demanded that the skeptical view of the world give way to its description through the eyes of faith. The materialistic aspect of man and human institutions, valid and hopeless on its level, sent Kafka hurrying into the burrow of faith, or rather, one should say, into the long corridors of faith. For the priest's parable which K abruptly rejected in *The Trial,* he was to test out in *The Castle* and find wanting. Faith was not really an escape, since somehow the spiritual existed side by side with the material, every person having only this curious relation to every other person that they alike were split into these two essentially unrelated aspects. The new explanation was only a new dilemma. If by definition of humanity itself, the flesh is unescapable, the spiritual must appear to function through the forms of the material. *The Castle,* therefore, is only Kafka's exaggeration of K's mistake (from the theological point of view) in *The Trial.* The quest for God is certainly more comprehensive than the desire for human justice, and the theological dilemma consequently more august. But psychologically, the new situation was less difficult. One knew that the good, unlike the evil, was incapable of revenge. The very fact that one's search was to find out if it really existed to man's perception made life indeed the safer; action banished the misgiving that action might be useless. The average man doubtless did not need to pursue the castle because he was reconciled to the contradictions that life had thrust upon him. Judged by his acts, he seemed to take them for granted, whether he found them within himself or in the outside world. But I think Kafka was right in assuming that this was a view of the situation from the outside; or, at all events, that if it was the true situation, it could not last. Look inside any common individual and he does not have so marked a compulsion to act for the good as led to downfall in *The Trial.* And, therefore, we may imagine Kafka arguing, if the impulse for the good be completely divorced from the practical, if it be taken only as man's quest for the disembodied perfection of God, there can be no revenge from the sources of evil. What he did not see was that he has made life ultimately useless and boresome.

It escaped him because his talent as a novelist was a distraction from the dilemmas of his mysticism. The fascination of the immediate creative task postponed his consciousness of ultimate implacable despair. It reduced the traditional dilemma of mystic communication: that mysticism posits the impossibility of communication at all. If he had lived in the Middle Ages, he would have repeated the thin allegorizing which was the best the medieval writer could achieve in human characterization. But the very skepticism of his age, by obligating the sort of novel in which the human personality must be first presented in all its immediate richness and inconsistency, enabled him to postpone recognition of the fact that *The Castle* was bound to remain another unfinished work. Kafka indeed sensed the inconsistencies in our personalities more keenly than most writers; for they were locked in permanent contradiction within himself. The new interest, furthermore, in the introspective novel with its apparent indifference to the external world of material values must have normalized for him the malady of his personality, by affording him an appearance of escape from the level of *The Trial,* satisfactory for the time being. He could, as a novelist, thus take for the spiritual, as contrasted with the materialistic, the working of our irrational impulses as contrasted with our ordinary habit of living on the conscious surface of experience. By abandoning the consciousness under the joint auspices of the new technique of fiction and his understanding of the mental processes of psychotics, he could delude himself into believing that the presentation of the world as thus transformed was the world of spiritual reality. Doubtless the process was chiefly unconscious. But the result of the process was that, for the time being, the hostility of the actual lost its actuality, became transformed into the cold distance of the objective world as it appears in dreams, as, to the dreamer, it is the actuality hovering on the fringe of consciousness that is the dream. In the dream, for the time being, appears to lie the reality; and to Kafka's satisfaction, if it did not possess the full-blown perfection that faith could hardly require this side the grave, it was at least harmless and impersonal.

Kafka has only transferred his doubts into a realm where they may be handled without emotional disturbance. The locus of *The Castle* is an isolated village high in the mountains. The atmosphere is that of the feudal pre-Bismarckian world, remote and ambiguous. The castle is even higher up, most of the time hidden in the mist and storm of the mountain top, and inaccessible because of the state of the roads. But in the village also, the snow cuts off easy communication and reduces clarity of vision. Winter drives people indoors so that the scene (unlike that of *The Trial*) is never populous. When one breaks through the drifts to reach the peasant's door, it is opened as though suspicion of the stranger were confused with dislike of the cold. Even within the inn, though men crouch resentfully, they are half hidden by the shadows. The author appears to have been as much affected by the cold as his characters are. For he describes all this as though himself experiencing the same partial anesthesia. We scarcely realize, so extreme has the numbness of our sense become, that we are back in the competitive world of *Amerika*. The conviction in *The Trial* of implacable doom has disappeared. But the fact that everybody works for the castle, even though the spiritual must take this inconsistently materialistic form, guarantees to men non-competitive qualities also. Kafka's theology has succeeded in enriching his presentation of men and their social relationships. They are, at last in his novels, fully human, to the imagination of the normal reader, in that they now show what impresses us as being a realistic complexity. They are both aggressive and considerate, both selfish and unselfish. The reader follows their conversation or the description of their actions with the same lively interest in the immediate situation which is certainly the essential characteristic of life itself, and the presence of which in this novel of Kafka's is the secret of its esthetic worth. But the esthetic satisfaction of the narrative has another ingredient in that this liveliness is entirely visual and verbal. The story has the coldness of the Grecian urn, the remoteness of the silent moving picture. Whatever happens we accept without any emotional involvement of our own. If our own emotions could be aroused, the book's flavor would become ironic as we read on. For it turns out that this flash of action and conflicting motive is a chaos. Men seem to act from compulsion and their attempt to understand their action only leads into a maze of speculation. By implication, *The Castle* is a parody on the introspective novel, the elusiveness of our so-called 'stream of consciousness.'

In this benumbed world of Kafka's, though the act is always clear, its meaning and justification remain forever doubtful, and acts, therefore, cannot have coherence when taken together. Now that life is presented in both its spiritual and material aspects, it becomes a bedlam of concrete particularities that lead nowhere. If we go within the single act to discover its motives, the act disintegrates. But it is the same when we pass from act to act. They fail to integrate into a pattern unless the perpetual repetition of Sisyphus' toil can be so described. The reader, for instance, gets the impression that K comes to the village bearing a definite letter employing him as a land surveyor of the castle. But as the book progresses, one begins to doubt whether K received such a letter or only came with the hunch that a job was vacant or thinking he could bluff his way. Nor do the castle officials succeed in clearing away the uncertainties. Possibly a letter had been sent some years ago, but they are positive that there has not been a valid recent communication, and no such official is needed. Yet K, on his side, may well feel that a higher official (if he could reach him) may be better informed; the only guarantee that the bustling official he meets really acts for the castle is his appearance of self-assurance. Even this cannot be trusted, since if one got to know him better (as K did Amalia's brother), the arrogance might only hide his own inner doubts. For Amalia's brother, though he poses as a messenger of the castle, has no assurance that he is accepted as such on the hill. He can only try, becoming in human eyes a hypocrite, in the hope that the castle may reward him for his good intention by a sign that never comes. And since his good intention is often disproved by some human frailty, he lives in perpetual doubt of his deserving the reward he seeks. All this is clear as ecclesiastical symbolism. The existence of the spiritual itself has been reduced to the suspicious dimensions of an intuition within one's own obviously insufficient ego. The individual intuition of the divine has only the verification that other equally fallible persons seem to share it. For, if there is no inspired Bible that Kafka can trust, it goes without saying that he is not aware of the possible existence of an inspired religious institution. The castle is obviously a criticism of the organizational hierarchy in the Roman Catholic Church culminating in the inaccessible recesses of the Vatican. But since Kafka begins by positing the absolute separation of spiritual and material, the book is a broader criticism also of the notion of spiritual hierarchy among men. It is primarily the Jewish-Protestant-mystical tradition that is failing him. Its belief that the inner light, the indwelling of grace, is the only assurance of the possession of divine authority is what paradoxically he can no longer either believe or disbelieve. He cannot reject it because it seems tied up in his own personality and that of other men with the restraining influence of conscience, a reversion from the cruel deed, a reaction against pride into humility. But above all, he cannot reject it because it is associated with his need to secure peace through an act of submission to absolute spiritual authority. Yet his only means of approach to it are through the dubious contradictory channels of the materialistic and the sensory. He attempts vainly to discover just what demands the authority seeks to impose. No act of compliance appears to win its approval. And there is therefore no certain evidence that the authority exists.

Equally devastating is the book's implied attack upon the pragmatic philosophy which is the ultimate lay application of this Protestant tradition. The book acknowledges the validity of the act as clearly as it makes a parody of the 'will to believe.' Always the act is there; what is wanting is any test of its 'working.' From this point of view *The Castle* comes near to being a refutation of James' *Varieties of Religious Experience.* He gets close to shattering pragmatism by bringing into the open its explicit metaphysics, and showing that it rests on the absurd foundation that, despite our inner doubts, we believe because others act as though they do, and belief, thus secured, seems to do us good. Kafka's own mysticism is, in fact, merely an emphasis upon this assumption which the pragmatist makes only to neglect. The pragmatist has been able to neglect it because he has been distracted by the exhilaration of wallowing among particularities which seem to add up to progress. But the misery and poverty of modern life, Kafka saw, have reduced the exhilaration, indeed have transformed it for most persons into despair. At this point he seems to have become aware that the pursuit through the medium of philosophy of this assumption, that the good is what works (when what works is so evidently the evil), lands the thinker in the theory of the useful make-believe, the philosophy of As-If. Though inclined to the same conclusion, Kafka hesitates to accept it. He recoils altogether from formal philosophy into that variant of functioning pragmatism which is the writing of novels and that peculiarity of its theory which accepts without a protest lack of coherent pattern in both our emotional and intellectual life. Pragmatically, the only certainty in *The Castle* is the efficacy of public opinion. Faith has become a superstition in a world where nothing else but public opinion would seem to work, even though it works to the disaster of the well-intentioned. For, as though to prove he had not forgotten *The Trial,* Kafka introduces one coherent episode: the fall of Amalia's family. They are socially ostracized and reduced to beggary for a number of reasons (for nothing is simple in Kafka), but essentially, I believe, because Amalia's father believed in progress, has tried to improve the fire department, and therefore had sought to relate the spiritual to the material aspects of life. His spiritual urge became corrupted into personal pride and ambition, and the revenge of the public upon his pride was the restoration of the hopeless chasm between the two facets of the human personality.

How hopeless it was Kafka seems now to have realized. Once more, as though fatigued by the useless repetition of the same motions, the book breaks off in mid-course, leaving K as far as ever from the castle, which still stands upon its mountain top, sometimes visible to our senses through the mist. But we remain ignorant whether its material appearance justifies our assumption of spiritual power within. Perhaps, as Kafka suggested in a later story, our vision of God is as perverse and inaccurate as would be a dog's assumption of ideal qualities in its master. Kafka had lost his struggle to attain religious faith. The later stories like 'The Burrow' ignore it. Fantasy and hallucination now are the last resort of a man who never had faith in humanity and could never secure a faith in God. His had been the symbolic prototype of the personality traditionally dominant in Germany, and found especially in the middle class that voted Hitler into power. But he was forced to wander into death and madness alone. For Hitler had not yet offered the fantasy of a fantasy in his confraternity of the doomed, who for the time being were able to distort their doom into the hallucination of a glory. We who are more happily situated than Kafka can draw from his novels the desolate pleasure that there too we should have gone if we had been unable to believe in the potentialities of democracy and the common man.

6

Ulysses and the Impasse of Individualism

For some readers James Joyce's *Ulysses* is the great modern novel. Indeed, persons who get this far in the erection of a hierarchy of the best in fiction usually go the whole way and call it the greatest novel of all time. Their reasons for so doing are not irrational. Starting from the assumption that the three best novelists of the twentieth century are Thomas Mann, Proust, and Joyce, they find that *Ulysses* has as good esthetic form as *The Magic Mountain* but is without the pretentious over-elaboration of Mann's style, that self-conscious obtrusion of the author's feeling of superiority to his characters and egoistic control of his narrative which permeates the book. Spontaneity is lacking, that zest for creative writing which seems to take charge of the author's personality in the execution of his plan, however consciously prepared in advance of writing. It is precisely this overwhelming love of writing that is a chief delight in reading Proust, and, despite the appearance of most careful arrangement of material in Joyce, he manages to give the same impression of not manipulating his characters like so many marionettes, but of watching them as they act under their own motive power. But Proust surely sacrificed a sense of proportion in indulging to an extreme this second aspect of the creative process. *Ulysses,* by contrast, combines excellence in both style and form,

Reprinted, with adaptations, through the courtesy of *The Virginia Quarterly Review;* copyright 1941 by E. B. Burgum.

and might well be judged, by one who likes categories, the greatest modern novel.

Whether this attitude be correct or no, *Ulysses* is worthy to rank with *The Magic Mountain* and *Remembrance of Things Past* as one of the three novels which most ably transfer into fiction the idiosyncrasy of a period in western culture which has seen two devastating world wars. But these three authors have another, equally significant element in common. Their work must be taken as a whole, and, as a whole, it becomes a study of a process of social change, which, except in Mann, is without qualification one of degeneration. In Proust this is obvious, because all his novels were planned as a single whole to its exposition. But when Joyce's different works of fiction are assembled in the order in which he wrote them, they too are discovered to form a similar whole.

Most critics would not demur to such a statement. They would approve an interpretation of Joyce's literary career which views him as beginning in *Dubliners* with the traditional acceptance of the objective world as the valid abode of reality, and as later shifting into a more and more complete transfer of the norm of reality into the subjective world of dream and unconscious impulse, which reaches its purest expression in *Finnegans Wake.* With such an interpretation I should agree. But I am inclined to differ with many of those who accept this interpretation when it comes to the particular work in which the transfer of focus is made. I prefer to believe that Joyce rejected a realistic attitude not in *Ulysses* but after it. That other beautiful work of Joyce's youth, *The Portrait of the Artist as a Young Man* (and what masterpieces both of these works would be held if they had not been overshadowed by *Ulysses*), though still accepting the validity of the outer world as ordinarily conceived, is the foil to *Dubliners,* since it is concerned with the young Dedalus's subjective reaction to his adolescent experiences. From this point of view, *Ulysses* combines the two without the sacrifice, yet, of the customary focus. Mr. Bloom (through his very introspection) reproduces that view of Dublin, that sense of objective reality, we got in *Dubliners;* whereas Dedalus brings the subjectivity of the *Portrait* into the larger work. But since it is Bloom and not Dedalus who dominates *Ulysses,* the referent for reality has not yet shifted. In this connection the otherwise unimportant play *Exiles* should be recognized as the connecting link between the *Portrait* and *Ulysses.* Its hero is a Christian first draft of Bloom, while Stephen Dedalus, who was the hero of the *Portrait,* becomes in *Exiles,* as in *Ulysses,* the character of secondary importance.

One of the reasons, perhaps, why we refuse to face the fact of Joyce's essential objectivity in *Ulysses* has been its great influence as the most important, if not the first, novel in the English language using the 'stream-of-consciousness' technique. The publication of Joyce's novel gave this new style of writing a prestige it has only recently begun to lose. We are consequently led to forget, I dare say, that scarcely one-fifth of *Ulysses* is anybody's 'stream of consciousness.' For the greater part, what Bloom and Dedalus experience in their seventeen hours of a Dublin day is taken over by Joyce and presented in the style he thinks appropriate to convey the collective tone of the particular group (and its particular problem) in the particular chapter. Thus is established a complex but definite 'view of Dublin,' of which Leopold and Molly Bloom and Stephen Dedalus form only a part, although it must be admitted to be the principal part. As sensitive a formalist as Joyce would not have been satisfied with a novel composed solely of three contrasting streams of consciousness. And it is absurd to take the notorious final chapter as a submission of the whole narrative to Molly's simon-pure but disconcerting stream of consciousness. We, as readers, do the summing up, surely, even if we do it with the aid of her necessary final information. We, by ourselves, get the unifying thesis that is not found in the personality of any single character, but just as certainly follows from our acquaintance with them all.

But suppose we examine the streams of consciousness that do appear. We must not forget that the method they involve is not ipso facto a mechanism for escape into the inner world of fantasy which an individual may carry around with him. It is not, after all, a stream of unconsciousness; rather it is the apparently dissociated flow of conscious ideas, images, perceptions, which are evoked by external stimuli exciting our various senses and directly or indirectly making contact with the body of our previous experience. The unconscious may become involved, but to the extent that an individual can achieve a scientific attitude or that approximation to it that we call a common-sense view of things, his stream of consciousness, affected of course by certain idiosyncratic interferences, will nevertheless tend to present a fair picture of objective reality. As far as deference to actuality goes, there is no necessary contradiction between this sort of subjective novel and the objective method. Molly's stream of consciousness at the end of the book distorts the facts of her life less than Stephen's does his in the third chapter. The distortion becomes extreme in the 'nighttown' chapter, passes over, indeed, into a more successful stream of unconsciousness than *Finnegan* attains; the whole day's experiences are translated into fantasy under the direct pressure of anxieties and desires previously repressed by the consciousness. They are mostly Mr. Bloom's. But save for this climactic chapter, Mr. Bloom's stream of consciousness is almost abjectly literal. He is ordinarily an individual who has taken seriously what many of us call the best in modern society: the skepticism of a Voltaire, the belief in democracy, the desire for social reform, the respect for science, the striving, as far as personal limitations will allow, for the right sort of relationships with his fellow men. If these are the central traits of the chief character of the novel in his conscious observations and contacts, we need not fear that seeing them through his stream of consciousness will mislead us as to the facts of Dublin life.

If there has been a second reason for mistaken emphasis, the master himself has been responsible. All these years we have been sitting at Joyce's feet with Mr. Gorman and Mr. Budgen and Mr. Gilbert. Authors are likely to be bad critics of their own work because their perspective is distorted by the urgency of some immediate problem of expression. We have paid too much attention to Joyce's conscious statements about his meanings and intentions. Too much of our criticism of him has been an amplification of remarks he himself dropped in the hearing of the rapt and ecstatic few whom he carefully and not altogether naively admitted to the presence. But the effect has been misleading, because what Joyce preferred to talk about was the chapter upon which he was working, or some interest, like place names, not vital to the central meaning. Joyce happened to have theories about the interpretation of Homer's *Odyssey*. Therefore, we have been drenched with full details about the *Ulysses* parallel until we have lost sight of the central fact that it is not simply a parallel but a parallel in reverse. Here, of course, lies the significance. The opposite of everything that happens in *Ulysses* happens in the *Odyssey*. Mr. Bloom is the opposite of the crafty, conquering warrior-king. He meets in his wanderings with contempt or indifference. He appears to resist Circe but he has really lost the capacity to become normally excited. He returns home, knowing that his wife is faithless, that the suitors have been victorious, and that he has lost a son. The parallel in reverse makes glaring the decay in our time of the individual, the family, and the community as integrated social units. Other learned interests in *Ulysses* are not, as in this instance, misused, but are simply irrelevant. Thomism was an influence, and a painful one, upon the substance of the *Portrait*. It was probably the fundamental source of Joyce's insistence upon esthetic structure. But once we get beyond the *Portrait*, Thomism recedes and Freudianism comes in to take its place.

Joyce's cynicism, too, should be put on a broader base than that of simple bitterness of reaction to childhood faith. It was a disillusionment with every possible source of faith, political as well as religious. The Parnell influence is quite as deep-seated in the *Portrait* as is the Thomist. Joyce was of that unfortunate generation born too late to believe in Parnell and too soon to believe in Sinn Fein. His was a world in which aristocracy was either dead or foreign, the poorer classes still besotted, and the middle class not yet risen into power within the Irish Republic. Indeed, the belated rise of the middle class in Ireland was fated to be only the ghost of its heroic rising centuries before in England. Through some fortunate conjunction of personal circumstances, Joyce recognized, as few of his contemporaries did, these devastating truths of practical life. In so doing, he also recognized the belated romanticism of the literary revival: the unpractical restoration of the Gaelic language; the poetry that sought to build a mysticism upon mediaeval survivals; the drama that for the most part could do no better than indulge in droll banter at the superstitions of the peasants, the irresponsibility of the workers, or the quaint provincialisms of the Irish temperament. Joyce saw that he must escape from Ireland if he would understand Ireland, if he would escape the illusions which concealed from his contemporaries of the literary world the stultifying actuality of the situation—which was that their own middle class position did not warrant the complacency made possible by the shallowness of their social perceptions.

Ulysses is Joyce's rejection of this new bourgeois world that seemed to be decaying in the very process of birth. Stephen is clearly the embodiment of Joyce. He rejects this world with an impotent savagery which in Joyce himself is softened into irony because channeled into creative expression. But Mr. Bloom is Joyce too, his non-creative side, masochistic in the absence of any confident talent, pummeled by the thousand contacts of a disintegrating world of business that is too indifferent to him for active hostility. Mr. Bloom is what Joyce might have become if forced by want of creative talent to remain the man in the street. This explains the strange sympathy the reader feels for this helpless creature of habits and aborted good intentions. It is the sympathy Joyce could feel for his incompetent practical self, since the very act of literary expression saved him from that aspect of himself.

But there is another reason why Joyce does not treat Mr. Bloom as sadistically as Stephen Dedalus does. It is that Joyce, thus freed (as Stephen was not) from his weaker side, is in a position to recognize that Bloom is the victim of circumstances beyond his control. Bloom, like all of Joyce's characters, is particularized in great detail, but this should not obscure the fact that he is only an extreme example of the corruption of the personality in a disintegrating society. Ireland, with her long history as one of the earliest of colonial possessions, had become no more than typical of a well-nigh universal process of decay. If Ireland could show the extreme form of this decay, who better could serve as a glaring example of it in the individual than a petty bourgeois canvasser of ads for a newspaper, already qualified as outcast by the unhappy fortune of having been born a Jew as well as an Irishman? Mr. Bloom is generically the little man, the average man of the middle classes.

Here once more it is necessary to dissociate from Joyce's pedantry a common interpretation of *Ulysses,* for the whole thesis of father-son relationship which Stephen presents in the library has been given more significant connotations by Joyce, the author than by Joyce, the critic. Shakespeare, says Stephen, wrote his plays to satisfy on the level of fiction the true spiritual relationship between father and son, which he had not been able to achieve in his own life. Whether or not we have parents living, whether or not we have living sons, what we require is not the blood relationship so much as the certainty of spiritual kinship. As he talks, we know that Stephen is expressing his own inner need, no matter whether his theory is fantastic or plausible as criticism of Shakespeare. What I have been saying is only an extension of this idea first to Joyce himself, to afford him the same excuse as Shakespeare for literary expression, and second, to the whole fabric of modern life through the narrative content of his own novel, *Ulysses*. According to this new Ulysses, the father-son relationship which the Greek Ulysses could adequately recover, in spite of all his wanderings, has vanished from modern society. That men may have physical sons makes only the more conspicuous their loss of the spiritual relationship. It is obvious that the quest for it by both Stephen and Bloom ends in failure. In the 'nighttown' chapter, the fantasy of Mr. Bloom's emotional orgy (for he has been drinking mostly by proxy) foreshadows the impossibility. The drunken Dedalus does not even recognize the identity of Mr. Bloom when at the highest moment of the lonely man's expectation, Mr. Bloom leans over to establish the contact in a whisper of his name: 'Mr. Dedalus! . . . Stephen!' Instead, the phantom of Bloom's own son, long since dead, arises to seal the frustration. But this failure on the level of intoxication (and how universal it is the grotesque parodies of friendship at any bar may testify) must be repeated on the level of sobriety. And so Mr. Bloom, now sober himself, sobers Stephen with food and coffee. The very style Joyce has chosen intensifies the futility of the attempt, for they talk to each other in the stilted question and answer, in the cumbersome impersonal jargon, of a scientific catechism. Stephen now recognizes Bloom with barely concealed aversion, and leaves him, though it is far into the morning and he has nowhere to go. But the ironic anticlimax for poor Bloom, Joyce mercifully discloses to the reader alone. When he gets into bed with Molly, who has shared the afternoon with her lover, she is dreaming how pleasant it would be to seduce a younger man like the handsome Stephen Dedalus. If the wretched man had succeeded in his quest for Stephen's friendship, the reader knows it would have been only to be cuckolded once more.

Doubtless this is the immediate theme of the novel. But it must not escape notice that Bloom's unsuccessful pursuit of Dedalus is only the supreme failure of a day that has been a failure from beginning to end for everybody. In the morning Molly has been reading a letter from her lover while Poldy cooks her breakfast. When his own attention later wanders to other women, it is lack of courage and not virtue that holds him back. He is in a state of vague erotic suspense that he can never pull together into a focus. In the park when Gertie flirts with him, the normal outgoing emotion gets corrupted into self-pity. His sympathy for the woman in childbirth likewise becomes a perversion of his own desire to create someone who will love him. He is equally unsuccessful in his casual contacts. When he passes through the library, no one accosts him, but Buck Mulligan calls after him, 'The sheeny!' At lunch he listens at his table while others sing at the bar. When later he takes a drink, the appearance of friendship disarms him; he breaks into praise of the Jews, and almost gets into a fight. Though he starts a collection for Dignam's widow, he receives so little credit for anything that in the published list we are not surprised to find his name buried towards the bottom and misspelled as 'L. Boom.' In 'nighttown,' what little aggressiveness his heightened emotion gives him, shows itself as maternal protection for the drunken Stephen. For the most part the series of Freudian reveries into which he translates the day's experiences reveal how thoroughly mauled and hated by Dublin he feels himself to be. It is an orgy of masochistic vision.

Mr. Bloom, none the less, is only an extreme example of a universal Dublin experience. Stephen so loathes Mulligan's hostility and Haines's English imperviousness that he refuses to return to common living with them. He is disgusted with his father, who after the loss of his money has become a sentimental toper; and he has refused his dying mother's request for a prayer. The head of his school is an Irish Protestant who underpays him and shares with him the single common bond of hatred for England. Nor has Stephen any greater interest in his students; they are alienated from him by the useless pedantry of their lessons. His father-son theory is received with polite credulity by the literary lights of Dublin, for whose talents he has scant respect. Only when he lies in the street rejecting the Bloom he does not recognize, does he come into unreal temporary reunion with his mother as he drunkenly sings phrases of an old song he once heard from her. He seeks his mother as Bloom seeks him, but he deems Bloom's friendship a degradation.

Indeed, all relationships in the book are either superficial or unsuccessful. We are living in a society where rejection is the norm and men have lost the fundamental basis for companionship. What Mr. Daiches calls 'public truth' has disappeared. There is no common ground of attitude that can be taken for granted. Otherwise, why is the chapter on the viceroy's progress included? The viceroy rides out, ironically enough, with the humanitarian objective of dedicating a hospital in the suburbs. But he has become an empty symbol of order and unity. What his progress denotes, rather, is the complete disunity of the Irish people. For he is greeted in every conceivable way: with sycophancy by those who profit from the English occupation, with hatred by those who remember Parnell; with indifference by the merely curious, with attention only by those who are distracted by magnificence. Some turn their backs on him in passive disobedience; others thumb their noses or mutter unflattering comments in acts of frank but ineffectual rebellion; still others do not recognize him at all until it is too late. The literary style of the chapter (which, as distinguished from anybody's subjectivity, is always the clue to the emotional meaning in *Ulysses*) is the falsetto gentility of the society columns of our newspapers. For all his splendor, the viceroy is as solitary in a hostile world as the haughty young intellectual or the wandering Jewish salesman.

Only in drink or reverie can the illusion of friendship be secured. The universal drinking is not mere local color but a pathetic attempt to create the warmth of some common ideal which can bind men together and satisfy their essential need for comradeship which the actual world, with its cult of competition and individualism, has long since broken down. Someone raises an old Irish song, and the tears fall in sentimental, wasted recognition that the feeling of simply belonging together, which once no man was poor enough or wretched enough to lack, has vanished from the contemporary world. Nor does anybody get consolation from looking ahead, save that among Bloom's useless reveries there float vague images of a better life. When he imagines a prosperous and happy 'Bloomusalem' in the fatuousness of his 'nighttown' dreaming, the grotesqueness of the ideal of progress becomes only the more sharply apparent. In the world of Dublin as it is, to which in *Ulysses* Joyce remains so wilfully and completely anchored, friendship is only pretended and men are withering from the lack of it. Molly Bloom, who has appeared complacent with her leisure, her music, and her secret lover, is no happier than the rest when we look beneath the surface that Joyce ever keeps ironically before us until the final chapter. She too is starved and restless for lack of love, and can find it only in the unreality of illusion. She has already disclosed that she married Bloom years before, not because she loved him but because she felt she could use his placid nature for her comfort. But infidelity has not quenched her romantic craving. She takes refuge in evoking a false memory of those days in Gibraltar against a background of soldiers and blue sea when both of them were young. She pretends that a valid affection existed between them then, and in her dream cries 'yes I will Yes' in a belated and now impossible sincerity of acceptance to an imagined Bloom's offer of his heart.

This cry of Molly Bloom's with which the book ends is as ecstatic and positive as it is unreal. It matches her husband's earlier fantastic and faltering whisper of Stephen's name. But hers is an affirmation and not a weak request; and it is an affirmation of the acceptance of a proffered love. As such, it contrasts with virtually everything that has actually happened in the book. For elsewhere the positive, in Stephen and Buck, has been the surly 'No!' of rejection. The reality of this universal rejection, whatever qualification of tone or intensity it may take on, is thus immensely heightened by the book's ending upon this resonant note, this delusion of rich, full, unqualified acceptance. We cannot take Molly's 'Yes' in any other sense than as the ironic summation of all the sorry existent 'Noes' of a Dublin in social disintegration. Like a keystone that marks and finishes the arch of a book's form, this single final word summarizes everything in a contradiction of its real meaning and emotion. The energy of the affirmation points its falsity. But it also frees the reader for the time being from his participation in the book by leaving him helplessly suspended between the buoyancy of its falsehood and the hopelessness of the true situation.

What one does with the book, therefore, will depend upon one's already formed attitudes. Those who have the certainty of despair will stay with it. The esthetes, enchanted by the marvel of its technical perfection, will find themselves translated, like true saints of decadence, into the world of dreams with Joyce. But those who reject decadence will at least have profited by the encyclopaedic description of it. Nor will they allow this final word of *Ulysses* to shake them loose from the cumulative significance of its discouraging but realistic detail. They will remain conscious of the despair and not be decoyed by the false final hope of the illusory. Nor will they permit themselves to be distracted by another stylistic device that Joyce uses occasionally throughout the book, when he attempts to qualify the gravity of the tragic spirit by the distraction of the animal spirits of the grotesque. It is as though he felt on occasions that the meaning of the book could be palliated if not altogether denied, by a robust excursion into the Rabelaisian. It is as though he sought to make the disorder, which I have interpreted as particular to our period, a universal one which the artist's esthetic consciousness of the grotesque can perennially surmount and vanquish. The Rabelaisian exuberance of *Ulysses* strains at the leash of its theme and seeks to obscure it by the restless, strident irrelevancy of its application. It would give an illusion of vitality to drown by its clamor the stern sad meaning I have isolated.

Now this, I take it, is a very different application of the Rabelaisian spirit from that found in the original. Joyce, in so far as he is a Rabelais at all (and only at a few moments does this form of escapism show itself) is a Rabelais disillusioned, intent upon making his disillusionment universal and impersonal by the gusto of its statement. Thus, the individual spirit of the artist would seek to exempt itself from involvement in the spectacle of the universal bankruptcy of individualism. With Rabelais it was otherwise. He ended his book also with a single word of dubious affirmation. It was not 'love,' however, but 'drink'; and it was an honest ambiguity, not a contradiction. Rabelais commands us to 'drink' because life is truly glorious, and we may ignore its endless possibilities, its immense range of activities now first revealed, since we are safe in the ecstasy of the new immediate interest. We may safely drink to forget the frivolity of boundless aspiration, but we drink also to redouble the expansive powers of the individual spirit as it explores the newly found possibilities of the life about us. Only too well has the Western world obeyed Rabelais's injunction. The Gargantuan spirit of the awakened individualism of the Renaissance has long since become a Frankenstein monster which has now turned from devouring others to devouring himself. Now, after four centuries of drunken individualism, we awaken from our intoxication to find that our ecstasy has cost us love and comradeship and the glory of a common purpose. If Rabelais is the literary record of the birth of individualism, *Ulysses* illustrates its final bankruptcy in the hopeless isolation of the individual spirit.

It has been left to others than Joyce to find a way for Molly's cry of acceptance to be wrested from the world of dreams and restored to the realm of actuality. It has been left specifically, I think, to the novels of André Malraux and John Steinbeck.

But before he turned his back upon the social actuality, for reasons of personal salvation, and entered into the dream world of *Finnegans Wake,* Joyce did us the service of revealing without essential compromise, not merely the Dublin of 1904, but the distraught spirit of the war-torn world as it very largely is at the present time.

7

The Paradox of Skepticism in *Finnegans Wake*

THOSE who have felt the urge to read *Finnegans Wake,* but have run away from the first encounter like boys after wild honey, may now take courage. Messrs Campbell and Robinson have worked out a method for dissecting the hive with a minimum of risk down to the very cell, so that anyone may try the sweet for what it is worth. The authors of *A Skeleton Key to 'Finnegans Wake'* are modest about their accomplishment. As their title suggests, they have given in their 350 pages only the skeleton of the structure of the book. But the lay reader who uses it is bound to have a reaction of bravado. In some respects *Finnegans Wake* turns out to be easier to read than *Ulysses.* With the exception of a handful of Russian, Sanskrit, and Gaelic terms, the foreign phrases used are within the comprehension of any reader with a moderate command of foreign languages. For the style of the novel, whatever the basic language, is grounded in popular speech, whether from the apothegms of folk tradition or from contemporary slang, and generally employs the full grammatical sentence. What, then, are the difficulties? Only the immense patience needed to keep the attention relentlessly fixed upon Joyce's unique word formation, which is a new language in itself. But so fanatic a

Reprinted through the courtesy of *The Virginia Quarterly Review.* Originally entitled 'The Interpretation of Joyce'; copyright 1945 by E. B. Burgum.

patience is hard to maintain as the suspicion grows that the book will not reveal meanings commensurate with the effort to translate them into comprehensible English.

The authors of the *Key* seem to a certain extent in agreement with this attitude, since they have afforded virtually no translations of Joyce's language; and those who expected from it a glossary will at first be disappointed. The *Key* does not explain, for instance, in any systematic way, that 'exsogerraider' means both 'exaggerator' and 'ex-soldier-raider' or that 'chalk full of master-plasters' means 'chuck full of masterpieces of chalk or plaster, i.e. merely casts or fakes.' Their plan is more practical. By reproducing in the running summary of a passage the easiest of these expressions, they introduce the reader to Joyce's way of thinking, and thus facilitate his reading for himself, if he has the time, the energy, and the growing inclination. They have realized that, once one is not reading in the dark from phrase to phrase, but has the aid of knowing the general structure of the book, the translation is bound to come easier.

Finnegans Wake, they tell us, illustrates in fiction the philosophy of Giambattista Vico. This Neapolitan of the early eighteenth century was the first to give a systematic exposition of the cyclic view of history. But his interpretation of it was more like the later one of Spengler than that of Marx or Hegel. His four cycles (theocratic, aristocratic, democratic, and chaotic) merely repeat themselves in new material. Human history, when viewed as a whole, shows no progress. It reveals no accumulation of truth, only the repetition of conflicts between opposites which may terminate temporarily, but are never resolved. The four cycles may represent the limited development of a certain style of personality, of thinking and acting, but one style is not better or more advanced than another, and each disappears in its turn in the endless circle of being. Thus there may be different styles of conflict between man and woman, age and youth, death and waking, love and hate; but the conflicts themselves are essentially permanent.

The authors of the *Key,* however, do not emphasize the fact that the novel elaborates the endless repetition of conflicts rather than their grouping into four cycles. It is to be inferred, nevertheless, from their division of the book not into Vico's cycles, but into family relationships: the parents, the sons, the people, and the return to the parents. The cycles of Vico appear in what seems to me a loose parallel to these divisions. The first of them, which presumably concerns the Finnegan material, covers only chapter one of the first book. But since Finnegan is a hod carrier of contemporary 'democratic' Dublin, what predominates in his portrait is a class representation as though Joyce felt that the 'theocratic' age survived principally among the illiterate lower classes. The greater part of book one brings forward one H. C. Earwicker, a tavern keeper of Dublin, whose spirit permeates the entire novel; and it is through this lower-middle-class person that the aristocratic cycle seems to get a burlesque perpetuation. The tavern keeper has two sons, Shem and Shaun, and the bulk of the narrative is perhaps devoted to Shaun. But the two sons do not so much represent themselves as they become involved in their father's affairs, both as his enemies and as the repetition in a new generation of his qualities. Shem repeats his introvert and creative side and Shaun, his practical man-of-the-world characteristics. The book of the people also is really given over principally to three appearances of Shaun (as Shaun, Jaun, and Yawn), no longer in relation to the family, but rather to the outside world. Though the democratic period seems disintegrating into the chaotic in book three, the latter period reaches its culmination only in the short final book in which Earwicker's wife becomes indistinguishable from the river Liffey. The novel, therefore, does not in any systematic historical way represent Vico's four periods, but is rather limited to the democratic giving place to the chaotic. Finally, the different types of personality associated with Vico's periods appear throughout the work. H. C. Earwicker, for instance, reappears (with different names but the same initials) dozens of times. Though doubtless these reappearances can be grouped into the four types, they stress the infinite individual variations within the types, and so still further weaken any taking of the book as principally an exposition of Vico.

These compromises of Vico are the consequence of a second (and, it seems to me, a more important) level of interpretation of the book, as an illustration of the psychology of Jung. The authors of the *Key,* in their introduction, limit their interpretation to the Viconian level, following the tendency of Joycean criticism to overstress his interest in systems of thought. Actually, he was too good and too modern a novelist to be content with writing mere allegory. He sought to humanize Vico's abstractions, and found in Jung a method which seemed to him to avoid the necessity of sacrificing our ordinary demand for characterization. Since Jung believed that the history of the race remains as a deposit in the unconscious of each individual, to expose the unconscious of a single contemporary tavern keeper would present in acceptable fictive form the history of the race as Vico saw it. This emphasis upon the Jungian level of meaning in the novel is, in fact, the one which permits us to make *Finnegans Wake* the complement to *Ulysses.* The structure of the two books lends plausibility to this point of view. Just as *Ulysses* gives twenty-four hours of the stream of consciousness of Leopold Bloom, *Finnegan* covers a similar interval in the life of H. C. Earwicker. Just as in the 'nighttown' climax to *Ulysses,* Bloom passes into a state of fantasy which is the equivalent of a dream state, so in *Finnegan* Earwicker almost wakes up in the least climactic passage of a book that has no climax but only innumerable moments of tension and release. Certain parallels, it is true, are unescapable. Both heroes are of the lower middle class, as though Joyce believed the transition from democracy to chaos brought the limitations of this group into the center of attention. And both works end with the dream-state of a wife. But here the parallel is deceptive. The norm in *Ulysses* being the world of consciousness, Molly Bloom's affirmation of life, her emotional tone of active hope, is only the falsehood of her dream-fantasy. But the sad, slow, final dreaming of Anna Livia Plurabelle seems to carry the wisdom of passive acceptance of vicissitude and disappointment as the law of life, superior to both the human conscious and unconscious because it is also the wisdom of the river, the law of nature.

This beautiful final passage, then, is the consummation of the book's meanings, and the bridge, therefore, to all the variety of symbolic interpretations by the way. Fortunately, it is written in a simplification of Joyce's special diction, and may consequently perhaps receive the approval it is due. 'A way a lone a last a loved a long a the' the book ends in what is also a beginning. This final sentence summarizes human existence as a series of contradictions, alone yet loved, along a way that, though long, has an end to it. But the final 'the' carries like a coda back to the opening page of the novel, to symbolize the rising of life out of death like the Phoenix, the renewal of conflict after the tranquillity of chaos; just as the river Liffey, after it has reached the loss of identity in the chaos of the ocean, will resume her individuality (different yet the same) as evaporation and rainfall re-create her at the source. For the individuality of the Liffey is measured by the opposition of her banks in the same way as Anna Livia is defined by her relationship to husband and children, and vice versa.

These conclusions, so emphatically championed by the tone of this last chapter, are confirmed by *Ulysses*. And, if there is any validity in invoking the psychology of Jung, a correct deduction can only be reached by taking both works as a single unit. Since Jung believed that the psyche is a composite of both conscious and unconscious, it is necessary to inquire whether the two novels representing these two aspects of the personality contradict or supplement each other. As far as philosophical meanings go, they seem supplementary. The conflicts in *Finnegan* are similar to the rivalry and indifference in personal relationships (what I have called the failure of friendship) in *Ulysses*. The father-son relation fails for Earwicker as well as Bloom. And the apparent contradiction between Anna's renunciation and Molly's ecstatic 'Yes' to life disappears when we see that the preceding action of *Ulysses* has already accumulated a denial of Molly's affirmation.

This beautiful fabric of interpretation is weakened, however, by certain other factors. Molly's 'Yes,' however unrealistic, testifies to her 'unconscious' belief that conflict ought not to be the law of life; and a similar belief that comradeship is a valid end men must continue to crave not only motivates Bloom's pathetic activities, but stimulates the reader's compassion for him. Since this novel is confined to the contemporary world, it sets up the presumption that in some other society these genuine demands of ours may be fulfilled. The minor figure of Dedalus introduces the only qualification, and affords the transition to *Finnegan.* For in Dedalus, the urge is weakening before a growing acceptance of the isolation of the individual. Finnegan pushes to a culmination this disillusionment of Joyce and Dedalus. Since our own period is now recognized to be essentially similar to every other, Joyce is no longer willing to support a hope he has come to regard as wholly fantastic. A devastating cynicism of style would have followed if he had pictured other men as still seeking this unattainable end. He now disassociates both himself and his characters from such a goal. But his Irish sense of humor led him into a rejection of any overt cynicism, and provided that the book, save where Anna Livia is concerned, be read with two simultaneous levels of emotional reaction: the tone of the action of his characters which is one of cool objective description, and the tone of Joyce's reaction to these activities, which is one of wit and humor, ranging from a delicate banter to burlesque, from the crudest nonsense to the most precise anatomy of inconsistency.

The first level he achieved by his use of the theory of the unconscious. Thus he could eliminate from his character the craving for ends and attachments which Bloom so keenly felt, the sense of free will and coherent activity which seems the very definition of the individual ego; and he could instead make our activity appear as incoherent, as automatic and impersonal, as it usually seems in dreams. Thus, perhaps, he violated his allegiance to Vico, who believed that men make their own destiny (under the illusion that they are getting somewhere). Holding no such illusion, Joyce could now depict men as acting bereft of both foresight and hindsight. Only in the Anna Livia chapter is there an exception. The river, old and near the sea, can dare to look back in a generalized way upon the uselessness of past conflict untroubled, aware of both past and present as a single whole, now that neither has any meaning in the face of death.

This change of approach to his theme is abrupt enough to disturb the symmetry of my interpretation. But there is evidence for going still further, and concluding that one part of Joyce was suspicious of all logical patterns, whether Vico's or Jung's. The authors of the *Key* seem to me to admit as much when they call these sentences 'Joyce's world affirmation': 'As Anna was at the beginning, lives yet, and will return, so we dream our dreams till Pappy returns; existence renewing itself. We will not say it shall not be.' I put aside the mystic naturalism which can so easily confuse the particular with the general, the eternal with the ephemeral, and Pappy with the Messiah. For the last sentence shows that we cannot take this belief any more seriously than its opposite. When Joyce dares not deny the possible validity of a belief, he is admitting that he has no criterion of evaluation, and that the dream may as plausibly be the truth as the truth a dream. But if this assertion of complete skepticism actually states Joyce's 'belief' (and I am ready to believe that it does), then the whole fairly elaborate logical structure of interpretation I have been making does not represent any ideological belief of Joyce. *Finnegan,* then, becomes only a single example of esthetic form to give pleasure, one out of countless forms that are possible and possibly true. Its contradiction would be equally possible; and the only argument against it is the psychological one, that Joyce did not choose to write it. And so, if it is permissible to make any philosophical interpretation of the book, I should prefer to regard it as only in certain of the bare bones of its structure, either Viconian or Jungian, but essentially a reflection of that Hindu attitude which views life as aimless activity. Closest to the spirit of *Finnegan* are those Javanese temples (described by Keyserling) every inch of whose outer walls are sculptured until the building is a single mass of intertwined vines and living figures. But at an important point the parallel breaks. The oriental confusion is erotic, somehow comradely, where Joyce's figures are in constant disagreement and rejection, as befits a western version.

But since the conflicts in *Finnegan* are unconscious, they are as empty of hate as of love. Once one is into the book (and no longer looking at its structure as a whole), it sets up an uncanny remembrance of Kafka, both on the emotive and the intellectual levels. In both writers, characters seem fragmentary. They make contacts, but do not really meet. Their lives are a succession of states of immediate sensation, into which the past breaks like a startling (but in Joyce, a constant) interruption. When one turns to analysis of structure, it is curious to find a letter playing the same role in both *The Castle* and *Finnegan*. It is important in the lives of the characters, yet impossible to validate or interpret. But the difference between the two books is as striking as the resemblance. Kafka and his characters, as though there were a still deeper level of the unconscious, are troubled by the elusiveness of truth, which they believe exists somewhere (in this respect there is a parallel with Joyce's uneasiness at the failure of friendship in *Ulysses*), but Joyce in *Finnegan* not only takes for granted that truth is a delusion; he pokes fun at every method which seeks to validate it. If the method is philosophical, you have the burlesque of the quarrels of Catholic and Protestant theologians. If the method is factual, you have the matter of the letter and that of Earwicker's trial, which form the backbone of whatever plot the book may be said to have. The attempts to authenticate the letter not only satirize the lack of common sense in pedantic scholarship; they attack our entire assumption that documents can be validated. The uncertainty as to what happened in the park is equally complete. Did Earwicker commit an act of exhibitionism before some girls as the three soldiers report (or were they soldiers) or did he make perverse advances to them or was it all a frame-up? The reader feels as hopeless of reaching a decision as he does in *The Castle.*

But Joyce doesn't care. Kafka was infinitely saddened by this insoluble situation, and his attempt to get out by following the stages of Kierkegaard's mysticism only made worse his despair since the literary expression which he followed was of the lowest stage. But the fact that Joyce utilized a combination of Vico and Jung not only enabled him (the one philosopher here compromising the other) to admit that the truth might be an illusion, but thus to discard the seriousness of the quest. The prime contradiction in the book is that between the author and his subject. Most of the work is a welter of laughs, ringing out like the discordant chimes of some strange musical scale. They are the belly laughs Joyce utters as he frees himself from the burden of the general plan of the book to plunge into the dialectic absurdities of the particular, into the infinite variety of human folly and inconsistency, now and ever before. Since the chief pleasure of reading a novel lies in the immediacy of the flowing impressions, the appeal of *Finnegan* is the laughter set up by recognizing the sound and meaning of a contradiction. Thus it is very difficult for any key or synopsis to give the flavor of the original. For the purpose of simplification, only one of two or more possible interpretations of a passage is likely to be given. The choice the authors of the *Key* tend to make represents the intellectual rather than the emotive content, though what strikes any naive reader at once is the burlesque element. But Messrs Campbell and Robinson seem bent upon discovering a religious mysticism in Joyce, when he comes as near to a complete skepticism as any author of our skeptical period. The authors of the *Key* (on page 148) paraphrase a short poem as follows: 'Then he traced a little poem about God who is our Home, the consolation and protection of our youth.' But the original reads:

> My God, alas, that dear olt tumtum home
> Whereof in youthfood port I preyed
> Amook the verdigrassy convict vallsall dazes,
> And cloistered for amourmeant in thy boosome shede.*

Here the meaning is certainly not religious nor mystical, but profane and scurrilous. 'My God' is less a reference to deity than a profane expletive, the exasperated tone of which turns to boredom in the 'tumtum' (which also means 'sometime'). Similarly, the bosom shade protecting the boy in the last line is also the shed in which he became acquainted with the bosom of girls. In fact, the essence of Joyce's style is to be found in this particular type of dialectic paradox, where a religious or respectable or serious meaning is buried beneath the cynicism and skepticism of its opposites. For where, one asks, was God when this boy was in the shed?

Difficult as it is, the style of the book, therefore, is an appropriate vehicle for its philosophy of life. When one value is as good as another, when doubt has become so complete that even doubt cannot be taken seriously, living has become a hoax and the pun the appropriate verbal reaction to it. Mr. Earwicker, when all is said and done, is Humpty Dumpty, and *Finnegans Wake* is Joyce's laughter as he sees the king's horses trying to put him together again, as he solaces himself with depicting the kaleidoscope of their shifting incongruities. This theme of the novel is symbolized in the microcosm of each word construction as it comes along. For Joyce's linguistic method is ordinarily to bring together into an apparent relation things which turn out to have only the relation of contradiction, that is to say, no

* Joyce, James, *Finnegans Wake*, New York, 1939, p. 231. By permission of Viking Press.

relation at all. With time and effort, any reader could master these difficult coinages, and spend endless hours reading and rereading the text, feeding his vanity and his superciliousness by his mastery of this very superior kind of double-talk. It is not the nature of the language that causes the intelligent reader to turn away. Rather it is the habits of thinking and feeling the language sets up. A little of it is exhilarating. But after a time our normal expectancy that we live in a world, characterized by its reasonableness and coherence, and essentially capable of order and harmony, must disgust us with Joyce's continual denial of everything that makes life possible and dear to us. The laughter cannot erase the bitter cynicism from which it is distilled. The elegiac beauty of Anna Livia's dying cannot atone for the useless anarchy of living that has gone before.

8

Virginia Woolf and the Empty Room

In 1924, when her reputation had become secure, Virginia Woolf issued an oblique justification of her work. It was in the form of a demand that the English novel recover its traditional simplicity of purpose. A novel, she insisted with refreshing common sense, is essentially a story written to widen the circle of our friends and acquaintances. It is intended to satisfy our natural curiosity about the Mrs. Browns we chance to meet in railway coaches but are forced by the circumstances of travel to leave as anonymous as their names. It breaks through the limitation of our actual relationships to people by extending them on the level of probability. Unfortunately, popular novelists like Arnold Bennett, she said, instead of finding out more about Mrs. Brown herself, were distracted into collecting the thousand and one irrelevant details about what had come to be known as her 'background'; while others, like Mr. Wells, swept her negligently into a boisterous picture of human progress. Mrs. Woolf rejected both of these prevalent conceptions of fiction, which in academic circles are called the naturalistic novel and the novel of ideas. She pointed to the rise of a group of younger writers, including James Joyce and herself, as proof that the restoration of purpose she demanded was already taking place.

In contrast to her novels, Mrs. Woolf's essay was a casual performance, reflecting only one aspect of her practice. A reading of her fiction shows that she drew back as definitely from the excesses of a different sort that developed among the writers whom she admired. She agreed with Joyce, for instance, that 'internal monologue' and unconscious motivation deserve attention. But she refused to burrow so deeply into the inner life of her characters that their contact with the external world became obscure. In her best works, *Mrs. Dalloway* and *To the Lighthouse,* she fixed as the center of interest that area of the personality where the unconscious elements mingle with awareness of the world outside. But if her focus was similar to that of Proust, she refused to distract her reader, as he did, by long analyses of the complex relations behind its apparent clarity. She wished to keep uppermost the sense of movement, of constant shift of actual content, at this focal point. Proust's absorption in philosophy and esthetics might be infinitely more profound than Mr. Wells's flashy dabbling with politics, but both were open to the same theoretical objection. Philosophy of art and philosophy of life she accepted as inescapably the concern of modern man, but the novel should present them as such, as part of the social intercourse of sensitive intelligent people, matters that they talked about when they came together. It was this coming together that she emphasized. Whatever philosophy she needed would be determined empirically by her observation of living men and women, and emerge as the structure of her novel. Form was to be discovered in life and not deduced from airy speculation. The plot of the novel was its discovery, and the theme its general statement. Mrs. Woolf took for granted, like an educated Englishman of her day, the existence of a law of order and sanity in the external world. It was the novelist's privilege to be able to give a sharp direct representation of human relations free from the indirection of abstract statement.

Mrs. Woolf did not articulate these critical ideas partly, it is to be presumed, because their very nature led her to be rather absorbed in the application of them; they developed gradually in the process of her writing. But primarily, I think, she did not express them because she could not bring into her own consciousness the difficulties a writer of the 'twenties faced when he sought only to tell a simple story. The superficial gaiety of her essay is as much a keeping up of her own spirits, as its negative approach is the distraction of an amiable polemic against those writers who had taken the easy way. For certainly, though she is elsewhere a master of the ironic, this paradox here escaped her, that her writers of simple stories were much more esoteric and difficult to follow than Mr. Bennett and Mr. Wells with all their irrelevancies. Even though we accept (as I for one do) her definition of the novel, she never squarely faced the question why writers from Flaubert down to herself who sought to follow it had done so only at the cost of the most excruciating effort. The history of pure fiction shows a constant increase of unintelligibility.

Before she reached this point, she let theory go and buried herself in practice. But once more her practice furnishes a clear answer. The recurrent theme in all her fiction is the hostility of life itself to her ideal. The flaws in the conceptions of fiction she opposes are unfortunately found to be only reflections of similar flaws in society at large. When the writer centers his attention upon that area where the inner life of the personality meets the impact of the external world, the focus of co-ordination he seeks can hardly be said to exist. The consciousness has not only lost touch with the unconscious within; it has secured no more than the conventional co-operation of other persons for the achievement of its external contacts. Having thrust the rich human interest of love and friendship into the background, our personalities have shriveled into the dimensions set by professional ambition, and our relations to the external world have been debased into professional rivalries and shallow social conformities. The order the novelist achieves is the clarification of this actual disorder, and he best attains it when he stands at this focal point where the integration should most strikingly show itself. Consequently, Mrs. Woolf's novels, like her essay, take the negative approach of concern with an ideal that has disappeared, that perhaps (as Proust believed) had never existed on the level of actuality. But there could be no doubt, nevertheless, that it remained the central need of the human personality.

The recurrent theme of her fiction is therefore the loss in the modern world of the Renaissance ideal of the well-rounded man, what our psychology terms the man of well-integrated personality, a loss which affords the novelist the melancholy opportunity to depict people groping for human contacts they are unable to make. What Wells and Bennett were doing as professionals in fiction, substituting the bandying of facts or ideas for human contacts, she realized had become the prevalent practice in the world at large. In place of men and women, conscious of the need for love and the amenities of culture, men, at least, had come to take nothing but business seriously, and to regard business itself as a hostile competition. Mrs. Woolf's interest in feminism was not at all a demand that women get the privilege to shrink their natures within these bourgeois limits, but an assertion that women, bereft as they were of their rights, still retained a more adequate conception and practice of the true ends of living as an older and healthier tradition had understood them.

Her position is an unmistakable inference from the most autobiographical of her novels. In *To the Lighthouse* she accepts Mrs. Ramsay's attitude toward her husband's research as a literary critic. While granting it a measure of respect (for, after all, he is not selling beef), she does not, as he does, conceive it to be the most important of life's concerns. There is more irony than Mrs. Woolf's sheltered position enabled her to be aware of in her making her hero a specialist in culture who worries, like any businessman, lest some competitor surpass his output and take over control of the market of ideas. Mr. Ramsay lives, as she puts it with a revision of Browning, in a mood of vexation because he has only reached the letter 'Q' in the dictionary of literary knowledge and somebody else may get to the letter 'R' ahead of him. But as a Victorian woman (here the paradox of her feminism enters), his wife can only submit and repair the damage to the social fabric from his irritability by a pressure of vigilant tactful suggestion under rebuff, which ultimately exhausts her and causes her untimely death.

I can only take Mrs. Ramsay's death as Mrs. Woolf's unconscious symbol of her own failure to reach her objective. The ideal of right relationships was an obsession with her. Our inability to establish them is, in one variation or another, the theme of all her important work. Early in her career she nurtured the hope that since the tradition of culture had never lost this aim, it might be restored to society. But the longer she writes, the more certain she becomes that society is moving further away from such decencies, and, unlike Proust, she cannot renounce her fealty to the actual world for any compensation in the ideal world of creative writing. She cannot renounce the necessity, that is, for right relationships, too, between the ideal and the actual. If the objective world drifts further from the amenity of these insights, she cannot herself escape the knowledge that she remains a part of that world. The accident of death is the sole escape the inexorable nature of things permits. While her consciousness continues to be absorbed by this problem of human contacts, the idea of death lies more deeply concealed in her unconscious than her habits permitted her to explore. But it was only waiting to come to the surface, when other ties had been broken, as man's final relationship to nature itself.

Mrs. Woolf's initial attempts at fiction had not been promising. Her experience in both living and writing seems to have been inadequate. The value of *The Voyage Out* is the illumination its rather startling failure sheds upon her subsequent writing. If the book escaped without difficulty the fallacy of Mr. Wells, its effort was painful to avoid the temptation of Mr. Bennett. The theme was clearly the hesitation a girl of spirit and breeding felt at yielding in marriage to one of the traditionally dominant sex. It is probably the most important theme for the novelist who wishes to write from a woman's point of view. But Virginia Woolf was unable to accept its challenge. She failed to go within her heroine's personality where the struggle was taking place and where alone her vacillation between marriage and independence could be solved. With so repressed and sensitive a heroine, everything on the surface was either trivial or misleading unless the novelist obtruded an interpretation. Unwilling to inject an evaluation, she was as yet unable to relate her introspective theme to the objective level on which she persisted in standing. She did not give even so much of the subjective struggle as would have rationalized her heroine's falling prey to tropical fever by associating the weakening of her physical system and the impact of her spiritual dilemma. The reader can scarcely sympathize with a girl who from the outside seems merely eccentric and self-willed. Under such circumstances the accident of sudden death was invoked to create a meretricious sympathy for her and a meretricious solution of her problem.

It was to remain insoluble: Mrs. Woolf never returned to so troublesome a theme as love, which, according to her conventions, demanded either marriage or rejection. Henceforth her locus is middle age, when the necessity for decisive action has receded into the past and her heroines need only accept the comfort afforded by conformity to routine. Her theme becomes the regret that persists beneath this placid surface for the intimate contacts which have been refused, or the possibility of making which has not been recognized in the past, and the feasibility of which in the present is beyond both one's energy and imagination. The regret itself, furthermore, tends to be transferred into a sphere where the desired contacts if they are normal, should be less close and passionate than love, the recollection of friendships among children, or that love, sublimated beyond sex, a mother feels for a son or a daughter for her parents. And in this more tepid region, it involves unwittingly the dilemma of women who have drawn back from love: that they seem to expect from other types of contact a parallel intensity. Mrs. Woolf treats these conflicts as though they were the fatalisms in which time enmeshes us; as though the inexperience and the inversions of our early years deprive us of the insight that alone can produce intimacy while the insight of the years has lost the opportunity to apply it. Keen as she is in recognizing the Victorian responsibility for reducing men to a state where they do not even see the existence of the dilemma, she is not similarly aware, until it is too late, that the dilemma itself is the imposition of Victorianism upon the well-bred girl of a later era.

In *Jacob's Room,* sex fades into the background, where it strikes a note of no greater intensity than the pathos of being misunderstood. Jacob's mother, lonely in widowhood, consoles herself with the innocent friendship of another villager with an invalid wife; and is criticized by public opinion. But the main theme has shifted into another region. In Mrs. Woolf's code, widows do not have affairs with some new man, or marry again, or fall in love with their sons, as Freud supposed. Having nothing but their children to focus their emotion upon, however, they feel the insufficiency of the maternal relation with a helpless poignancy which they must conceal and children are in no position to recognize. They have no choice but to watch their sons grow out of the obtuse dependency of childhood into a closer relationship with strangers. They see them leave for Oxford, and strive to share by letter and occasional visits the new world their sons are unaware they desire to enter. If before the estrangement of maturity is complete, war cuts sons off in sudden death, what a mother has left is the physical contact with their now useless personal possessions. Jacob's room, which she has never before seen, is empty. On the floor a discarded shoe (symbolizing the careless rejection of intimacy) brings into full consciousness the fact that she has never really known her son, and whatever of palliation there may be in the knowledge that death has put a stop to the vanity of her desire.

But, within the limitations of her insight, Mrs. Woolf has become for the time being capable of flawless execution. Since the reader sees the mother as much from the outside as she her son, his own emotional reactions to the theme are neutralized this side of sentimentality. The mother has lost what she discovers too late she has never possessed. But since the reader has accepted the postulate from the beginning of never possessing at all, of being content to view from the outside, the book leaves him with only an echo of the mother's desolation. He has not presumed the more intimate contacts the mother has found more and more eluding her. This method of letting a few details symbolize emotions which cannot be directly presented is reinforced by dividing the material into a few large panels of exterior description whose relationships can be subsumed. The acceptance of the convention of the surface as a technique frees the reader from any disturbing identification with the impossible demand of the theme that surfaces ought to be penetrable.

In *Mrs. Dalloway* the relation is reversed. An objective technique is discarded in favor of the introspective method, while the theme accepts the conventionality that to live upon the surface of the proprieties is at all events to keep living, to repress the fear of sudden death (although one's heart is weak), to attain at least a mutuality of superficial contact with others through poise and graciousness. Mrs. Dalloway is an aristocrat trained in self-control. But contrary to the tendency of modern fiction, Mrs. Woolf has given her a richer personality than the widow living on a modest income in a provincial town. On the surface less dependent upon others than Mrs. Flanders, she is more so underneath. And now that Mrs. Woolf has worked out her own conception of the focal point, these more profound meanings can be more precisely expressed.

The theme is stated at the outset as literally as is possible to the stream-of-consciousness method. When a debutante, Mrs.

Dalloway had the choice of marrying the clever, reckless Peter Walsh or the well-connected but stodgy Mr. Dalloway. But she has never been able to free herself of a vague dissatisfaction with her choice of security and convention. Her husband's neglect of her and his contentment with his sinecure in the government, where he has no real responsibility but meets all the important people, have become less and less endurable. She has supported herself through the knowledge that she might have made a different marriage and the fantasy that it probably would have been a more rewarding one. When she reminds herself on the first page that Peter Walsh is back in England and calling upon her that afternoon, she is eager to renew her youthful pleasure in his company with the sense of latent possibilities in her own personality it carried with it. But when Peter actually sits before her fingering his jackknife in the old vulgar, nervous way, admitting that his life in India has been wasted, weakly asking her sympathy for his divorce after an impulsive marriage, she realizes that her alternative choice would have been worse. She becomes aware that a faith necessary to her life has proved a delusion.

But Mrs. Woolf decides to intensify her heroine's despair. At a reception that evening, a psychiatrist casually remarks upon the suicide of a patient in the afternoon, while Peter Walsh was calling upon her. He was an ex-soldier, shell-shocked in the war, of the odd name of Septimus Smith. Though she has never heard of him before, the doctor's tone seems both shallow and cruel. He has built a wall of convention around himself which shuts him off from understanding either other people or himself. She feels in the indifference of this fashionable doctor an intensified version of her husband's indifference to her. To reject sympathy, it now seems, is to continue to live in illusion, to remain unaware of the bitter lesson of experience. She now senses a spiritual contact with a man she has never seen. It may be another illusion; it is certainly a contact of despair, but it goes deeper than proprieties into the reality of things. Septimus Smith in his act of madness was responding to an insight such as hers, only more penetrating and more intolerable. Her defenses are temporarily shattered by this emergence of her unconscious need of a similar suicide, and she disturbs the social pattern by leaving the drawing room. After an interval, habit reasserts its power and she returns to the shallow safety and the apparent reality of polite conversation. But the reader is not certain for how many more years she will be able to endure its futility.

Such is the story that is told with a technical mastery unparalleled in English fiction. Her use of the method of interior monologue is more pure and subtle than that of Joyce. It is also more economical, because she never loses sight of the importance of external contacts, of our normal demand for the elimination of conflicts between the inner and the outer world. The theme of the novel, it is true, is the growing consciousness of an inability to eliminate such conflicts. But interior monologue in Mrs. Woolf is never a static mélange of images, from which the protagonist (unlike the reader) learns nothing. It reflects a process of development within the personality, not a retreat from life, even though the development of this relation between the individual and society be an awareness of the impossibility of an adequate and desirable one, leads, in fact, to its opposite, a dissolution of the bonds quite as disastrous as the illusory integration of escapism. The end desired may not have been reached, but one has the negative assurance that illusion has been torn away.

Mrs. Dalloway proved that the society novel need not remain within the shallow limits of Henry James's deceptive circumlocutions. But Virginia Woolf seems to have felt that there was a limit beyond which it could not pass. Interior monologue used very freely remains the method in *To the Lighthouse,* but it is distributed among several persons so that the whole picture has an objective focus in the social life of a family and its friends. The new story repeats the same theme in a locus less aristocratic and more intellectual. Since this is the social milieu where

Mrs. Woolf was at home, the style is no longer that of cool ironic contrast and ominous undertone, but of a uniform seriousness which is afforded variety by the astonishing breadth of serious allusion, and relief by overtones of ironic counterpoint. The entire range of modern sophistication (save in the sexual sphere) is represented. She did not forget that her brother-in-law was England's leading advocate of pure form in painting, nor that her father was one of the great Victorian literary critics. Within these areas she was as sensitive as Proust: indeed, more so, for she forbade herself the indulgence of satisfying any one of them at the cost of irrelevance. She sought never to lose the sense of the irresistible movement of life in a scene. To Lucy, the painter, watching from the shore, the trip to the lighthouse shows a sailboat with the hard outline of a Manet against the blue sea. But to the reader, this trip taken too late is the very heart of the theme, and Lucy's absorption in its pure form and color a proof of how outside our vital experiences our friends remain.

With the shift of the theme from the aristocracy to the intelligentsia of the middle class, there follows a shift in the nature of the new heroine's defenses. If Mrs. Dalloway was buoyed up by the necessity for complying with a code of perfect manners, Mrs. Ramsay is supported by the Victorian conception of the family. Her first duty is to safeguard its integrity as a social unit. She, it is, who must stem the invasion of bourgeois irritability and Philistinism within the family circle. Since men presume to have more important matters on their minds, the obligation is hers to keep people compatible so that there may be a real interchange of ideas and affections and the possibility of growth of personality. *To the Lighthouse* is therefore virtually a series of tableaux, Proustian in length but not in content, in which Mrs. Ramsay repeats the same function of liaison. She must check her husband's tendency to dominate the conversation; she must see that the young couple's courtship runs smooth and ends in an engagement; she must forestall the crotchety guest's complaints about the food; she must sit patiently on the lawn (since nobody else pays attention) so that the composition of Lucy's painting is not disturbed. It is not the ridiculousness or the futility or the outrageousness of such concerns that commands our attention but the desperate need for somebody to take them seriously. Mrs. Ramsay must continually sacrifice herself to an ideal of genuine human relationship that everybody else is too self-centered to keep in mind.

This positive theme dominates only the first section of the book. After Mrs. Ramsay's death, its negation becomes part of a larger theme of too late and too little. What Mrs. Ramsay has been trying to do, it becomes apparent, has not simply caused her death, but turns out to have been an illusion for which she gave her life. We learn too late not to try the impossible. The present demolishes whatever fantasy of the past was not then exploded but the memory has kept sentimentally alive. Meaningful human communication must always remain a fantasy. Mrs. Ramsay has been striving by exhausting effort to palliate a situation which her nearsightedness (as a symbol) made her fail to recognize was hopeless from the start. She had (when she put her glasses of experience on) a suspicion of the truth. But her brilliant intellectual husband (the feminism is not vindictive) has torn through life in complete ignorance. He had predicted with unction that rain would come to spoil the children's boat ride to the lighthouse. Like Nature herself, he had obtusely enjoyed demolishing their childish illusion of fine weather which his wife had been indulging. And the rain had come. But now, ten years later, he is still victim of the larger illusion which even his children have outgrown. Without Mrs. Ramsay, there can be no completion of the unfinished plan. When their father insists, with old-time wilfulness to do as he pleases, upon carrying it through, he seems to them to be sadistically willing vitality into a dream that is dead. They are all in the boat together, but they are farther apart in spirit than ever.

Mr. Ramsay had been partly right. There was no use in indulging illusions of fine weather. What he did not see was that it was of no use to oppose them either. It was the decree of nature that we are born in the ignorance of hope and happiness, of which experience may be trusted gradually to denude us. For all her sophistication, Mrs. Woolf, bred in the English tradition, could not surrender her English fidelity to nature, her belief in the reality of the objective world. She had begun, as Burke and Wordsworth had taught, by believing in the order of nature, to which men may freely submit because it reveals itself empirically in the established circumstances of living. When the facts made her doubtful of this order, she could not, like Proust, escape to a realm of ideal values existing only in the artist's representation of the external world. Her conception of Nature might change with experience of life, but her fealty must remain. And more and more, as the orderliness and beneficence of Nature and Nature's reflection in the human society became an untenable concept, she accepted Nature as necessity. The process that began in the delusion of hope and produced the melancholy knowledge that human contacts are never vital ended in the annihilation death offered to the individual passion and desire. But she would not break her rule of esthetic form to obtrude such reflections into her narrative where they did not belong. They were powerful enough, however, to demand expression. And the interim of ten years that must be filled in by her giving her reader some awareness of the passage of time afforded her the opportunity. There such reflections prepare the reader to take with less personal involvement the concluding section of the novel by the retreat for the time being into a cosmic perspective, too impersonal to be sardonic, and more definite, more tactful, more cumulatively impressive than the pompous afflatus of Hardy's pessimism.

After Mrs. Ramsay has died and the family moved back to London, night takes over the empty house, concealing its authority in the impish tact of gradualism. It restores a fictive sense of life to things. The wind sets creaking the door that Mrs. Ramsay once had opened, and rustles through her abandoned dresses in the closet. Finally, the darkness, like death, wipes out benevolently the individuality of everything. But daylight restores the facts and provides a melancholy insight. To walk along the beach no longer induces the Wordsworthian inspiration. Nature does not complete what man has begun, but with equal complacence buries the illusions that man has discarded, the hopes he has not yet found illusory, the crudities of statement and of conduct through which he has disclosed his fatal unawareness of the problem. 'With equal complacence Nature saw man's misery, condoned his meanness, and acquiesced in his torture. That dream,' Mrs. Woolf asks, 'then, of sharing, completing, finding in solitude on the beach an answer, was but a reflection in a mirror, and the mirror itself was but the surface glassiness which forms in quiescence when the nobler powers sleep beneath—to pace the beach was impossible; contemplation was unendurable; the mirror was broken.'

She had answered her own question. Death might mean the escape from the need for an answer. But Nature could not satisfy the active demand. The mirror it offered was another fantasy. Men who could not make contact with one another could not make contact with whatever plan or deity might exist behind it. Men must rely upon themselves. They must act, write stories, since to contemplate was fruitless. The restless wind, by breaking the glassy surface of the mirror, negated even the apparent validity of its temporary reflections. But Mrs. Woolf is still able to return to her customary defenses: better than this inhuman callousness, any human contact, however shallow, by use of which men can hide from themselves its more profound deficiency. The frivolity of the unknown old women, who have entered the house to clean it after its ten years' closing, is better. Their presence brings life back, even though it is not the life desired. Nor is it, on second thought, a new life healthily imposed by youth and vigor. These old women, down at the heels, their own lives factitious, are nevertheless wise (like Hardy's peasants) in comparison to their betters in their shrewd recognition of the unexpected demands of Nature and their submission to them. They are real in contrast to the death in movement of the night when the house has been in Nature's gently destructive hands. Their grotesque submission is better than the futile mockery of the boat ride they play their unwitting part at long last in making possible. And yet, by delineating the boat ride that follows (as well as by the suggestion of disdain in their description), Virginia Woolf rejects Hardy's solution. We cannot undo our sophistication and, like peasants, live in the twilight world of platitude. Lucy has the satisfaction of knowing that her picture is fit only to be hung in attics. She has the acrid consolation of the truth.

The truth, however, when it accumulated in all its terrifying bulk, was overwhelming. Believing with the English tradition in the reality of Nature, but believing also from her acceptance of humanism that man, though related to Nature, could not be subservient to it, her bourgeois empiricism afforded her no explanation of connection. She sensed that man should dominate the objective reality of Nature by understanding it, and she saw that a purely scientific understanding was not sufficient, since it shed no light on the important problem of human relationships. She felt obscurely that men could not understand their relationship to Nature while they remained unable to achieve and to understand their human contacts with one another. But she saw the problem as one of individual relationships, as the English evangelical tradition has always seen it, subsuming without inquiry the propriety of class gradation under the dominance of the educated minority, Matthew Arnold's 'saving remnant' and Plato's elite. But the times were changing, and the longer she lived, the more apparent it became that the elite no longer counted.

She found herself borne down by the disintegrating forces. The war and the postwar disorders seemed to her to show not so much that this class or this political system or this aggressor was to blame, as that the whole humanist tradition might be the fantasy of human egoism. Perhaps her esthetic love of order, of relatedness, though it had seemed guaranteed by the tradition of culture, was itself a delusion which Nature was even now in process of corroding. As she saw social distinctions vanish and vulgarity by its sheer bulk impose disorder (so it appeared to her), breeding and intellect counting for naught (since she continued to define them wrongly and look for them in the wrong places), her pessimism deepened. In her esthetic devotion to the sharp image, the waves became a more adequate symbol than the night or the wind or the mirror. We see them gathering off shore in apparent integrity and relatedness; one vast breaker after another rolling in rhythmic succession to dominate the waiting land. But when they get closer, they collapse neurotically into froth, and all we can follow are the thin sheets of water evasively scattering back whence they came over the sand. You look at the dry sand later, and the waves have left patterns. But one who has tried to follow their actual movement knows that the patterns are the static deceptive recordings of an active degenerative movement. They will soon be wiped out again. It is not the power of Nature that is a delusion, but her plan. Art, in sanctifying upon the urn the apparent order of the movement, becomes the final illusion.

She was still enough the artist, even so, to insist upon a pattern for her pessimistic admission that dynamic integrated patterns do not exist. *The Waves* followed *To the Lighthouse.* But the cost of her stubbornness was that ingenuity took the place of insight. Like Proust and Joyce, her attention now became absorbed in what she would have earlier called the irrelevant. But she concealed the fact (as they did), by reproducing with all the more precision the pattern that was lack of pattern which she had found upon the shore. A new finesse in the use of interior monologue now gave a static form of exterior juxtaposition to the casual fickle reality of human intercourse. If in *Jacob's Room* she used a few simple panels of observations from the outside, now she would cut her panels thin and compose them of introspections which show our interior monologue to be as defectively integrated as our external contacts. We begin to see that we are composed of conflicting impulses which scarcely add up to a personality. But the possibilities of this theme remain an allusion. The stress continues on the theme of individual isolation. We now see that each one of us is from birth a hopelessly separate person. Betty Saunders had once thought that her son escaped her own disillusionment in their relationship; now we learn that for the children also there is no escape.

The panels are etched with a precise and delicate stylus, and afford an insight into the child mind which (like Mrs. Woolf's best work invariably) is without parallel in English fiction. But each interior monologue of the half-dozen children in the group discloses that he is seeking to pursue a private end (though with greater wilfulness than accomplishment) while, like any outside observer, he assumes the intimacy of friendship with the others from the fact of physical proximity. Only the shy child is aware of the illusion, and from her penetration into the pretense of the game, she gets the reputation of being the one who is unco-operative. As she grows up, she gathers further proof that she was right. Maturity is to strain and to break even the specious tie of being physically together. It is to accept in practice an alienation our social conventions are perhaps instituted to conceal. We leave for the remote ends of the earth; we develop special interests and professions; we marry persons unknown to the group: so that our chance reunions (our American college reunions, could she have known them) only prove by their hollow ring that we have never really known each other.

The structure of the novel makes the disillusionment almost physically painful to the reader. The thin panels flow in rapid succession, but instead of her weaving them, as Joyce did, into an intricate pattern of confusion, she allows them to scatter in manifold directions which it exhausts the eye to follow. Such a structure, however justified by her theory of the correspondence between life and art, is bound to be esthetically distasteful. By its very consistency, it reinforces the abstract idea of futility with the unpleasant accompanying emotion of scattered effort and disintegration. The ordinary plot of tradition begins with ignorance and confusion and attains integration. This structure reverses the normal. Beginning with the appearance of order, it leaves us exhausted by the effort to follow the winged seeds blown from the physical unity of the pod farther apart in every direction by the indifferent wind.

But events, impinging upon her Victorian respect for the reality of nature and the external world, were tempting her to supplant an individual by a social approach to her theme. Unlike her great contemporaries, there was a limit, which had been reached in *The Waves,* beyond which she refused to pass in her use of interior monologue. She would not employ it to set up an elaborate structure of solely interior imagery to distract attention from the objective disorder. Her one gay and reckless excursus into fantasy took the curious form of an apparently objective history of English culture. But the social awareness that had grown strong enough to produce this *tour de force* of optimism in *Orlando,* now dictated a rewriting of *The Waves* into a sociological novel, to correct the fantasy of triumphant feminism in *Orlando. The Years* was the new testimony that Mrs. Ramsay's generation had gone forever. The specious security of the Victorian family (like the children's intimacy in *The Waves*) had disappeared with the obvious dissolution of the once stable, prosperous Victorian society on the shores of the present.

Daughters of men of title, now dead, their houses sold, accept the situation candidly enough in *The Years,* and try to adjust themselves. They work with such energy as their breeding has left them to earn their living, and live in dirty, noisy Soho. But they cannot effectively adapt themselves to new circumstances. They have neither the energy nor the philosophy. The values they had accepted on faith from Mr. Ramsay, without ever bothering to read his books, are not practicable in the new environment. And they have, like Virginia Woolf, on other grounds than theories of fiction, rejected the daring suggestions which Mr. Wells had been so noisily and eccentrically proclaiming. They have been used to finding their philosophy practiced in their conditions of living, and these have left them stranded among other conditions from which their training has too successfully protected them. They are unable to draw a different kind of stability from their new contacts with the working class. They feel no possibility of communication of strength and friendliness from the way the working class bands together and takes the hard knocks of life. Indeed, their intellectualism, their respectability, the limited gamut of their values, distort the crude energy of clerks and charwomen into a menace where it might have become an ally and a protection.

And so, when the Second World War developed into a catastrophic climax to this confusion, Mrs. Woolf did not find the story of her dog Flush more than momentarily distracting. There were still new facts to be faced, of a kind that could not be ignored. To spiritual disorder was added the stark physical destruction of the London that was as real and loved as flesh to her: St. Paul's bombed, into which she had sometimes sent her characters for a moment's meditation; Buckingham Palace, whence some royal personage had driven in *Mrs. Dalloway* to symbolize the permanent decency of the English tradition, struck by a German bomb. She took her own trip (did she not?) to Hampton Court, like those the children remembered with unalloyed pleasure in *To the Lighthouse,* even though she had then preferred to recall the trip not taken. Here once Elizabeth had held court to heroes in the great serene rooms or talked to poets in the gardens along the Thames. Now there were only a few pensioners hidden in obscure servants' quarters, widows of men who had once increased the greatness of England, now in chill obscurity of exile from useful activity. But no fires burned in the huge ovens. A chill emptiness hung everywhere within, while the old English flowers blossomed in indifferent profusion of beauty outside along the Thames. The faultless Gothic fabric of the building was intact and spotless, but unused. Its dead perfection must have seemed to her to mean that only the dead past could any longer seem to live in England, like the illusions of childhood her novels have bravely torn apart. But destruction willed by human savagery defied Nature's beneficent palliation. The time had come to try that final act of communication which Mrs. Dalloway had pondered but the sanity of Septimus Smith's madness had dared. The time had come to asseverate her ultimate recognition that Nature remains tranquil and dominant in the end. This congruity between her life and her novels she would, as an artist, secure. She would leave her problems for someone else to solve.

9

Aldous Huxley and His Dying Swan

In *Grey Eminence*, prompted by the state of the world and his own soul, Aldous Huxley abandons fiction and writes a biography of the confidential agent of Richelieu. The story is in one respect only the transference of Huxley's cynicism from contemporary events and its confirmation as an empirical generalization of the equally sordid events of the seventeenth century. This turn to history at the same time conceals Huxley's flagging powers as a creative writer, and restores his flair for journalistic appeal. A narrative of diplomatic intrigue, of secret meetings in the dead of night, can be trusted to carry itself. The spectacle of a dirty-bearded bare-footed monk, received with deference by kings and cardinals because he is the unscrupulous agent of the power of France, is worth a Hollywood scenario, and probably will get one, shorn of its cynicism.

But in this book, cynicism is only part of the picture. Father Joseph was a mystic as well as a politician, and Huxley labors monotonously over the contradiction that seems to be involved. He accepts with respect and a little wonder Father Joseph's renunciation of cleanliness and other comforts of the body, his spending long hours in prayer and few in sleep, dedicated in such moods to the escape from sin and reunion with God. What puzzles him is the reason for his abandoning so admirable a life for the sordid affairs of the world. He is not inclined to blame any inner weakness before which the finer urges retreat. He regards such weakness as inherent in human nature, and blames instead, though ever so tactfully (lest he alienate his readers), the Roman Catholic Church. The church, as he sees it, is an institution that must promote such degeneration of motive and hypocrisy of conduct. If the state is frankly an organization to further the base materialistic interests of men, in proportion as religion becomes similarly organized, it becomes subservient to the state and corrupts the spiritual values it is supposed to strengthen.

Huxley's argument can be accepted as valid only if one assumes that every joint activity of men is corrupt because it is in some measure concerned with practical means or ends. It is a melancholy reversal of the Romantic tradition of philosophical anarchism, that man's self-reliance should now appear no longer the source of social amelioration, but the final refuge of virtue in retreat. Huxley's pessimism takes for granted the failure of the ideal of progress. It goes back to earlier Protestant suspicions of the integrity of organized religion, and assumes that the individual soul has the power to resist depravity only when freed from external control. Since contemporary Protestantism is beneath his notice as an instrument, the tolerance of desperation stimulates Huxley's interest in Father Joseph's possibilities as a mystic. But when he turns his tired rationalistic eyes upon the spectacle, it becomes evident that he has shifted his aim from ecstatic union with God to the annihilation of desire. He is forced to go to the Hindu mystics because the West affords no adequate precedent for so negative an ambition. Even the classical tradition of Stoicism is too positive in its emphasis upon the full-rounded integrity of the individual personality. Huxley is still enough of a Puritan to retain some notion of self-discipline, though the aim is for a trance-like state of apathy. He has become the literary spokesman for those pseudo-mystical sects, the cults of Yogi and Gourdjieff, which, like the Mithraism of the decline of the Roman Empire, are beginning to reappear in the decay of European culture.

If one wished to borrow Huxley's cynicism, he might point out that Huxley's new religion only substitutes a more subtle contradiction for the one he finds so painful in Father Joseph. It permits him to continue a not altogether spiritual contact with the world through the writing of books. It does not obligate him to renounce physical comfort; only to take his attention alike from the miseries of the poor and his own prosperity. His books, indeed, become propaganda for the creation of disciples among the well-to-do by justifying in them a similar indifference to the sufferings of others. They thus leave the road free for the extended dominion of a fascism which is bound sooner or later to invade whatever temporary security the new doctrine may have afforded its adherents. But such reflections scarcely need to be pressed. If it is clear that Huxley is now advising this spiritual appeasement of fascism, it ought to be equally evident that he has become too dull and awkward a writer to remain influential. The swan is dead.

Perhaps if material comfort and reputation had not come so easily to Huxley, his style might not have been destroyed and his judgment warped by these spiritual torments. His failure is rooted in his original alienation from the workaday world, and its disastrous consequences he now seeks to avert through making that alienation the more thoroughgoing. His new religion is the rationalist's substitute for suicide. His mysticism is the last resort of a personality too lacking in self-confidence to accept the world on its own terms and so weakened by the moral decay he can vividly sense in others that an aim for nirvana is needed to forestall the collapse of his own defenses. His rapid degeneration is the last chapter in the Romantic agony, as Mario Praz has described it. An account of Huxley's career is therefore desirable not merely because it may give an understanding of these subjective factors, but because the disturbances he is now trying ineffectually to reduce are typical of the intellectual of the 'twenties and because his prescription of a cure might otherwise appeal to esthetes with a conscience today.

At the beginning of his career Huxley laid bare with a charm of style he has long since lost the sensitivities he now finds it necessary to shield. In *Crome Yellow,* you will remember, the hero, though a dwarf, was a man of title, the head of an old country family. He has therefore been able to purchase immunity from the ridicule of ordinary men. He has married an exotic Italian girl of similar proportions and similarly ancient family. They have surrounded themselves with servants who are also dwarfs, changed all the furniture in the ancestral mansion, and filled the hunting stable with Shetland ponies. After several years of happy married life, the couple are blessed with a son. They set to planning forthwith how to transfer to him their own unusual sensitivity and the comfortable recognition of their superiority to the common herd. But to their dismay, as time passes, it becomes only too clear that the laws of nature have asserted themselves against the creation of a better world. Their son grows up into the usual vulgar dimensions. They pack him off to school, as custom requires, but on his holidays the degradation becomes more and more apparent, and it is impossible for his mother and father to escape a sense of strain. On one vacation he brings home with him some school friends. After dinner, under the pretense that the younger generation will have its own affairs to talk about, the parents retire to their rooms. But the father, stealing downstairs when the laughter has become too raucous, observes that his son and his friends have made the little family butler drunk, and are forcing him to dance upon the dining table. He steals upstairs again, and as he lies in bed with his wife, they recall the early years of their romance, and hum once more together the street songs of her native Italy. When he rises to give his wife her sleeping potion, secretly he doubles the amount, and when she is sleeping soundly, slits his wrists in the bath after the old Roman fashion, until the surface of the water is still in arabesques of red and gold.

This narrative of an incident that is supposed to have happened several generations ago is inserted into the middle of a trifling novel of our own period which sags badly under the strain. But the contrast between the two stories is important not solely because it is a contrast between the golden potentialities of the past and the actual crudity of the present, but because the repetition of one character in both stories makes the contrast the more emphatic. The character of the dwarf's son recurs in a youth of another name who is as callous as the son would have been to the telling of his story. It is week-end on the estate of which these dwarfs were once the masters, and which is still owned by their descendants. A low racing car explodes its way to the portico. A tall young Nordic leaps out. One girl in particular of the week-end crowd attracts him, but they are forced to spend a boring evening while their doddering host reads them this story of his ancestors. At bedtime, since the night is hot and everybody save their host is modern, the young folks decide to sleep on the roof. During the night the blond hero leaps the barrier separating the sexes, and the next morning, after a careless farewell to his chance friend, he is speeding on his way to similar exploits at the next country-place.

In this story Huxley wrote with a depth of emotion he was never afterwards to achieve and a directness he has never cared to repeat. Later he was often to restate (but with the substitution of aggressive bitterness for this plaintive demand for sympathy) his assumption of the world's rejection of quality. His later expressions were careful to conceal his consciousness of the personal affront involved. Even in this early work it is obliquely put. But here his sense of the world's wounding him is still too fresh and keen to be controlled. It is barely concealed by the delicate irony that plays about the figure of the dwarf and by the framing of the dwarf's story within a situation which is treated with the biting irony of the later work. The contrasting styles reflect his struggle as a creative artist to free himself from both attitudes. But the nature of this double narrative makes it only too clear that the dwarf represents his essential self while the cold detachment of style in the frame predicts the rallying of his consciousness to disguise the fact. In later works this conscious attempt to control emotion was to promote its expression in perverse or ambiguous transformations. The esthetic quality of *Crome Yellow* is the immediate consequence of the separate and therefore lucid representation of these contradictory demands of reason and feeling, which he can never resolve, and the separate treatment of which here permits emotion its direct representation within the protection of the frame. The structure of the story facilitates its frank appeal for our sympathy in behalf of the weak man who believed himself strong against the strong man who did not know that he was weak.

The subjective reason for Huxley's identification with the dwarf is doubtless that he symbolizes Huxley's sensitivity as a young man in a world that has been taken over by the blond giants. In spite of the ironic style, the dwarf's conviction of his superior intelligence and sensitivity is clearly that of Huxley himself. It is as though he has not forgotten that in his own person he is the mingling of the distinguished blood of the Arnolds and the Huxleys. In his frame, science and culture celebrate the fruit of their reconciliation, which, like the union long ago of the White and the Red Roses, should bring forth a Renaissance in that New World both Matthew Arnold and Thomas Huxley had predicted but which they had fought each other vainly to possess apart. In this instance, to the confusion of idealistic philosophy, history had not repeated itself. The nature of the objective scene made the fact only too apparent that the genetic effort this second time had been a useless gesture. The world was in no state to join hands in a new Renaissance. To Huxley, instead, had been bequeathed the ironic impotence of a Henry Adams with the generations of the Presidents behind him, dwarfed by a world too crude and too hysterically superficial to recognize his symbolic value. *Crome Yellow* is his half-suppressed cry of humiliation, caught in the protective framework which was later to become the whole picture. But one such exposure of his intimate feelings was all he could afford to make. The defenses immediately sprang into action, and *Crome Yellow* was never repeated. Henceforth he was to distract attention by assaults of satire upon his enemies. And so, armed with malice and common sense, Huxley turned his back upon his dwarfs and proceeded coolly to demoralize his blond barbarian. He would fight brutality of body with the brutality of intellect. The strategy was to be what has come to be known as the war of nerves. But to his amazement, the barbarians liked it. They felt at home in such an atmosphere and declared him one of themselves.

It was after the First World War, and they were ready to grant not only that they were a lost generation, but that Huxley was their spokesman, for England at all events. People of education, who had believed themselves the rather exceptional heirs of progress, similarly felt they had been deceived. But though vanity may be assailed, it can never be annihilated. Under such an attack, it sets up in the personality an uneasy division of labor with self-abasement. Huxley became symbolic. He had only mistaken the nature of the symbolism. The blond hero was no longer typical. After the war he had grown up into the Webley of *Point Counterpoint,* and he was despised or laughed at for his delusions of grandeur. Huxley found himself the idol of the sophisticated in a shell-shocked generation. He represented the droll camaraderie of those who reject the loyalty of friendship and are taken for a fraternity only because they share similar habits of thought and conduct. They satirized in others the traits they sought to ignore in themselves. Needing to forget the past and lacking courage to face the future, they followed whatever novelty of sensation might afford the pleasure of not being taken seriously. They proceeded to shock the conventional by any act of nonconformity, and when they found out that conventional persons no longer cared, they satisfied the craving for conventionality in themselves by satirizing their own frivolity in others.

The satire of this period, unlike neoclassical satire for instance, did not have any coherent ideational basis. In a general sense it doubtless expressed the lack of some useful and accepted orientation of society. It grew out of loss of faith in the old ideal of social progress, but it had no substitute to offer. It was content to advertise the hopeless inconsistency of human conduct. The spectacle of social disintegration had the saving grace that one might go down laughing, feeling one's own superiority because of the insight that permitted the laughter. This joyless cynicism also afforded a temporary relief from anxiety because it seemed the only appropriate action. Indeed, this source of support to the ego appeared to offer possibilities of unlimited satisfaction. When standards have become the whims of the moment and are no longer worthy of respect or free from criticism, the revelation of inconsistency can approach the infinite.

Because chastity had been taken seriously by the Puritan tradition, now that the war had wiped out its authority, love became the especial target of the new ribaldry. Persons who, if they had belonged to the American Legion, would have celebrated the new freedom by brawling, showed their cultural superiority by enriching the inheritance from Bohemia. No novelist excelled Huxley for wry delight in broadcasting the flippancy of the sophisticated. Free love in Floyd Dell never lost something of the sincerity of ingenuous first romance. Though Hemingway sought with laconic determination to be as sophisticated as his neighbor at the bar, he could never lose consciousness of the wounded idealism beneath the surface. But Huxley's novels remained garrulously on the surface, and mirrored the commonplace. He was as witty and frivolous, as droll and as daring as one could wish. When remorse seeped in, he molded it ruthlessly into an attack upon those who seemed to lack its crippling influence. He hated every manifestation of power but his own attempt. Normally, however, he provided the rare intoxication of the literal. Life was too distorted to require the distortion of art. His portraits were transcriptions of what everybody saw but could not write, and gave the satisfaction of the *roman à clef* in every gesture and conversation. Both *Antic Hay* and *Point Counterpoint* were composed with the elder Quarles dictaphone and will remain invaluable social documents of the period. But this gay and accurate display of the variety of contemporary frailty could not entirely suppress an undertone of melancholy, which was equally faithful to the real situation. The roisterers, at the end of *Antic Hay,* having left their last party, in lieu of anything better to do, get themselves driven around the park in a taxicab. The episode is an adequate symbol of the disintegration of social purpose in the 'twenties of which Archibald MacLeish has recently complained.

Huxley did make an effort to recover some aim for living by an intellectual acceptance of D. H. Lawrence's philosophy. He recognized that Lawrence was striving to popularize an adequate understanding of the nature of love, which barely survived in the 'twenties, but has been an important current of thought both immediately before and since. The emancipation from Puritanism of the first decades of the century had a progressive as well as a decadent aspect, as the researches of Freud have shown. Within the novel, this growing consciousness that love had been misinterpreted by the bourgeois tradition led Sherwood Anderson into a mysticism which was at all events free from both the pruderies of the Puritan and the new vulgarities of the sophisticated. In England, more stridently and physiologically, Lawrence fell to praising the majesty of the erotic instinct. The need appears to have been too vital in Huxley for the slightest criticism of Lawrence as man or theorist. In fact, of all the characters in *Point Counterpoint,* the only one who is seriously misrepresented in both flesh and spirit is Lawrence. He could have been more easily satirized than anyone else by Huxley's usual process of description of surfaces. Yet in his case Huxley becomes the respectful disciple. In Mark Rampion he pictures Lawrence, not as he was, a nervous, red-headed little man, continually hectored by women, but as he earnestly wished to be, hearty, robust, well poised, William Morris without either his Victorian flatulence of style or his Victorian temper. Lawrence preached his ideal the more extravagantly, the more conscious he became that neither he nor anybody else was practicing it. But he was trying to practice it, and Huxley's pen mellowed into admiration for this real nonconformity which was beyond his own capacity. The 'thirties have taken sex more wisely than either the Victorian or the Bohemian periods. In the light of our present attitudes, Lawrence's religion of sex betrays its neurotic source in its oscillation between a self-centered sensuality and a self-obliterating passage into the spiritual unity of kindred spirits. But for the time being it was a necessary attack upon the assumptions of asceticism. And Huxley's admiration for him testifies that he could not entirely suppress the social conscience of his ancestry.

It nevertheless remains true that Huxley's attraction to Lawrence was not strong enough to affect his dominant attitudes, once the master was out of sight. He reverted to the asceticism of the Puritan tradition, though he had lost the reticence. All expressions of love seemed a vulgar invasion of privacy, and he became perversely eager to advertise them. The followers of Lawrence are actually treated with less indulgence in his novels than an old rake, like the painter Bidlake, who continued the decent hypocrisy of the Victorians about their secret vices or discreet violations of accepted conventions. His admiration for Bidlake may appear flavored with the shyness of adolescent inexperience, but it is also the nostalgic admission that Victorian ways have gone forever. The real source of his scorn for his contemporaries is not that they failed to live up to Lawrence's ideal of love as abjectly as the master himself, but that they have lost the prudent self-control of the Victorians. But Huxley controlled this atavism more sharply than his admiration for Rampion, lest the contradiction in his own personality become too apparent and his conservative side appear too conspicuous at a time of social revolt. If one looks beneath the surface, however, this vacillation of Huxley's between the old and the new morality, between license and standards, made him once more representative of the sophisticates of the 'twenties. Like them he retreated from a difficulty he lacked the capacity to resolve, and for distraction vent his scorn upon the inconsistencies of other men.

So Huxley was satisfied, for the most part, to describe a decadence he shared, and in its own terms. Quite generally the social degeneration was being recognized by novelists. Huxley's distinction from Proust and Joyce was his refusal to penetrate the surface. He is closer to the esthetes of decadence like the earlier Huysmans of *Against the Grain,* though he prefers a more crowded canvas. A thorough investigation might be disturbing, but the immediate perception of the disorder was intellectually fascinating. To make an intricate pattern out of it, as so many of our estheticians have advised, was to escape for the time being from the reality of its pressure. Obedient to the injunction of Somerset Maugham's *Of Human Bondage,* Huxley followed the casual narrative of *Antic Hay* with the pretentious structure of *Point Counterpoint.*

He constructs the form of his new novel with the aid of the conservative reflection that class distinctions are vanishing. The basic melody of the book, which occasionally appears in its simple form, like the bars of a folk song distorted into a jazz symphony by a modernistic composer, is the old Victorian society represented by the painter Bidlake. Its orderly hierarchy of social groupings, under the aegis of bourgeois convictions of propriety, is now being violated in the wanton cacophonies of melodic variation. Openly and secretly members of different classes intermingle, dissatisfied with the values of their normal groupings. Huxley is primarily interested in the twists of temperament seen against these contrasting backgrounds. But the assumption of the narrative is pretty much that the eccentricities are a consequence of this lowering of the barriers. The weakness of old values is symbolized by the drawing room of Lady Tantamount. But if she tries ineffectually to make freaks from other classes at home there, her daughter is more at home in Bohemian circles, and her husband is only at home in his laboratory. The possessing classes like the Tantamounts appease and tolerate, but almost everybody else seethes with jealousy. Little men of the lower classes like Illidge who, in Huxley's conception, have profited by the generosity of the well-to-do, despise the hand that soothes them. Lower middle class hatreds are more violent and directed chiefly at the Illidges below. Spandrell has come to hate society because his mother violated Victorian convention by marrying again after his father's death. The immediate cause, to be sure, for Spandrell's brutality is given a Freudian explanation, and his degrading seductions of young girls claims the immediate attention. But Huxley also depicts the social consequences of his warped individualism. The blond hero of *Crome Yellow* has matured into the fascist leader, Webley, obviously modeled upon Sir Oswald Moseley, whom Spandrell hates as a kindred spirit encroaching upon his own right to do whatever he pleases. But it is curious to note that if Huxley takes grim satisfaction in Webley's murder, it seems to him an equal act of justice that little Illidge should lose his life also. Discontent among the lower classes he views as the pretensions of mediocrity. When Illidge consents to become Spandrell's tool for the murder of Webley, and loses his own life too, two enemies of society have disappeared. Huxley views Illidge's death superciliously as almost a matter of course. But it is worth pointing out that he identifies himself with Spandrell sufficiently to leave him alive, even though the difference between Spandrell and Webley is only that the fascist's depredations have taken a political instead of a sexual direction. Both are essentially sadistic demands for domination. The only domination Huxley fears is the one that might limit his own independence as an intellectual of the middle class.

Despite his interest in counterpoint, Huxley does not clarify the social meanings of these actions. One feels, nevertheless, that the dilemma of Father Joseph is latent in them. A view of life so permeated by the individualism of the bourgeois tradition, so blind to any humane interest beyond that implied in Lawrence's conception of love, suppresses for the time being the conclusion that, if good results from practical activity, it is through the ironic accident of two evils annihilating each other. The destructive elements still preponderate. The present stands in Huxley's eyes between the threat of fascism to individual liberty and the decay of middle-class privilege. When matters get too bad, one goes abroad to forget. The intellectual, like Philip Quarles, can still escape by looking on. He can still bury the undemocratic implications of his own superciliousness by interposing the writing of fiction between his real self and living, even though he is conscious his novels are second-rate.

I must return to the form of *Point Counterpoint*. The novel overflows with the persiflage of wit and anecdote. Yet its variety of incident, the criss-cross of relationships among its characters, does not add up to a plot. An incapacity to solve the social problems I have been alluding to is without question the cause. The consequence is an esthetic failure since the pattern promised by the title is never achieved. Only minor conflicts are resolved in a murder or a rupture of friendship. No development takes place in the totality of relationships. These remain what they were at the beginning, a chaos of contrasts. The melodic theme, as it were, gives rise to a set of separate studies, which have the curious charm of repeating now and again certain minor themes; but there is no attempt to weave them all into a single fugue. For an example of real counterpoint in fiction, one must go to a work whose title is more significant than a purely formal label. The title of Gide's *Counterfeiters* denotes the presence of a dominant idea which permits a truly fugal construction. In Gide the theme of counterfeiting is repeated on different levels. While the boys are distributing counterfeit money, their fathers are disseminating counterfeit justice in the law courts, their mothers counterfeits of Victorian morality in their homes, their brothers counterfeits of love in their adolescent skirmishes, and their friends among the literary critics counterfeits of criticism aimed only to increase their reputation and income. The counterpoint enters when these parallels begin to react, and the parents, for instance, blind to their own hypocrisy, are horrified at their sons' crimes but proceed to shield them. Perhaps in an over-ingenious way, counterpoint also enters when the author confides to his diary within the narrative his first impressions of this universal duplicity, which only the complete plot of the book of which he is a part is finally to clarify. The process of writing becomes an exercise in the use of literary insight to escape the hypocrisy of the theme and to lay bare through its gradual discovery the real structure of the personalities behind the façades. In place of this really contrapuntal construction, Huxley's circles merely overlap, and the minuteness of the overlappings sets up the illusion of their being in gear and movement.

Point Counterpoint represents the culmination of Huxley's creative ability; just as Gide's *Counterfeiters* is the single adequate fulfilment of a more penetrating talent. The plot of Gide's novel is the successful resolution of an inner conflict. The process of discovering hypocrisy in others frees Edouard, the novelist, from the tendency to indulge it in himself. Albeit circuitously, the movement of the book is toward the serenity of candor, the establishment of consistency between the inner and the outward life. But Huxley can only throw the conflicts he is aware of into the satire of juxtaposition, leaving the possible solutions adrift in the aimless narrative. The glitter of this accomplishment postponed the necessity for a settlement. Neither love according to Lawrence nor the mechanism of composing novels about its nonexistence could bring him tranquillity. He was forced to conceal his defeat by projecting it upon society and issuing more and more bitter denunciations of whatever in modern society is not Victorian. Too distraught to be any longer clever, he sought to break his dilemma by main force and sent his malevolence crashing through the wreckage of what had once been a restrained style and a certain ability to create character. He turned to issuing novels of propaganda exposing what he had come to hate as openly as Spandrell. If Jonathan Swift had once loathed the society of men because it was cruel to so many other persons, Huxley now assaulted it because it was becoming a menace to himself.

Undeniably, Huxley's insight into society was growing more acute at the same time that society itself was being transformed with varying degrees of celerity in different places. The disorders of the postwar period were giving way to attempts at regimentation which were most successful in the fascist countries. Huxley recognized that the pressure of industrial organization was to the same end everywhere. But instead of emphasizing the economic causes, he preferred to find the real cause in the disastrous effects of science upon the personality. In *This Brave New World*, science is blamed for herding us into offices and factories and substituting stereotyped banalties in place of thinking. According to Huxley it has deprived us of that sensitivity of feeling in every human relation which the long literary tradition of humanism had exalted and encouraged. But it has been unable to secure complete domination. As a compensation for these rigid conformities, our suppressed emotions burst forth in irrelevant or avenging acts of violence, both literally in the mob spirit and habitually on the level of phantasy in the satisfactions of sensational journalism which play up the excesses of the criminal minority. Though *This Brave New World* is in a measure a penetrating satire of our industrialized mode of life, it was Huxley's personal tragedy that he failed to see the possibility of any but a fascist adaptation of scientific discovery. Any co-operative movement is suspect to him as a form of regimentation; and his only alternative, if suicide be discarded, is the salvation of some form of personal escape.

The difficulty that faced him was not the choice between a spiritual or a physical form of escape, but success at either.

Hatreds become delectable needs of the personality, and Huxley's first attempt was a failure. In the novel I have been mentioning, he retreated physically like Lawrence into a parody of primitivism. He abandoned society for the American desert, though he counterfeited the eremitic tradition by taking along a checkbook. Yet, like the moth, which presumably is controlled by base mechanical instinct, Huxley's hero cannot restrain himself from revisiting this world he hates. Newspaper reporters hound him for an account of his experiment in retirement. The humiliation of this exposure of his sensitive feelings to the mob is more than he can stand, and he commits suicide.

Huxley, apparently determined not to imitate his hero, tried escape again in *After Many a Summer Dies the Swan.* He no longer feels compelled to dwell long in this novel upon a description of the society he rejects. He takes us back once more to the American desert. Since he has no intention of forcing his hero to work for a living by any vulgar grubbing in the earth, he introduces two ameliorative devices. A little shame-faced at being dependent upon the lower classes for domestic services, Mr. Propter expects to reduce the number of servants to a controllable minimum. He expects in due time that most of the work will be taken over by the operation of a mechanical gadget in the form of a domestic model of a machine to harness the energies of the sun. In the meanwhile he is content to harness a little of the energy of a despicable millionaire who very much resembles William Randolph Hearst. Modern society, when reduced to the personal dimensions of Mr. Stoyte, becomes a fairly compact and manageable object of hatred; so that the question of conscience is settled more readily than usual. Granted that Mr. Stoyte is villainous, granted, frankly (as Huxley does), that he is a fascist, Mr. Propter prefers the lesser of two evils. For Mr. Stoyte at least is willing to support Mr. Propter financially and otherwise to afford his unique mental gifts the special consideration they deserve. Communism, he is certain, would be blind to his exceptional qualities and forthwith corral him with the herd. It is difficult, perhaps, to believe that Huxley can be thus naive in arguing for self-interest. But he distracts attention to the figure of Mr. Stoyte, for whose benefaction he vouchsafes the immediate reward of a full length satire. His bestiality and hysterical fear of death are exposed with an equivalent ruthlessness. The process of evolution is pictured as in reverse. Mr. Stoyte is at least halfway back to the gorilla, and even after he has seen a noble earl quite reduced to a gorilla by a special diet that guarantees longevity, Mr. Stoyte jealously mutters that the animal seems to be enjoying himself. Doubtless all this is intentionally symbolic of the depraved aims and personalities of fascists. But perhaps Huxley is not conscious of the broader implications according to which the intellectual is willing to receive the support of what he hates and can conceive that the disloyalty of his hatred removes the stain.

The problem is not yet solved for Huxley. In *Grey Eminence* he recoiled from this hysteria of bitterness, comparable only to the pathological disgust of Swift on the verge of insanity. He suppressed his emotions the more firmly and buried his dilemma the deeper by resort to casuistry. Like this passage into history, his more recent espousal of mystic disciplines to secure good eyesight and peace of mind has banished the hatred by removing the menace of the present at the very time when it is most real. But it has not been able to restore the ruined style, that fragile and limited gift to create character, that play of irony upon the disordered surface of life, which once gave promise of the emergence of a novelist.

10

The Genius of Miss Gertrude Stein

When the name of Gertrude Stein is mentioned, even among informed readers, one query generally arises. She has told us often enough, it goes, that she is a genius. What is there in her work that has compelled others to accept her at her own evaluation? Much of her work cannot be understood at all, and the rest, especially the recent, is altogether too easy to fathom. The query evokes the first of many paradoxes. Gertrude Stein is not only a contemporary writer whose *Wars I Have Seen* appeared during the Second World War; she was also one of the most completely lost of the 'lost generation' of the 'twenties. And earlier still, her first book came in with that upsurge of confidence in the promise of an American culture which got under way shortly after the opening of the century. To appreciate either her significance or her limitations, it is necessary to revive the past.

This first book of hers, *Three Lives,* which was destined to remain her best and most influential work, was published in 1908. It came shortly after the first work of Theodore Dreiser and shortly before that of Sherwood Anderson, in other words, at a time when a new literary movement was exciting attention. And, although by no means enjoying as wide or immediate a reception as the works of these authors, it must be considered in relation to them.

To the public at the time, the new movement seemed primarily the revolt of the Middle West against the dominance of the New England tradition. The attitude of its chief spokesman in criticism emphasized its negative aspect. H. L. Mencken was intransigent in his attacks upon the Puritan ethics and the Victorian respectability which the provincialism of New England had imposed upon the rest of the country. But he also attacked the formal British usages of the New England literary tradition, and in his insistence that a new American language was in the making, he himself disclosed the positive side of the movement. It is now clear that the awakening of the Middle West to an awareness of its own cultural potentialities was a phenomenon of much wider significance. It marked the emergence for the first time of a culture, national in scope, and popular in both diction and content. Just as the American language of which Mencken wrote represented the coming of age of popular usage, the rejection of the mores of New England meant the recognition and acceptance as literary material of the problems and the values of the common man throughout the nation.

In literary history this line of development can be traced back to the pioneer work of Mark Twain. But his lively sympathy for common people receives direct expression only in *Huckleberry Finn,* in a novel presenting American life from the point of view of an underprivileged boy. Elsewhere his submission to the dominant middle-class fantasy of respectability forced him to write from a more shallow level of perception and distorted his style into humor. The effort which it cost to examine with serious candor the life of the man in the street at this period is recorded in the painstaking assemblage of detail in the novels of Frank Norris and Stephen Crane. By the turn of the century both author and audience had become familiar with the new material and language, so that Cather and Anderson and most of their group were able to work more freely. They could write not only without apology or superciliousness or fraudulent idealism, but with more economy and less sense of strain.

Gertrude Stein was affected by this new movement as every American writer has been ever since. But she can hardly be said to have been its active ally. As early as 1912 she moved to France, where virtually all her writing has been done. She soon abandoned the simple style of *Three Lives* under the influence of an exotic foreign experimentalism which contradicted the essence of the American movement. She remained cut off from any significant relationship to her own country until the end of the First World War brought her to the attention of a younger generation of American writers. Even then her influence was destined to remain tangential to the main stream of American writing. Those Americans who became her most ardent and faithful disciples were either dilettantes, unable to write, or writers like Carl van Vechten who continued to write without being affected by either her former or her new technique. Upon the best of these young writers her influence was only a passing phase in the development of their sensibility. Those who were beginning to write in styles as eccentric as her own, like E. E. Cummings, were more influenced by European sources than by her, and more influenced by her mood than her manner. The majority of our expatriates of the period, on the contrary, took for granted their inescapable Americanism and sought from Paris only so much of technical experimentalism as would enable them the more adequately to carry out the promise of an American novel along the lines already set by Anderson and Dreiser. Though the war had intervened to transform their temper, and the optimism that had dominated the work of the earlier group now gave way to the disillusionment latent in it, their attention remained focused on the common man and his language. Hemingway and Dos Passos returned from Europe not having become any less American in either style or attitude, but only the more sensitive to form, the more competent as writers. Gertrude Stein continued to live abroad, cultivating style for style's sake in the most refined European manner. But the Gertrude Stein who had influenced Hemingway was not the woman he visited in Paris, but the one who had long ago published *Three Lives.*

This was in a way to receive a foreign influence. For though Miss Stein's book was a most advanced expression of the American movement in its raw material and diction, in such essential respects as tone and plot and philosophy it seemed to belong abroad. When she wrote *Three Lives,* she did not share Anderson's optimism concerning the potentialities of the laboring class either as individuals who knew how to reach happiness through love or as the group that deserved to dominate society. Nor was she made melancholy like Miss Cather by any respect for those virtues of cheerful acceptance of toil and childbirth which the middle class had lost but poor foreign-born farm hands still retained. Nor did she trust, with Dreiser, in the will of the exceptional individual to rise above class and make his own place in the sun, or in the power of love to survive the failure of will in poverty or alienation. All of these writers of the new school involved themselves in some way emotionally with their themes. But Miss Stein seemed to revert to the scientific impersonality of *The Red Badge of Courage.* In reality she was reverting to the example of Gustave Flaubert. Without the precedent of his *Une Cœur Simple, The Gentle Lena* would probably not have been written. And *Melanctha,* the best of the three stories, is, if one may be pedantic, a variant of *Madame Bovary,* a Madame Bovary of the American Negro who is under bourgeois influences.

It is, indeed, the American ingredients of these stories that make the telling of them seem the more strikingly un-American. The fact that these domestic workers are of a different racial stock from the employing class represented by both author and reader, that they are German and Negro, increases the alienation already imposed by the difference of economic class. Miss Stein is thus not only rejecting the respect the new movement felt for the lower classes; she is also puncturing our earlier literary fantasy that this is the land of liberty and opportunity. She is presenting, in other words, the actual everyday attitude of the

American mistress towards her servants, and ruthlessly representing it as no better than, as identical with, that customary in benighted Europe.

For there are only four attitudes possible in the literary treatment of the lower classes, and each has its record in literary history since the Renaissance. When they are still politically unimportant and without self-consciousness as a class, they appear as unimportant minor characters treated humorously, as in Shakespeare and Fielding. When they have become of sufficient importance in the world of affairs and sufficiently aware of themselves as a group to force the attention of writers, but are not yet a menace to privilege, they evoke a melancholy pity as in Gray's *Elegy in a Country Churchyard.* But when their practical power as a class becomes imperative, they call forth the positive reactions of acceptance or rejection, of admiration or contempt. Such is the general tendency as the history of literature records it, though special circumstances may introduce variants in the case of individual authors or indeed national societies.

The fact, for instance, that the democratic tradition in the United States has never had to compete with and supplant an earlier aristocratic one has imposed an idealism upon our literature which, whether corrupted into fantasy or no, has prevented the growth of a literature of pity. For pity is the emotion which, unlike sympathy, flows from a primary assumption of one's own superiority, of the contrasting security of one's own position in society. Our American assumptions, on the contrary, have denied the validity of class distinctions. They have presumed quite ambiguously but none the less strenuously a law of progress that has riveted everybody's eyes to the top, taken serious attention from the bottom, assumed a better and bigger life for everybody sooner or later. We have generally treated the lower classes, therefore, with an affectionate humor, either, when they are for instance Negroes, because we have given them only passing attention, or, as in the more popular works of Mark Twain, because in the grand confusion of progress, poverty and graft and inefficiency and pain have been held only the passing shadows of a summer day. We have laughed at our own limitations, whether bourgeois or working class, because we have conceived them to be both unimportant and temporary. By the twentieth century, the masses had forced the reality of their special unsolved problems as a class upon our attention, and the reaction of the new movement had been in general the discovery also of their potentialities.

The significance of *Three Lives,* sociologically, therefore, is that it is one of the few pieces of writing in the United States to assume the conservative attitude which was common in Europe. Flaubert's servant, disappointed in her private life, having sunk herself for compensation into abject devotion to the interests of the family she serves, when this tie has been broken and she is forced to live alone in her last years, turns in abject senility to worship her parrot. Miss Stein's servant girls lead lives that are even more drab and stabilized and do nothing to strain the limits of her pity. Like the patient animals of the field, her poor people continue soberly their routine service to their betters until their final return to the soil. They are not potential Miltons kept forever mute and inglorious by the implacable circumstances of life. They are merely persons without talents who arouse pity when the compulsion of a democratic atmosphere forces them into the focus of attention.

Indeed Lena is so gentle and Anna so good that their stories become dull reading. If *Melanctha* is the best of these three, it is because Miss Stein, although accepting the conventional surface, gets beneath it; she no longer views her domestics as their actual employers must have done, but realizes that they have their problems too. These difficulties turn out to be similar to those Flaubert found on a bourgeois level, and *Melanctha* is a surprising analogue to *Madame Bovary.* In this story of two Negro girls, Rose Johnson, pursuing the ideal of a respectable married life, waits with cautious self-control until a man comes along who will provide the security of a home. Her friend

Melanctha, who is of a less calculating temperament, gives herself with a generosity that passes the limits of prudence. The two girls represent what the Romantic generation used to call the difference between the life of reason and that of instinct, what the contemporary American movement was criticizing as a desiccating Puritanism and praising (in the terms of Freud and Lawrence) as the wholesome spontaneity of love.

Miss Stein's position remained closer to the reaction from Romanticism in Flaubert. But her stress is less sociological. In place of hating the low values of bourgeois life, she accepts them without rebellion, and becomes more concerned with the struggle within her heroine's personality. For, though Melanctha is not corrupted into accepting the materialism of bourgeois standards, her fear of them prevents her from making any lasting relationship. It sets up a streak of perversity which holds her back from a marriage like that with Dr. Campbell, in which both the demands of love and those of respectability would seem capable of fulfilment. In other words, behind the action of her novel, through the portrait of Dr. Campbell, one catches a glimpse of the possibility of reconciliation between the demands of love and social responsibility which the Romantic tradition denied, but which our contemporary sociology sets up as a desirable goal. But Miss Stein averts her eyes and prefers to share the perversity to the extent of keeping her attention upon it. The relation between the two lovers becomes a plaintive version of the sado-masochism in that other tired Romantic, Stendhal. Love, in Melanctha, evidently draws back before any tie as a violation of independence, restlessly demands suffering to justify novelty, and confuses novelty with freedom. She wears herself out in the struggle and dies. But though the cramping conventions triumph, our pity remains with the woman who has sought, however futilely, a better life than a shallow conformity.

But as a student of psychology, it was natural for Miss Stein to be more interested in the personality of her heroine than in the situations in which Melanctha was involved. What is surprising is that she is content with so superficial a psychological analysis. She was writing on the brink of the period when Lawrence was to use the simplest proletarian speech to convey the subtlest emotive responses. Yet her psychology was more shallow than that of Sherwood Anderson, who had not studied under William James; for Anderson in *Winesburg, Ohio,* went much further in precise delineation of the hidden motives. Miss Stein actually anticipates his later retreat into naturalistic mysticism, with the Negro as illustration (though she rejects his admiration). She seems to have seized upon the weakest part of James's psychology, and to have been unaffected by the work of G. Stanley Hall and other contemporary founders of psychology. The new science was in process of discovering that the most apparently simple among us is a complex and subtle mechanism, that the nervous system of a child or a shop girl is as delicate and involved as that of a statesman or a millionaire. But James veered away from research of so democratic an implication. He became more and more fascinated by 'the periphery of attention,' more and more hypnotized by those areas where difficulties of investigation justified a recourse to superficial description, and description became a defense of mysticism.

Miss Stein has invariably chosen her own course; she has invariably contradicted the impulse to identify herself with any other person both in the pursuit of her own life and in the composition of her stories. So here, characteristically, though she followed the lead of the master when she grasped for a philosophy of intuition analogous to his account of the religious experience, she did not accept the religious overtones. She substituted the definition of instinct in the literary tradition of Romantic naturalism. She rationalized her shift, in all probability, by deciding that the artist is not a psychologist, but should remain nearer the surface of daily living. Though her rationalization was sound as an esthetic statement, it neglected to take into account the fact that the novelist can give so rich and suggestive an account of the surface that the philosopher and psychologist can read beneath it. Dostoievsky presents life as it flows, but in such a way that the psychiatrist can interpret his characterizations as case histories if he chooses. Miss Stein, like Maeterlinck, preferred a philosophy which permitted her to accept instinct as beyond definition and therefore to present Melanctha's instincts in all the vague mystery they held for Melanctha herself. So far as a theme obtrudes into the story, its presence is a penetration of the mystery. But Miss Stein subordinates theme to characterization, makes this shift in Flaubert's method precisely because she was rejecting *le mot juste* in favor of the suggestive word of Mallarmé and French symbolism. She wishes to evoke a vague state of pity to match the vague state of pleasant revery in the *Afternoon of a Faun.* And whether such is a desirable aim when dealing with a more poignant human material or no, it must be admitted that the result Miss Stein aimed for she beautifully secures, by using the stylization of Melanctha's own natural speech to create the mood of helplessness. The ambiguity with which Flaubert's theme is handled becomes a desirable ingredient for the weaving of her own more objective pattern.

So it is appropriate to the purpose that Miss Stein's stylistic intention should be as definite as her psychology is vague. Though aiming to reproduce realistically an illiterate Negro's limited awareness of herself, the style of Melanctha is not realistic. It does not reproduce the actual vocabulary or cadence of Negro speech. The actual diction is the Anglo-Saxon element in standard English enriched by the addition of modern proletarian idioms as Negroes use them. The cadence of the sentence is also basically proletarian. It is the cadence which Negroes share with other half-educated Americans when they are trying with clumsy self-consciousness to explain or understand something. The characteristic of this ordinary speech (as anyone who has eavesdropped at a street corner will recognize) is explanation by repetition. And the Negro element is that this repetition proceeds without verve or passion, but with somewhat of that slow drawl, on the verge of a whine, which marks the speech of people who have ceased to expect anything from life save drudgery and mistreatment.

'I ain't a bit better than just lots of others of the colored people. You certainly have been unlucky with the kind you met before me, that's all, Melanctha. I certainly ain't very good, Melanctha.' 'Hush, Jeff, you don't know nothing at all about what you are,' said Melanctha. 'Perhaps you are right, Melanctha. I don't say ever any more, you ain't right, when you say things to me, Melanctha,' and Jefferson sighed, and then he smiled, and then they were quiet a long time together, and then after some more kindness, it was late, and then Jeff left her.*

But a little later in the story,

Sometimes now and again with them, and with all this trouble for a little while well forgotten by him, Jeff and Melanctha with him, would be very happy in a strong, sweet loving. Sometimes then, Jeff would find himself to be soaring very high in his true loving. Sometimes Jeff would find then, in his loving, his soul swelling out full inside him. Always Jeff felt now in himself, deep feeling.

Always now Jeff had to go so much faster than was real with his feeling. Yet always Jeff knew now he had a right, strong feeling. Always now when Jeff was wondering, it was Melanctha he was doubting, in the loving. Now he would often ask her, was she real now to him, in her loving. He would ask her often, feeling something queer about it all inside him, though yet he was never really strong in his doubting, and always Melanctha would answer to him, 'Yes, Jeff, sure you know it, always,' and always Jeff felt doubt now, in her loving.

Always now Jeff felt in himself, deep loving. Always now he did not know really, if Melanctha was true in her loving.†

These passages, nevertheless, set up the disturbing impression that the style over-illustrates the meaning and pushes the reader

* Stein, Gertrude, *Three Lives,* New York, 1933, p. 142. By permission of the Modern Library.

† Ibid. pp. 164-5.

to the brink of boredom. However sympathetic to her intention, the cultivated reader feels pulled apart by the contradiction between the inclination to read fast because the meanings are so apparent, and the demand to be read slowly which is imposed by the mere order of the words. There is a discrepancy between the vagueness of the unconscious or intuitional nature of the meanings and the deliberate intention with which the symbols representing these meanings are assembled into a pattern. The story moves as slowly as Miss Stein appears to think is characteristic of the mental operations and expression of semi-literates. The energy of the author which might have gone into psychological insight spends itself in the building of a pattern of words that is much more complex than the meanings require.

Though Miss Stein has started with the authentic patterns of simple working-class speech, she has elaborated them much as the writer of a symphony may ring the changes on a folk melody. Words are repeated in different parts of successive sentences as though they were notes in music. The fact that the sentence is always a simple grammatical unit only emphasizes this planned variation in the placing of its elements. Predicate becomes subject or, by inversion of position, replaces the subject. A clause at the beginning of one sentence shrinks to a phrase at the beginning of the next, and swells into a clause with a phrase within it in the third. In the second passage quoted, the first paragraph is built around the word 'sometimes'; just as a musical passage may seem to grow out of a single chord. The last two paragraphs are similarly built around the word 'always,' and, although the relation of the word to the paragraph sets up an overtone of irony, since the permanence of its idea is so used as to convey both the foreboding of its dissolution and the resistance to its meaning; yet at the same time the reader comes to look for its reappearance almost without regard to meaning as an element in the elaboration of a pure form, like an abstract painting by Picasso. The result is a story which is wilfully planned not to reach an emotional climax or an ultimate idealogical conclusion; just as an abstract painting may be so designed that the eye cannot find itself drawn to an indisputable focus of attention. In addition to the distraction from Flaubert's theme, promoted by our interest in the perverse contradictions within Melanctha's personality, our attention is turned from Melanctha's inner state by a concern with Dr. Campbell, and from the psychology of both by this persistent absorption in pure design. But the interest in pure design is itself qualified by its inescapable involvements with meanings. With such material, apparently, you cannot produce the companion piece to *L'Après-midi d'un faune*.

The escape to Paris solved this dilemma which had kept her from joining the tradition of Mallarmé. For the cult of symbolism in one form or another was the dominant movement there in all the arts, and justified her abandoning her proletarian material in favor of sophistication. New associations promoted her swing from Melanctha to the opposite extreme (in superficial respects at least) of Jean Cocteau. But the decision which her imperious egotism dictated was not reached without a struggle. *The Making of Americans* is a Herculean effort to find literary value in the story of her own family. These well-to-do German-American Jews who preferred to live in a proletarian suburb where they would be the most important people are scarcely more complicated in her account than the poor people who work for them and live in the neighborhood. The fact that there were more of them than in the earlier stories introduced an arithmetical complication which Miss Stein sought to clear up by philosophy rather than psychology. But the philosophy was hardly more august than the statement that, though we are all different, we are at the same time somehow the same. 'There is then always repeating in all living.' The aphorism is only too well illustrated in the texture of this book. An empty verbosity, unrelieved by any successful distraction into pure pattern, quite buries the reader's recollection of Miss Stein's original intention to confess her 'interest in ordinary middle class existence, in simple firm ordinary middle class traditions, in solid material unaspiring visions, in a repeating, common decent enough kind of living, with no fine kind of fancy ways inside us, no excitements to surprise us, no new ways of being good or bad to win us.' But the very extravagance of repetition with which this simple intention is spun out into a novel of great length testifies that the bad new ways were tempting to that part of her which was not 'repetition' of her family but of that other 'family' of the literary geniuses. And she must have found these bad, new ways more satisfying, for the great bulk of her work for the next twenty-five years registers an obsession with them.

The new direction produced works which were less boring only because those with the patience to take them seriously found it so difficult to make anything out of them. Just enough meaning would break through to revive one's flagging energy. Buried in these immediate difficulties, most readers neglected to note the originality of her new intention. For within the field of literature, Gertrude Stein became the most extreme advocate of pure form. The symbolist movement in literature (as opposed to painting), it is too often forgotten, did not aim to set up an awareness of the objective form of a work of art but to stimulate, through the work of art, a subjective state of emotion detached from all practical associations, and of a particular quality as a whole. Symbolism was less interested in the work of art than in its effect and emphasized, not the particular stimuli by which the effect was secured, but the over-all particularity of the final effect itself. In this turn away from the tradition of Mallarmé, the analogues to Miss Stein's new work are not the poems of Valéry but cubism in sculpture and abstract painting. Her aim was to use words like notes in music, and with no little acumen she recognized that the word as sound cannot compete with the musical note, that she must seek for her music not in the tones of the individual words, but in the cadence of their repetition in combination. It was not sound that was to count so much as position. Thus, she strove to divest her prose of verbal meanings not by discarding, like the symbolists, literal definitions in favor of overtones of emotive response in words, not by discarding denotations in favor of connotations; quite in the opposite fashion, she tends to sacrifice the connotation in favor of the denotation when she cannot get rid of both; and the consequence is that she now strips words of their warmth of color or texture, uses for the most part the cold impersonality of denotative meanings so that her form becomes the objective source of a purely intellectual pleasure such as is produced by a game of chess or the solution of a problem in geometry. If meanings, whether logical or emotive, happened to become involved (as of course they must), they set up a different and opposing level of interest; just as, in following music, one may sense the taking of it simultaneously upon two unrelated levels, the one a detached intellectual recognition of objective relationships among notes, and the other, a warm subjective yielding to the pleasant assault of the sounds as they come.

In listening to music doubtless one should bring both levels together into a single experience. And it is possible that Miss Stein sought to do this in her new works, indeed succeeded, according to her private reading. If so, her expression has become so autistic that the outside world cannot interpret it. What the reader senses is an unsuccessful attempt of the one level to suppress the other. By elaborating the most subtle intellectual pattern of words, she is trying to control her confused emotions. But the process defeats its own ends: the rich private meanings cancel out into bare words without apparent significance, except when their cold meaningless pattern is broken by the unexpected emergence of emotions. Probably all sorts of surging emotional conflicts are in constant association with this conscious cerebral willing of pattern; and they relate to the attempt at pattern in various ways; sometimes they seem to dictate a change of the type of pattern needed to conceal them. A portrait by Miss Stein, dead and meaningless as it is to the reader, was undoubtedly to her a highly exciting experience, but it would require the combined aid of a biographer and a psychiatrist to explain it. Here I am only interested in so much analysis as will shed light on the nature of pure form.

Now I take it, the portrait of Hemingway is one of the easiest examples to interpret. The conflict between the two levels is fairly constant and apparent in it, and though there is an attempt at pure form in the one paragraph, the whole portrait approximates our customary conceptions of form, and is obscure chiefly within its separate segments.

> He and They, Hemingway
>
> Among and then young.
> Not ninety-three.
> Not Lucretia Borgia.
> Not in or on a building.
> Not a crime not in the time.
> Not by this time.
> Not in the way.
>
> On their way and to head away. A head any way. What is a head. A head is what everyone not in the north of Australia returns for that. In English we know. And is it to their credit that they have nearly finished and claimed, is there any memorial of the failure of civilization to cope with extreme and extremely well begun, to cope with extreme savagedom.
>
> There and we know.
> Hemingway.
>
> How do you do and good-bye. Good-bye and how do you do. Well and how do you do.*

Although this portrait may seem incoherent according to the usual rules of interpretation, and the phrases certainly do not make sense by themselves, upon second reading one becomes aware of a certain consistency of emotional undertone. The sequence of 'nots' collects emotively into a pugnacious rejection of Hemingway. At the same time certain apparently unrelated

* Stein, Gertrude, *Portraits and Prayers,* New York, 1934, p. 193. By permission of Random House, Inc.

references assemble into such a definition of Hemingway's personality as to justify rejection. Lucretia Borgia, crime, the head hunters of Australia: these references combine to suggest a sadistic ambition in the young author who is surely 'not ninety-three' and 'not by this time' famous, but is governed by an ambition (as wilful as Miss Stein's); for does he not insist upon getting ahead and heading away in his own way? In fact Miss Stein's dislike of Hemingway is so intense that she has to restrain its violence by the prosaic anthropological pun which forms most of the long paragraph, the nature of which we should not suspect if we were unaided by the little pun within of a similar complexion in the phrase 'a head (ahead) any way.' With the aid of the double meaning of this phrase we can also ferret out the double entendre of the entire paragraph; for Hemingway's conception of 'a head,' or good writing, is closer to the barbarians of Australia than to the civilized literary tradition of the English who are trying to restrain them (like Miss Stein, shall we say, Hemingway). Confident that such pride (in another person) must go before a fall, exhausted by her vituperation, and wishing to cover it up, Miss Stein brings her (so un-English) belligerency under control in the coolness of the final suggestion that matters may not be going so well for him as he supposes. How does he really do? Her question answers itself. But at the same time it is a salutation, a return at parting to the specious urbanity of formal greeting.

But one wishes one knew whether she had written the title first or last. For the title reduces the whole portrait to the plaguing naughtiness of a romping child. It is not only a new kind of attack upon Hemingway suggested chiefly by the cadence. The implied thumbing of the nose at Hemingway and the savages is also, probably unconsciously, Miss Stein's dissipation of her own savage attack into a mood of childish frivolity.

Indeed this reversion to a little girl's attitudes of mind and body is repeatedly found in the work of this period. It serves as a *divertissement* to distract the reader's attention when deep-seated emotions begin to break through to the surface. Subjectively, it represents a breakdown of the author's seriousness in grappling with her material. When she finds that the form she has been seeking arouses to a pitch beyond control these passions she does not wish exposed, she solves the conflict by forgetting it. She controls the emotions by abandoning the form she has been pursuing, and substituting a pseudo-form which does not involve them. In a similar way, children break off meaningful games either because they are tired or because they sense the approach of a meaning too much beyond their experience to handle; and turn to a meaningless jumping up and down which has the pseudo-form of automatic repetition. What would in other cases (to one not habituated to form and control) become random movements, bereft of content, are thus simplified into 'pure form.' This stylization of the romping of little girls is psychologically identical with Miss Stein's ultimate of sophistication as an artist. Meanings having vanished, words become mere counters to set up the tranquillizing effects of the ritual of sheer movement.

It will please those with a sense of the incongruous that such a sophistication of pure form is utilized by Miss Stein in her portrait of Jean Cocteau, one of the most decadent and esoteric of her friends among French men of letters. His passion for the perverse is rather inadequately described when Miss Stein writes

Part two and part one
Part two and part two
Part two and part two
Part two and part one *

But the passage is indeed the perfection of meaningless symmetry.

At other times, this automatic repetition is used when Miss

* This and the following quotations are from Stein, Gertrude, *Portraits and Prayers*, New York, 1934, through the courtesy of Random House, Inc.

Stein has not yet warmed up to her theme. The Cocteau piece, for instance, begins

> Needs be needs be needs be near
> Needs be needs be needs be

which introduces the line:

> This is where they have their land astray

which, though quite meaningless to the reader, reads as though it meant a great deal to somebody.

This breakdown of meanings, this tossing aside of a responsibility that has become too heavy for the author, may also take the form of a pseudo free association. It is not true free association because the next word is not suggested by the idea or mood of the present word, but solely by its rime, and is actually often a word of the same type in both sound and meaning. Again the example comes from the Cocteau 'portrait':

> He was as when they had nearly their declamation their declaration their verification their amplification their rectification their elevation their safety their share and there where.

Nevertheless, it must be remembered that, though these practices psychologically represent an evasion of the author's traditional responsibility, esthetically they are also precisely the opposite; they represent an approach to the author's goal of pure form. For, just as the painter senses the danger to pure form involved when he paints a violin, even though he distributes its parts here and there over his canvas, so Miss Stein was aware of the danger that readers might be distracted into trying to find meanings in words like 'declamation,' abstract though they be. An analogy with algebra may have suggested that pure form in words might be achieved if the words could have no other content than to suggest relationships. Since they would then be so related that no relations beyond those of cadence were possible, pure form would be actually reached. And one should not be surprised that Miss Stein's contrariness impels her to reach it in an essay which any other author would have supposed obligated a maximum of fairly precise meanings, an essay, 'Composition as Explanation.' She sums her essay up in a climactic passage that reads:

> Once or twice and for this then they had that and as well as having it so that and this and all and now and believe for it all when they and shall and when and for and most and by and with and this and there and as and by and will and when and can and this and this and than and there . . .

Perhaps Miss Stein is only utterly confused. Perhaps she is trying to say that these are all words very important to writers whose business is with the association of images. What the passage really says is that such words have become an obsession with her; just as an English teacher may become obsessed with grammar or punctuation to the complete neglect of content in a freshman's theme. Unfortunately for lovers of pure form, all that has been left to enjoy, the sheer cadence of words (in this the most meaningless of her writing), is the most unpleasant to the ear. The grouping of sounds is unpredictable, and one who tries to read the passage is constantly forced to correct a false start. The method has revealed its bankruptcy in the very passage which illustrates its perfection, and its bankruptcy in its own terms.

Twice at least, the humorless labors her genius imposed upon her melted away under the sedative effect of the one theme for which her method was unreservedly suitable. On one occasion, in *Portraits and Prayers,* she uses these child rhythms to a beautiful effect. In 'Play,' the theme which advises a return to the joyous irresponsibility of childhood seizes upon the form as altogether appropriate.

> Play, play every day, play and play and play away . . .

But here, it should be noted, the repetitiousness ceases to be automatic, and stylizes by subtle shifts of cadence the sense of freedom in those who have not yet had to face the obligations of maturity.

The idea that people should play and 'remember to play again another day' is universalized in the second example. *Four Saints in Three Acts* (written in 1927 though not produced until 1934) presents religion as the highest form of play, the play in which maturity consummates itself. If such a line as 'Ring around a rosey' suggests that maturity should not be taken as a contradiction but as an extension of the juvenile attitude, this play about saints defines life as a play in lines like 'Let us come to this brink' and 'Let all act as if they went away.' Compere and Commere and the chorus who utter these lines have a dual role, both to play with the saints and to play with interpretation of the saints' words and movements. But the action of these representatives of religion also presents the highest ideal of living as a dignified kind of play. Religion, the polite dance of their incoherent conversation informs us, is the façade of dignity which the discipline of art imposes upon the uselessness of our activities. Maturity only intensifies the gravity with which children assume responsibility for their parts in the game.

Everything constructive in Miss Stein's middle period crystallizes in this discovery of a new relation between art and life. Previously she had recognized that art ought to be pure form without meaning. Now she sees that her denial of purpose in living should have been extended also to include that overzealous purpose to attain the purposeless in art of which she had been guilty. She had forgotten in her own psychology the truth of the little child she had once been, that the end of life is play. With what stolid tenacity had she gnawed in *The Making of Americans* at whatever of complicated philosophy might lurk within the idea that 'there is then always repeating in all living.' Now she saw that if she, with all her genius, could make nothing of the venerable conception of the one and the many, nobody should try to. Like her, they had all been laboring beside the point. Her mistake and the world's had been to take the truism for something more august and explicable than a simple fact. If life is meaningless repetition, we might at least, like children, accept the fact without the tension of further inquiry. To reduce maturity to the dimensions of play would at one and the same time demolish the pretensions of philosophy (as she had previously put psychology in its place) and leave pure form victorious in life as well as art. If she were to reject popular conceptions of the purposiveness of life as she had done those of art, the breach between art and life was healed. She was ready at last to accept the universe. As she herself had stated with dogmatic finality, 'A rose is a rose is a rose,' and no use to explain it.

She should have heeded the lesson of the Dadaists, one may imagine her thinking, and trusted more to her genius. Her intuition had been overwhelmed by the hectic labors ambition had imposed upon her. Distrust of her genius had thrust this self-defeating perfectionism upon her. If life lacked purpose, there was no point to passion, whether that of love or genius. Her genius must be freed from passion as she had long since freed herself from love. Without passion, form was possible; people might then relate, not as she and Hemingway had related, but with grace and dignity because their relatedness had become a façade. There would then be no contradiction between form and content; the form would appropriately become a façade when the content had lost all importance save for its inevitability as material for the satisfaction of the form. Joyce, obsessed by the error that he would profit, whether as an artist or a man, from his reading of Jung and Vico, by this pursuit of meaning to disprove meaning, had of course fallen victim to meaning. No wonder, then, that his mistakened conception of form fairly provoked a content of emotional disorders. The hilarious, the angry jostling of his characters in *Finnegans Wake* implied a striving to meet and merge even as the form of the novel logically proved the impossibility. What was a pattern for, if not to permit people to remain tranquilly within themselves in the very appearance of their meeting?

But at the same time that *Four Saints in Three Acts* would eliminate the incongruity of so much cerebral effort as Joyce required, Miss Stein's genius informed her that the patter of the Dadaists resembled the random activity of children rather than their conscious pleasure in erecting the façade of the game. If writing was not simple automatic activity (as she declared she had never believed it to be), neither was living, properly conceived. The pleasure in the long run was not in chaos but in order. Intuition was not enough, as Melanctha had long ago discovered. If Melanctha had only known that life is a game, and nothing more (a revelation that descended perhaps more frequently upon persons with a steady unearned income), Melanctha would have avoided tragedy. The mistake of the Dadaists in art had been hers in life, their complete subjectivity. If relatedness was obligatory in life, so must it be in art. The Dadaists might have brought life and art together as she was doing, if they had only known that this relatedness which is form need go no further than an appearance.

Four Saints in Three Acts would present all this with the clarity of Composition as Explanation. She would not write a philosophical piece, as so many of her misguided contemporaries were doing. She would not fall prey to the temptation to verbalize the situation (as I have been doing). The only purpose of the façade was to order living. And the only façade she would accept was that of art for art's sake.

Such a façade set up an interesting equilibrium between its own compulsion and the anarchic compulsion of instinct. Once you saw this, once you saw the essential contradiction between the control imposed by the façade and the real aimlessness of living, you had escaped domination by the voluntary nature of your submission. But this could be achieved, outside of life itself, only in the area of art. Any other approach detached the façade from life (as Pater had feared), gave it an independent development into a philosophy or a theology, introduced a purely theoretical set of values which negated the nature of life. Doubtless the façade was inevitable, but there was no point in wasting one's energies like Flaubert in a conflict between rebellion and the obligation to submit. The wise are not philosophers or psychologists or statesmen, but children and saints and (as the superior intuition of Virgil Thompson suggested) Negroes who possess the gravity of children. These people escape bondage by the simple act of accepting its reality. Life is a stage (had not Shakespeare almost hit upon the truth), and men play meaningless games upon it with a sobriety hardly in accordance with the facts.

Behind this slow ritual of the religious dance that maturity imposes upon us always nevertheless, one catches echoes of the gay innocent laughter of the primitive in us. The façade is only a pose we hold with a straight face. The genius of this play is its presentation of both these contradictory aspects of living simultaneously. Many mechanisms of form and style are employed to guarantee that frivolous hints at the absurdity of our seriousness should show through. Lest the philosophy she was implying become a source of value, an end in itself (when the only proper end is life as art which permits art to become life), she wilfully confuses everything. The static nature of repetition she would emphasize by the paradox of using that literary form which is least static. She would use the dramatic form in which people actually meet and clash and make up, to show them actually never clashing and making up and therefore never really meeting. To show that thinking is normal human activity as long as it remains an aimless conversation, there would be people talking like Dadaists. Since mathematics by itself is similarly a random activity, she would have four saints in her title, but fifteen in the play itself. She would announce three acts in the title, four and a prologue in the dramatis personae, and then repeat three of the four acts in the text until all criteria for counting are gone. Having thus cut the cerebrum away, the way was clear to prove the soundest adage of art, that it involves, like life, the whole of what is left of the personality. She would make her play a dance in which the latest conceptions repeated the most ancient Greek, a grave spectacle of that useless rhythm of speech and gesture and movement which is living. But to show the delicacy of the equilibrium, she would present the false sobriety of the surface as always on the point of being shattered into hilarious laughter, that laughter you sometimes see in Negroes (not Melanctha), and in children when your mature back turns upon them. Strangely enough, everyone in her play seems on the brink of hilarious laughter, awaiting a cue to return to the happy chaos of spontaneity.

Indeed, as though this aspect of the play were prophetic in a manner not intended by the author, her own façade unexpectedly fell away, and she was surprised to discover that she needed it no longer. In the early 'thirties she began to write very much like an ordinary person. At first she assumed it was because she was adopting the style appropriate to that dear but ordinary person, her secretary, Miss Toklas, whose 'autobiography,' she decided to compose. But when all her own books from this time on got composed in very much the same style, she must have known that she had at last found herself. The exhilaration was an intoxication and she became anaesthetic to all but the inner bliss of the new experience. It did not occur to her that the intelligibility of new style came after the Depression when she was in dire need, for the first time in her life, of earning an income. But the motive, I think, was not altogether so crass. She had proved her genius to herself by such performances as *Four Saints in Three Acts.* The Depression only promoted a relaxation of the effort. Everybody was beginning to write in readable fashion or not at all. The cult of unintelligibility had been scattered by the first puff of the social disturbance. Their stomachs threatened, writers and artists were discovering that they had been taking too much for granted, and their styles changed as they began to look for a dinner. They craved the comfort and the security of that contact with other people which they had formerly despised.

Once more Gertrude Stein was a leader, and once more she led in her own direction whither nobody followed. No other writer of note became quite so commonplace. I put aside her lectures upon literature which remain obscure not because of her language but because, to our amazement, she has nothing to say. Her real self comes out in her rediscovery of America. What she had said of herself in the *Making of Americans* now proved to have been simple candor. She was a naive middle-class person, kept from pretentiousness by somewhat of the humility of the foreign stock, liking to talk, to travel, to meet people, above all liking a good old-fashioned dinner, liking to gossip about how big the trees are in the Yosemite, how nice a stranger was in the Union Station at 'Frisco, like any other American girl who had passed through college, but had really never understood what William James was talking about, and had lapsed into a matron with more money than culture, with money enough to do as she pleased, but pleasing to do only the simple things, except perhaps where cooking came into the picture. One qualification of course persisted. Miss Stein was also a genius, and so she had one pleasure, not typical, not shared, though she was happy now to share it; she could overhear strangers on the street whispering with a mingling of awe and intimacy: 'Isn't that Gertrude Stein, the genius, passing?' Since she was now indubitably a genius under the ultimate accolade of sales, and bid fair to become a popular author, there was no further reason for façade, for reticence, indeed for any concern with pattern. She could be as garrulous as she would. Her new style was more coherent than the old (for how otherwise could she be so easy to understand?), but now it turned up echoes of comfortable Jewish usages and the unaffected colloquialisms of American housewives (or clubwomen off guard) talking to one another. But when she began to think, as she sometimes did in the midst of this recounting of her adventures in rediscovering

America, or when she had a lapse into self-consciousness, the old defenses would rush in and twist this speech into the old elaborate patterns.

When the Second World War came, she did not react to it as she had to the First. That earlier intrusion of actuality had indeed pulled her out of her strange utterance, forced her into contact with run-of-the-mill people. But she had then taken it as a temporary lark, a vacation from the strain of art, a lapse from the façade into a gay and novel irresponsibility. She had driven her car the length and breadth of France, gallivanting over the country, scarcely aware that men were dying as she chatted with her soldier hitch-hikers, and felt herself at one with them in the bravado of her escape from the dour obligations of art. Though she was now silent about the blood and the suffering, though she continued to state the theory that all wars are alike, she knew at the same time that this second war had killed the nineteenth century at last, which was the form her intuition took of its being quite a different and more serious war than the last. And because it had killed the nineteenth century it was closer to her, since she had been engaged in that work for a long time. As to whether it was the Nazis or the Allies who were doing the killing, she may for some time have remained confused, for she had friends in both camps. But when the American soldiers came over, she knew the Nazis and even her old friend Bernard Faÿ must have been wrong. Since these brave and open-hearted lads were rescuing her from the uncertainties of the Occupation, there could be no doubt that they were the rescuers of civilization. Thus simple persons, uninterested in politics and unaccustomed to the larger issue, feel the impingement of events in proportion to the violence with which it disturbs the daily chore. A surge of patriotism swept through her. She went down to the station to gossip with her countrymen, and invited them home to dinner irrespective of rank. Under the pressure of events, the paradox that had hounded her life dissolved at least for the time being. She could now frankly be herself, frankly indulge her secret craving to be common and ordinary like the bulk of mankind. She had reached the goal that had been closed to her (when years ago she had written 'Melanctha') by both the spirit of the age that had now passed and the demands of her ambition which had long since been satisfied. According to the harsh judgment of criticism, she could no longer be considered a writer of importance, but she had become a woman of the people. It lay with the unknown events of tomorrow, whether she would be obliged to resume the protection of the mask.

11

Ernest Hemingway and the Psychology of the Lost Generation

ERNEST HEMINGWAY'S first published novel was *The Sun Also Rises*. But if chronology be determined by content, his second novel, *A Farewell to Arms,* has prior claim. It is the story of a soldier in love in the First World War. Hospitalized for a wound in the knee during the Italian campaign, this American officer falls in love with his nurse after the usual manner of soldiers. His intentions are not altogether honorable, since war leaves men no alternative but to gather rosebuds before they fall. The casualness of such friendships, bound to be ruptured as the furlough ends and death or distance calls, debases love into the sensuality of the moment; and youth, ardent for ever more varied experiences, responds. But before experience has accumulated into the cynicism of habit, there is a period of flexibility. If events permit the acquaintance to continue, acquaintance may make the heart grow fonder. So it chances with these two. The long convalescence encouraged a qualitative change. With each meeting, sensuality is further absorbed into a richer distillation of mutual interests. The crude barbarism of war, the disintegration of retreating armies, no longer holds the officer in its sinister spell. It fades into a background for the integration of love. The indifference to conventions induced by the war survives only in the rejection of the importance of the marriage tie, though the girl's initiative in this rejection is perhaps intended by Hemingway to suggest a fear that events may make the relation temporary after all. So, in fact, it turns out, to the soldier's consternation. Both woman and child die in childbirth; and he leaves the hospital for a world that has become empty of warmth and meaning.

On the whole this novel is written in a more awkward style than any other work of Hemingway's. Only in the scenes given over to the war does the writing reach his usual level. If the well-known scenes of the Italian retreat are better told than the love affair, the hindsight of the critic may now find in this discrepancy a prediction that Hemingway will never be able to express any profound and positive emotions. But the crude impulsiveness of the dialogue between the lovers, even the colorless banality of much of it, at least registers his determination to avoid the sentimental.

Despite these faults, *A Farewell to Arms* remains an outstanding example of good fiction of wartime in its freedom from the emotional meretriciousness which the hysteria of war often stimulates. Against a conviction that war, however necessary, is like racketeering, a dirty business in which one would prefer not to be involved, the narrative proceeds on an even keel, of facing the facts without turning either toward a specious idealism to cover them up or into an opposite reaction of pessimism, which would expose an incapacity to cope with them. Indeed, ideals of any validity are but an occasional echo in this novel amid the clamor of the egocentric. Enough that one is doing the job assigned at a great personal inconvenience and with no little show of manliness. But the spare time of the soldier is his own, and he will turn in it to the predilections he cherished at home. And though pursued at an increased tempo, they are not always vicious. The novel has become a classic statement of the psychology of the soldier of our generation both in his new profession and in his private life. It shows that the healthy attitudes of peace may survive the devastating attack that war makes upon our normal standards, holding before the reader this possibility in anticipation of its denial in the *Brick Fox-holes* and *Shore Leaves* of the Second World War. At the end of the book it is not war but chance that plunges the soldier into gloom.

When, however, the book as a whole has been deposited in the memory, a shift of interpretation is likely to occur. And it is identical with our reaction in real life to the memory of such an experience. By involuntary association, the frustration in love, though not logically related to the war, is bound to become so psychologically, and we blame the war for personal consequences for which it was not responsible. The strangling of hope in love, which had in fact been a relief from despondency in war, not only in effect lands one where *Shore Leave* begins, but all the more bitterly since there is no escaping this false association. For these reasons this realistic novel, which shows no trace of symbolism or nuance of larger meanings, becomes a single sufficient symbol of the frame of mind in which modern wars leave the citizens of the democracies. What in the novel is the escape from the cynicism set up by the retreating armies into the awakening of love that dies to reduce the soldier to a more intense cynicism: this becomes the statement of an emotional pattern which some of those who fought in the First World War (and some of those in the Second) accepted as symbolic of a quite different content. What such men 'loved,' what afforded them hope in contradiction to the sordidness of the immediate task, was their belief in its social ideals. When, at its ending, they became aware that the settlement of the peace spelt the death of their hopes or, more selfishly, provided no opportunity to translate their abstract ideals into a job and security for themselves, then hope collapsed, became a vain memory, just as love died in the novel, and left men adrift in a world they had not made.

From this point of view, *A Farewell to Arms* gives the history of those basic emotional reactions which culminated in the maladies of the postwar generation, and marks Hemingway, from the outset of his career, as pre-eminently the novelist of the 'lost generation' of the 'twenties. More specifically, he was the novelist of the expatriate Americans. For the 'lost generation' as a whole did not know it was lost. Most of the American soldiers returned, concealing their dubieties under a show of recklessness. But, absorbed into the American Legion and fortified by the false hopes of a revival of prosperity, they recovered from their discontent and lived in fantastic expectations until the Depression brought them to their senses. The expatriates had been in their senses all along, to the extent at least that their cynicism formed an emotional pattern which, though not consciously related to the real consequences of the peace, actually corresponded to them as they were disclosed after a time by the economic collapse of both Europe and the United States, the rise of fascism, and the outbreak of the Second World War. It would be idle to say that their frame of mind had any overt justification in so accurate an understanding of the international situation. Their freedom from illusion, nevertheless, was in conformity with the underlying facts, and provided them thus much of a sound basis for facing the ills of the world: that they were determined never again to be fooled by false promises.

Meanwhile the cynicism that was uppermost in this minority of veterans produced a new type of American personality, which it was Hemingway's distinction to translate into fiction. In a general sense this new personality was a variant of a change of attitude common to the postwar generation everywhere. Everywhere, save in the United States, men felt restless, at cross purposes with themselves and the world. A grudge had grown in them because the war had disturbed their normal expectations from life at an age when these were keenest and most promising. Not knowing precisely who or what was to blame, they had an impulse to blame anybody or anything. But, sensing the folly of such petulance, they sought to control it by camaraderie with the like-minded. Many of them who were well educated sought relief also in a hectic pursuit of new theories, esthetic movements, any intellectual activity that offered the illusion of an aim in life. By such a show of activity they often succeeded in concealing their despondency both from themselves and others. Sometimes, indeed, they projected their inner conflict upon the world at large, and then took ironic cheer in the discovery that their projection conformed to the facts. Vaguely they craved the aid of some revolutionary movement which the perverse anarchism of their spirit would embrace only to reject, after their manner in personal friendship.

Such a personality is caught in a conflict between rebelliousness and a sense of its futility; and the American variant of the type, as seen in the difference between the characters of Hemingway and Aldous Huxley, was an emphasis upon rebelliousness which demolished class distinctions. The men in the English writer's novels for the most part have accepted their hopeless state. Typically, they submitted to the aggressiveness of women and were horrified at the fascist implications of aggressiveness in men. Their inner turmoil was less intense. They seemed to take a sad pleasure in awareness of their impotence, of their being borne this way and that by less reliable breezes than Shelley had in mind. When they acted, if it was not a fling to the opposite extreme of sadism in love and fascism in politics, it was a febrile splutter which soon burned out. Their normal state was to be as receptive to sin as a saint to virtue.

The American variant, on the contrary, is best defined as the degeneration of the frontier tradition. Indeed, Paris was to these expatriates the last frontier, where nothing counted but the assertion of the individual spirit. Since the American of those days always had money enough to pay, or friends who had, his ego could expand, find friendship everywhere, and meet no opposition except from his friends. Still fundamentally aggressive, he was involved in constant quarrels and reconciliations, and he accepted the equality of women by treating them as though they were men and expecting to be treated likewise. Unlike the Englishman who despised the poor because he was afraid of them, his American counterpart felt superior to distinctions of class or education. Where the Englishman satisfied his ego by the range of his ideas alone, the American demanded also range of friendship, and was therefore a more active person. But activity actually diminished the intensity of any single interest, whether an experiment in painting or the pursuit of love. It was a method by which he concealed both his inner conflicts and his hatred of them. Since he refused to play the passive role of the English sophisticate, his unhappiness was a more positive state, and apathy a sign of exhaustion rather than the consolation of self-pity. But both were fundamentally alike in the deeper apathy of distrust of their own abilities.

In either case, very few of these turmoils got through to the surface. These expatriate Americans, in particular, had learned one lesson from the aristocratic tradition which the frontier tradition could not provide. They had learned the use of manners, as an attempt at control of the disorderly emotions within. Proud of their sophistication, they refused to acknowledge the aimlessness of their lives. They imposed upon their random activities so rigid a control as to provide an illusion of purpose, even of heroism, since the façade of manners enabled them to confuse a sporadic impulse with a profound emotion. Thus they were proud never to wear their hearts upon their sleeves, forgetful that it was not the heart at all that sought the limelight but some whim whose suddenness they confused with intensity and which would as suddenly disappear. To keep a stiff upper lip was their most valid rule, affording them a specious unction of manhood, carrying over into their frivolous peacetime pursuits the stoicism of the soldier to grin and bear. Actually the inner turmoil broke through the purpose of the façade by becoming stylized as a part of it. For this code of manners had overtones of irony and indeed of hatefulness; so that there was always in it a contradiction between either the crisp assault of the phrase as sound and its careful understatement of meaning, or the pugnacity of meaning and its apparent check by the firm control of the utterance.

This façade of language, in fact, whose intonation seemed so aristocratic, was, when analyzed for more essential elements, actually derived from the other end of the social scale. It was only the typical speech of the proletariat, taken over and stylized, as the last step in a process long under way in the speech of the American collegian and his elder brother, the sportsman of the mature world. The underprivileged classes, both here and abroad, had long been in a frame of mind into which the war had driven these better educated and financed gentlemen from the best American colleges. They had long felt themselves without a future, at the mercy of forces beyond their control. No training in bourgeois mores, no seduction by bourgeois comforts, had purged away the pugnacious directness of their utterance. A mood of rebellion paralyzed by a deeper sense of insecurity spent itself in the short staccato sentence, in which the brevity of the utterance negated the intention of assault. The sentences in Hemingway are closer to the speech of workers in Lawrence than to that of Huxley's British sophisticates. They are American variants of the Lawrence cadence and interrogation, which reduces conversation to a verbal battle, but in them the restraint imposed by fear and helplessness is replaced by this conscious code of manners. Our expatriates found the atmosphere most congenial where rebelliousness was controlled by becoming convention in the ill-concealed cynical mood of revolt, the brusque grumbling, which still characterizes the language of the working class today.

Such is the type of personality and manner of speaking as presented with varying shades of emphasis in every piece of fiction Hemingway ever wrote. Whether his characters be Americans of wealth or racketeers, artists or soldiers or college graduates, they follow the same pattern of speech and emotion. Hemingway's greatness lies not in the range of his characterization or the suppleness of his style but in the astonishing perfection of these limited objectives. And they never later got a more profound statement than in his first novel, *The Sun Also Rises.* In the simple plot of this novel, Lady Ashley runs away from Paris to enjoy an affair with a new lover. But, as customary in her set, she is accompanied by other men: a young Jew from Princeton who cannot tear himself away from her though she has terminated his affair; and the interlocutor, who, disabled in the war, plays the role of disinterested observer. But in Spain she forces herself upon a young bullfighter, leaving all the Americans restless onlookers. After demoralizing his fight to satisfy her vanity by his attention, she has a change of heart, and, in a fit of remorse that she has ruined him, impetuously leaves to return to her fiancé in England and a second marriage.

This novel is important for other reasons than the verisimilitude of its dialogue or the typicalness of its plot. In the portrait of Lady Ashley, Hemingway goes deeper into analysis of personality than he was ever to do again. In the treatment of his heroine, he clarifies in the round the personality structure of the postwar generation. Perhaps since she is a woman, he feels more free to break through the façade she shares with his masculine characters and himself. In later stories he remains on the surface of his characters, and their real depth is to be deduced only from the development of the plot. But from his picture of Lady Ashley it is apparent that his characters are typically self-defeating and project this perversity upon their friends. Their *bonhommie* conceals a surly dislike of the very persons they pretend or desire to have as friends. And the differentiations among the stories is in the degree to which this conflict is carried and is permitted to show through. In most instances the action takes place within the limited democracy of the façade. But in *The Sun Also Rises* the inner conflict is for once thoroughly exposed in this shift from an irresistible attraction, with its desire to dominate, to the remorse of a renunciation when the desire has been satisfied and the damage done. In other stories the conflict is concealed since they tend to confine our attention to the particularity of the action, to the plot, and at best to insinuate rather than elaborate the motivation. But this conflict within the personality nevertheless remains, to reduce any ideological belief in democracy to a precarious sig nificance, since it is bound to be distorted by some interference from the anarchism of this inner discontent.

The only fiction of Hemingway's, therefore, which vies in quality with *The Sun Also Rises* is to be found in his short stories. This absorption in the façade, this need to live on the surface, is especially suited to the limited demand for meanings inherent in the shortness of the short story. For this reason, the technique of his stories is structurally similar to that of Katherine Mansfield, emotionally a masculine counterpart to her feminine quality. His material is more melodramatic, his conclusion more abrupt, his theme more bitter than those of the English writer. But these differences are deceptive, since in both writers intense emotion is either wanting or suppressed, and the theme is presented only by insinuation. 'The Killers,' for all the gruffness of the surface, is as casual in its indictment of American society at the moment when bootleggers were virtually in control of our local governments as the delicate shading of Mansfield's 'The Garden Party' is subtle in indicting the well-to-do for their crass obtuseness regarding the emotions of the poor. Indeed as the tone of the surface in a Hemingway story draws closer to that of Mansfield, even though the theme remains of a disparate intensity, the identity of technique becomes more apparent. 'An Alpine Idyll' is in the restraint of its style closer to Mansfield than either of them is to the casual manner of their progenitor, Chekhov. In both writers the mastery of the art of the short story lies in this contrast between the nature of the surface, which reflects the consciousness of the characters, and the contradictory meaning of the theme, which is slowly gathering from the denouement of the action. Writers of good short stories of this type will seldom be good novelists. Not having very much to say, they do their best work in the shorter form. When they try to elaborate they go against the grain of their talent, and ruin their most carefully planned plots by the intrusion of elements of which they are unaware.

This is not to deny the sensitiveness of Hemingway's artistry but only to define the limits within which he must work. For his next book proved him sensitive to esthetic problems as American writers seldom are, even in our present sophistication. The most significant part of *Death in the Afternoon* from this point of view is its interpretation of the bullfight as a game that is also a form of art, the nature of which is conditioned by the economic circumstances of the country. Hemingway praises the bullfight as the only game that takes the form of tragedy instead of comedy. To clarify what he means: in our own country, baseball is obviously comedy on the verge of farce (when Babe Ruth is around); and football, though it has the intensity of the tragic action, does not intentionally achieve the plot of tragedy. Bullfighting alone can do so without the derogation of human values, such as took place, for instance, in the Roman gladiatorial combats, because it is the bull that is the victim of a situation potential with tragedy, and rarely the bullfighter. But this value of the form of the game is dependent upon the significance of its theme. What gave it continued importance in a barren country like Spain was that it kept before men's attention their struggle with the brute forces of nature, to control them to their own ends, in which their human ingenuity gave them the assumption of victory, if they spent their best effort. In comparison one can see in the rodeo the rudiments of a game, sketches toward the style of a game, which miserably failed to develop its form. But the perfected form decayed in Spain with the decline of a feudal economy in the face of an industrialized world. Ideologically, when machinery enabled man to achieve the victory over nature without effort, the bullfight became an anachronism; and under the Republic the art became a mark of the decadence of the aristocratic society with which it had long been associated. But what Hemingway is chiefly interested in is the relation between these social conditions and the art of the game. At its height, the performance of a good bullfighter was measured by his efficiency. So long as the game remained close to its thematic significance, close therefore to the everyday life of the functioning feudal estate, the good fighter was one who could measure the precise instant when the bull had been sufficiently weakened so that the thrust of the knife behind the neck could take place without unnecessary hazard to human life, but before the bull's weakness had removed the conflict of wills and made the killing mere slaughter. It should take place at such a time and in such a direct clean way as to give the most vivid spectacle of the authority of the human personality. When, however, the bulls declined in fierceness, since the raising of them had become a luxury the country was too poor to afford, this aim became a pretense. The fighter, no longer facing a hard problem, must make it appear hard; style became involved, unnecessary twists and flourishes entered; it had become style for style's sake; and Hemingway, like a sensitive artist, recognized the degeneration.

Hemingway's admiration was perforce for the past; and one wondered for a time which horn of the dilemma a writer of so much esthetic insight would choose; whether he would align himself with the past, choosing the perfect at the price of its having become illusion, or accept the reality of the present with its apparent imperfection. Doubtless the influence of many forces, including the leftism of foreign friends, had a hand in his decision. But a powerful factor must have been the very quality of his bohemianism as I have defined it. He would remain with the present not so much because he wished to improve it, but because it provided fuel for his contempt. Sympathy for the underdog was there. He liked his informality, the casual democracy of his mores. But unwittingly, he liked even better their common grudge against the powers that be. If he could not have the perfections of a feudal art, he could at least hate the imperfections of the social system that had done away with it. The times, also, were forcing a decision upon him.

Rebuffed by prohibition in America, he turned to the wisdom of simple foreign-born farmers, who continued their old customs of wine making, unable to comprehend our divorce of law and tradition, even when it landed them in jail.

Suddenly he saw this oppression as but one aspect of a universal oppression of the free spirit, through which a handful of wealthy persons, who lived as they liked, were able to demoralize the poor. He turned against one part of his bohemianism, the pointless self-indulgence which it shared with the rich, and retained for the time only this genuine and spontaneous camaraderie, the equalitarianism which, by transcending class distinctions, actually put him with the majority, that is to say, with the poor. And he saw from his experience of all sorts of men, and perhaps from some hearsay of political talk, that society forms one great hierarchy, in which the idle rich live well, but all the others poorly in proportion to their distance from the top, until those at the bottom are crushed by the weight that bears indifferently down upon them. The spectacle stirred his emotions during the winter of the Depression, and the façade became rigid with contempt. The style of *To Have and To Have Not* is almost ugly, as though he could fight privilege and its agent, racketeering, only in the temper of the racketeer. Conscious for the first time of social justice and the good intention of the common man, he could present their defeat in modern society only with the brutality of men of ill will. The owner of a motor boat seeks no more than to give his big blonde wife and little girl a stable home, but he is forced to loan his boat to rum runners, and is killed when he tries to kill them or turn them over to the law. But the reader's admiration for this heroism is overwhelmed by the cynicism of the plot. He gets an impression that the common man fights a stout but hopeless battle for abstract principles of justice he alone respects and fears. The definition of tragedy has become the impotence of his courage and the illusion of his faith to challenge the injustice that unfortunately rules the world.

From the sidelines where the reader stands, death is preferable to surrender. The tyranny of the powers that be, offering their permanent challenge to the individual spirit, gives to the sacrifice of life a mystic sanction, provided it is sought with all the violence of dedication to a valid and ideal goal that man is capable of. Such an analogue of anarchistic attitude lurks in the latter writing of Hemingway, and doubtless is partly responsible for his interest in the Spanish civil war. But it never became clear in his thinking or wholly acceptable to his feelings. The control of the façade had become habitual and prevented the resolution of conflicts in so definite a theory of self-sacrifice. The type of personality he shared with the bohemians of the 'twenties disdained the philosophy of politics as an un-American retreat from living and recoiled from the violence of anarchism as a Latin excess. Even in this single book, in which, stimulated by the Depression in America, Hemingway drove wilfully through a simple plot toward this stark conclusion, he pulls his punch at the end. A coastguard cutter in search of rum runners might have intervened in time, so that the state cannot be dismissed as altogether bad or always inefficient. The directness of anarchistic thinking dissolves in this unanarchistic but quite American retreat into equivocation, and the simplicity of our pity for the hero is qualified by the ironic insinuation that chance cannot altogether be eliminated, however rigid the predestination may appear to be. It may be no more than the pip-squeak of a chance, since we do not expect much help from the coastguard, but it is enough to confuse the philosophy of the action under the guise of a Hollywood devise to increase the suspense.

Despite appearances to the contrary, Hemingway's confusion was increased rather than lessened by his attachment to the Loyalist cause in Spain. One doubts neither the sincerity nor the helpfulness of his public announcements of support. But novels are written from a deeper level of the personality than the rationale of pronunciamentoes. Indeed, what is fundamental to their orientation and its effect is governed by more complex (though not necessarily more creditable) factors than either reason or action. For action may be only a temporary solution of permanent conflicts, the existence of which fiction of any quality will expose. Such, I believe, was the case with Hemingway. From this point of view, his little play, *The Fifth Column*, is the prelude by the light of which *For Whom the Bell Tolls* should be read. It relates to the novel in a way somewhat analogous to the relationship I have pointed out between the portrait of Lady Ashley in *The Sun Also Rises* and the familiar Hemingway type. If it was easier for him there to give an adequate description of the bohemian of the 'twenties through the not altogether gallant device of the portrait of a lady, in *The Fifth Column* he similarly projects his fear of the meretriciousness of the bohemian support of the Spanish Republic by an attack upon a woman. The woman reporter is depicted as attracted by the sensations of danger rather than the ideals involved in the conflict, and as more interested in making a name for herself by her articles than in clarifying the issues. In proportion as this temptation may have existed in Hemingway also, his very determination to avoid it would increase the basic distortion set up by the bohemian habit of finding fault with one's friends. In addition there was the inescapable fact that his friends were losing the war and thereby causing him to do a great deal of rewriting. Under such circumstances his good intention was bound to capsize in an undertow of moody exasperation.

The result was that *For Whom the Bell Tolls* did not merely record the defeat of the Loyalists (as it had to), but turned into an indictment where an exoneration was intended. If the average American reader did not take it as such, it was because faulty reading habits encouraged a faulty political perspective. Approaching the book with an avowed political interest, accepting in advance Hemingway's adherence to the Loyalist side, predisposed to favor democracy but not having the slightest notion whether the Spanish Government was or was not democratic, the average reader found in the book the confirmation of a confusion analogous to Hemingway's, instead of the political guidance he had expected. Since the Loyalists aroused such contradictory reactions in him, he was inclined to leave the book with a feeling of relief that in such a doubtful case, our Government was probably right in holding aloof from aid. If, devoid of all political interest, he had approached the book solely as a good story, but with a capacity, rare in the casual American reader, to follow a text sensitively and interpret its meaning from the flow of the action, he would have found his confusion dispelled by a surprisingly definite conclusion. He would have perceived that it accomplishes precisely the opposite from what it intended, that it is derogatory to the cause of Spanish democracy, and therefore, by implication, sympathetic to Spanish fascism.

No reader can escape a certain awareness, to be sure, of the mood of despondency in which *For Whom the Bell Tolls* leaves him. But the significance of this mood is obscured by the sustained breathlessness of the action and especially by the interest in the personality of the hero. Robert Jordan's love affair distracts attention by the intensity of its description. Its passionate sensuality represents the very ideal of love according to the postwar generation (to which its accomplishment was in such shabby contrast), and those no longer trapped by its fetish of virility will dislike the histrionics of the masculine role. But if we are minded to analyze the cause of our melancholy, we find that it is not caused by Jordan's being killed, but by the fact that we are uncertain about the profitableness of his sacrifice.

Jordan is, indeed, the only character of Hemingway's creation whom he treats with unreserved affection and admiration. The qualification upon friendship in other instances is wanting here; there is no trace of detachment concealing an inward contempt. The old attitude once characteristic of his relationships with his fellow expatriates is now transferred to the Spanish characters (with the exception of course of his lover, who does not count in the essential action), to all of whom Jordan stands in contrast as a discreet representation of the ideal American. The distortion that characterizes his personality as lover disappears in his functioning as soldier; and, I think, it does so because Jordan as soldier and hero comes pretty close to being the accepted functioning American conception of the good soldier. He is one who doggedly does his duty, his not to reason why, sustained by the mystical belief (symbolized a little sadly in the title of the novel) that every individual is a part of a social whole, just as a peninsula is part of a vast continent. For this reason, even though Jordan realizes that the action of blowing up the bridge he has been sent to perform has become useless through changed events, when he cannot make contact and get permission from remote authority to change the order, he carries it through at the sacrifice of his life. He has not invoked his own powers to analyze a situation and act independently in an emergency, willing to accept responsibility for reversing the plan. Instead, he buttresses his rigid sense of duty with a mystical theory that any sacrifice of life that at all hinders the enemy, however ineffectually, must promote the good cause merely because it has behind it his wholehearted enthusiasm as a subjective potential. Perhaps fundamentally, on the subjective side, such an ideal approaches the anarchistic belief in the mystical value of self-sacrifice as an act in itself. But Jordan's ideal is conspicuously not anarchistic, in that this subjective state is made possible only by the sense of obedience to a higher authority. Doubtless such is the obligatory psychology of many a soldier in the ranks who must do as he is told because he cannot be in a position to understand the reasons justifying a command. But surely for an officer, and one on a special mission, where he has superior opportunities to gauge the overall situation, to act in such a way is only to conceal a dependency upon external authority for the very decision which affords the greatest sense of personal achievement through self-sacrifice. As such, the psychology of

Robert Jordan is, I should say, strangely enough that typical of the authoritarianism of fascism.

But Hemingway does not stop here. Against such a picture of Jordan, with whom he identifies himself as with no other character in his fiction, he puts the clearest assemblage of evidence that the higher authority is not to be trusted. The Loyalists have neither the materials nor the co-ordination necessary for victory. Lack of communications makes co-ordination impossible. But Hemingway gives the impression that, even with material, the co-ordination would not have become any better. The anarchism in the Loyalist higher command is a matter of temperament, and is reflected in the philosophy of anarchism prevalent among Spanish liberals. This confusion and contradiction at the top betrays their lack of a sense of duty like Jordan's, which would have imposed at least a rigid assent to some common plan. But when it is a matter of direction from above, when it is a matter of imposing orders rather than obeying them, this obverse of the sense of duty, the obligation to exercise authority, is by no means palatable to Hemingway. If he objects to the laxity of the anarchistic temperament, his rejection of the surly attempts of the Communists to achieve discipline, as he describes them, is even more positive. He pictures their hysterical insistence upon action and obedience as offensive to the dignity of the individual and equally benighted as planning. Nowhere at the top is there the wisdom and firmness that can command respect. Hemingway's bohemian background leads him into a perverse enjoyment of the picture. His idealism is outraged; that is enough; for he makes no conscious effort to suggest what type of command will avoid the laxity of anarchism on the one hand and the rigidity of his Communists on the other. He wallows instead in the subjective pleasure (in itself a kind of anarchism) of denunciation. And to intensify this mood of fighting the windmills of futility, he chooses to put Jordan in a situation in which his immedate associates are worse than the men at headquarters, even less typical of the Loyalist fighters. Jordan has to deal with non-Spanish gypsies in the mountains, who have withdrawn and ceased fighting when they have acquired for themselves booty in the form of mules and horses. It is exciting to follow Jordan's tact in winning back the support of these selfish dissident individuals, and it restores for the time being one's confidence in human nature. But the fact that the principal characters in the novel have to be wheedled and cajoled into a sense of duty by an American reinforces the gathering cynicism of the reader for the Loyalist cause.

One's cynicism is further intensified by the intensity of the spontaneous emotional reactions set up by episodes not directly concerned with Jordan's blowing up the bridge. These subtly accumulate to establish an emotional orientation of uneasy suspicion of the Loyalists and unconscious admiration for their fascist opponents. There are acts of horror on both sides. But those on the Loyalist side are made indelible by the manner in which they are treated; whereas those on the other are absorbed by the narrative and fade away. Jordan's lover, for instance, had been raped by the fascists. But since the memory is too painful for her recollection, it becomes a cold fact in the reader's mind, quite forgotten in the activity that enabled her to forget it, her ecstatic participation in her new and satisfactory love affair with Jordan. Utterly different is the reader's attitude toward Pablo's confession of his part in the murder of the anti-democratic officials of his village. His sense of guilt keeps the episode vivid to the reader, since it still preys on his own mind and forces him to recount most vividly the gruesome details. His weakness of character, as revealed in his later treachery to the Loyalists, not only lessens one's sympathy for his contrition, but makes one wonder how typical he is of the Loyalists in general. His present disloyalty toward the Republic comes to seem indicative of a tendency there toward disintegration that is stimulated not so much by the success of the enemy as by flaws in Spanish democracy itself.

Such a conclusion is strengthened when one realizes that there is no character on the fascist side who arouses as much detestation as Pablo, and no description of fascist brutality (when so many abounded in the actual events which Hemingway might have chosen) is inserted to palliate and compensate for our dislike of Pablo as a Loyalist. The fascists are not on the center of the stage, and Hemingway's bohemian personality, which seizes upon the flaws in any ideal he has grasped, by compensation tends to find a sentimental idealism in whatever is beyond contact. The fascists in the novel, who are not close at hand and therefore do not require to be described in any detail, approach the reader through an emotional haze which is not at all sinister but fundamentally agreeable. They are almost always depicted as gentle refined officers, who do what they must out of a sense of duty like Jordan's, but under circumstances where they can have confidence in the integration both of their philosophy and their army. They are the men who are destined (as it turned out, at least for the time being) to win. Serene in their conviction, they soil their hands as little as possible; and such is the author's perversity in planning his book that by the time one has read it carefully, they seem to deserve to win. Jordan's heroism, therefore, is put within a context of overwhelming detail that proves its folly as a practical code of action. In the larger context of the narrative, it is seen to be as futile as it seemed without qualification admirable as immediate subjective experience. And though it is given the emphasis of being the final action of the book, for any careful reader who cannot forget his accumulation of previous impressions, its position only makes its meaning the more melancholy.

Hemingway's attitude toward the Loyalists, therefore, is similar to that of the postwar bohemian toward his erstwhile friends. Any keen emotion of attachment carries its hidden counterpart of contempt. And any attitude toward persons, like the fascists, whom one dislikes in theory but does not know takes on a flavor of liking precisely because, free from this inner contradiction by not being known, they become vague and gentle images, which seem not so much unreal as ideal. Indeed, to a person of Hemingway's type, unlike the anarchist, the ideal will always be delectable because it cannot be realized either through life or death, either through social or individual action. Once you come into any form of contact with it, it ceases to be ideal. The ideal, consequently, fails, just as friendship fails, and the failure of democratic societies is analogous to this failure of friendship. Goodness drifts and is as impotent in the world of practical affairs as these men sense themselves to be in their personal lives. They project their own failure upon the world at large.

Anyone as interested in the facts of the Spanish War as the abundant detail of Hemingway's novels show him to have been could not, unless blinded by some prejudice, have avoided the most pertinent facts of all. Inefficiency there was on the Loyalist side, but no greater than on the fascist; and in the course of the fighting, the co-ordination actually increased despite the tremendous handicap of lack of material. What caused the loss of the war, as everyone now knows, was not the failure of democracy in Spain but its failure abroad. I well remember waiting, as I read the novel, for some hint of 'non-intervention,' some evidence of aid to Franco from the Axis and lack of aid to the government from the foreign democracies. The only aid the Loyalists are pictured as getting is the irascible meddling of French Communists and the haughty indifferent cynicism of the Russian observers. The tremendous support of Franco by the Axis through diplomatic pressure and armed intervention plays no part in the narrative. Yet only through these was Franco's failing cause snatched from actual defeat. As a political history of the war, the novel is almost wilfully misleading.

What kept such patent facts from Hemingway's consciousness was, I think, the rationalization of his esthetic interest. He did not wish to write a political novel, but one in which political events should form the setting for a timeless story of personal tragedy. He sought to escape the notorious deficiencies of left fiction in oversimplification of motive and plot. But to put the political interest in its place does not necessitate its distortion. It might, however, distract the author from awareness of the distortion. Nor does a timeless story require a theme that contradicts the correct political interpretation. But its contradiction may escape an author's notice in his herculean task of assembling all the purely 'human' detail needed to prove his broader 'human' theme. And in the process he may also lose sight of the interference with the purity of his theme by the idiosyncrasies of his own personality.

Actually Hemingway's theme obligates a wrong interpretation of political events, and is no more universal than a rationalization of the problems of the bohemian personality can be. For the 'human' theme of *For Whom the Bell Tolls,* the theme of Robert Jordan's dying, is nothing more than a special instance of the conception of tragedy that has dominated romanticism in its decadence. The belief that the ideal is constantly frustrated in a wicked world is, to be sure, older than the postwar generation. It stems from the precedent of *Madame Bovary.* To say, therefore, that inefficiency wrecked the Loyalist cause would be to make a political statement that though true would be a mere corollary to a larger philosophical reflection. Virtue is everywhere inefficient, impractical, unsuccessful, like the drifting of those men in Paris after the war, believing themselves so well intentioned as they studied art or drank with their friends, and ascribing their failure to the way of the world, to the hopeless state in which the peace had left mankind. The bohemianism of the 'twenties may have been of good intention. It was something to have sided with democracy, whatever the inner motives. But the traits of personality in the postwar generation made these writers, against their will, unreliable as the interpreters and friends of democracy.

12

William Faulkner's Patterns of American Decadence

WITH but the turn of the screw, Hemingway's characters become William Faulkner's. You have only to take away their sophistication, deprive them of that code of manners that could partly control a discontent not strong enough to prevent its installation. You have then only to interest yourself less with the surface than with the turbulence below, and you have Faulkner's stories of those Americans who never thought of going to Paris or, if they went, went too late. And, just as the charm of Hemingway is the astonishing ease with which he catches the clang of the surface, so the greater significance of Faulkner is that we are willing to sacrifice ease because it does not seem appropriate to so uneasy a content. We are willing to accept the elaborate introspective style of his best work because it takes us into the seething torment beneath the surface, more typical of the American today than Hemingway's reminiscences of Pershing's veterans and their women.

It is true that Faulkner's characters are not only all Southerners, but practically all from Jefferson County in the State of Mississippi. But while we enjoy the tang of their provincialism as keenly as the mannered colloquialisms of Hemingway's émigrés, we find that we pass beyond it into meanings that transcend the provincial. We recognize in these Southerners only an extreme form of typically American personalities. Their brothers and sisters are in the poetry of Jeffers and the novels of Steinbeck. Their traits, moreover, represent the American variant of a decadence that is common to Western culture as a whole; just as the abnormalities in Kafka emphasize by their exaggeration the pattern of decadence in the German personality. What makes us think of Faulkner when European writers like Kafka come to mind, as we do not recall Steinbeck in their connection, is not that Faulkner is any less American, but that he has a deeper insight into personality and a style of his own to express it.

The idiosyncratic evidence of decadence in the American personality, what distinguishes the American from most Europeans, is his more pronounced instability. His internal conflicts are more intense and closer to the surface, unchecked by the habit either of obedience or meditation. The one rule he consistently obeys is the imperiousness of his own whim. Self-centered and self-indulgent, he obeys otherwise only provisionally and when he must. Assailed by inconsistent precepts, unsupported by any dominant philosophy of life, he seeks solutions through flight, impatiently desirous of being somewhere else, whether it is back home or away, in future hopes or boyhood memories. Since he tends to disregard reason and live by impulse, he is either on the edge of violence in word or blow, or, if at all sensitive, fears his own violence and retreats into a restless brooding. Whether he carries it out or no, his obsession is to do something, to act. Though thus anarchistic by temperament, but lacking any philosophy of anarchism, he has only the rags of pragmatism to cloak his inconsistent reactions with the dignity of explanation. Generous because he is improvident, he lives in future expectations, and seeks the affection of others through some magnificent gesture of superiority and control, yet he is childishly incapable of accepting rejection without a tantrum. More like the southern than the northern European, he has somewhat of the Frenchman's verve and wit but none of his respect for the rule of reason; his impulsiveness is checked by doubt where the Italian responds to a superstition the American has long since discarded, and the Spaniard to an illusion of dignity our rough and tumble past has never bequeathed us. Thus lacking the habit of obedience which the Englishman still shares with the Teuton, he cannot conceive of being a little man when he is one, must believe he is defying in the act of compliance, boast most of sex when he is the world's worst lover, make the most grandiose plans when he is on the brink of bankruptcy. This is not the personality of the average American. But it is a description of that American Professor Turner once met in a western railway coach who wanted to live so that he could tell the world to go to hell, now that in a later generation he has experienced its impossibility. It is a description of the extreme to which the average tends today, when it has not been molded in a more favorable environment with the aid of a more constructive philosophy than that we have inherited from Professor Turner's Westerner. And it is, by and large, the structure of personality in these Southerners of William Faulkner.

In clarifying such traits as these, Faulkner himself also illustrates one of them, the inability to philosophize. By some form of rationalization or another, his great European contemporaries in fiction ordered and interpreted their material in such a way as to keep aloof or appear to keep aloof from it. Kafka is exceptional in his use of a method that compels participation in the degeneration he describes. Faulkner uses a different method to the same end. He employs the stream-of-consciousness method to force the closest emotional identification with his material. If there is any philosophy in his better novels, it must be distilled from the action by the conscious effort of the reader. He gives no running commentary of interpretation like Proust, no clear patterns of symbolic meaning like Thomas Mann. He does not smuggle into the stream of consciousness innumerable details and constant shifts of literary style, more characteristic of the author than the hero, such as scatter the emotional intensity in Joyce. By using the interior monologue in its purest form, so that the reader gets the fullest picture of the whole inner life of his characters and nothing else, no intrusion of the surface except what is obligated by its indissoluble connection to what is going on within, Faulkner in his best, his early, novels secures an intensity of emotional effect almost without parallel in the history of fiction.

After two desultory tries at novel writing, he suddenly compressed what had been gathering in his mind into the form of introspection, then new to this country, and published *The Sound and the Fury* in 1929. His particular theme is the decadence of a Southern family of good stock, where pride makes furious the awareness of decay, and decay has become visible in an idiot brother. The story corrects the implications of Poe's 'Fall of the House of Usher,' which, however moving as a short story, has turned out to be inaccurate in its symbolism of Southern history. No implacable destiny caused the Southern aristocracy, suddenly crumbling, to bury in the debris of its tradition its last helpless scion. That tradition, always illusory since it had never produced a culture, survived to corrupt the new. It remained as pride with an ever-decreasing hold upon fact. Economic deterioration of its agrarian base, following the pressure of Northern industrialism, was as irresistible as a gathering storm. Against it pride could only fume as it kept alive by compromise and submission. But Faulkner takes for granted the moral and social aspects of his theme. He is interested only in making vivid the effect of this decline upon the individual personality, in which pride is checked by fear both of the outside world and of the incompetence within. The individual spirit becomes locked in a conflict which it seeks to resolve either by retreat or by an attack upon the outside world.

Now the Compson who would solve the conflict by retaliation is Jason. Exteriorly he is brusque, ungrateful, untrustworthy, perhaps the most disagreeable creation of American fiction. He works in a store whose owner has hired him only to help a once reputable family which still lives in the shade of its rotting portico; but he shirks on the job and treats his employer as though their roles were reversed. He whines continually that he has never had a chance since a job in a bank, once promised him, never came through. He gambles away his salary by playing the stock market (like so many of his betters in 1928), rushing at the lunch hour to the post office for the latest report from the big city on his losses. When his sister, who had made a good marriage and moved away, leaving an illegitimate daughter behind, tries to send her money through him, he confiscates all but a few dollars of it. He abuses the daughter for the looseness his abuse has promoted in her, until she runs away with a circus dude. But he tries to get her back with the money he has stolen from her. And we begin to realize that behind this contemptible surface, however twisted and self-defeating in its expression, is a savage obsession to patch the walls of Usher, at last without doubt crumbling. He and he alone of the entire family is making some attempt to restore what they were once proud of in the past. Caught in the vicious circle of the family pattern, he only hastens their decline into a commonplace vulgarity. But he is struggling to maintain some command over his own destiny and theirs.

No one else in the family faces the issue as squarely as Jason compels himself to do. Uncle Maury spins schemes to get rich quick, while he lives in idleness at their expense. The mother rises from her sick bed, like an echo from the past whining its helplessness and contributing its confusion to each present crisis. She cannot believe that her last born, drooling in the kitchen or loping down the yard under the eye of a bright Negro boy, is no longer a child, although this is his thirty-second birthday; nor can Benjy himself realize it, nor does anyone else, except the Negro cook who made the cake, in the distraction of the day's happenings, with Quentin running away. The only philosopher of the family, the father, has long since died of alcoholism, led to it by his conviction that 'time is the mausoleum of all hope and desire.' 'Because no battle is ever won,' he said. 'They are not even fought. The field only reveals to man his own folly and despair, and victory is an illusion of philosophers and fools.' So he had been wise to drink, degenerating under his sons' eyes, until he spent the day over a bottle of whiskey at his place at the dining table in stockingless feet. It was an inheritance of such advice as this, such a spectacle of fatherhood, that Jason willed out of mind, but Quentin (the son, not the niece of the same name) could never forget.

And so Jason fought, while his brother Quentin went under. Yet Jason somehow had not thought of his brother as weak. He seemed rather to respect him with a trace of awe, as though he symbolized some possibility of fineness in the family tradition, too shy and fragile for maturing. For in Faulkner, as in so much modern fiction, the good intention lacks the strength for execution, is crushed beneath an unbearable weight of insight. To feel for what is good and fine can only mean to come face to face with how little of it there is any longer in the family and, by tie of blood, in oneself. In a family on the defensive against the world, knit close by its own morbidity, to be capable of love must mean the bitter folly of falling in love with one's sister. But as though to testify to the poignant spirituality of even such a love in such a family, to assure that the memory of it echo through the whole book and afford to the most crude and sordid failure in the present some atmosphere of tragic dignity, Faulkner inserts this story of what happened eighteen years ago, and inserts it through the purest stream of consciousness. We are immersed for the time being in its reality and return to the present of 1928 (if I may use Faulkner's later style to describe it) with that old tragedy still living in us, as though to prove that the most intense conflicts are within the spirit itself, invoked by the very presence there of love surviving nowhere else, but surviving there only to reject the temptation to incest at the eventual price of self-slaughter, and yet projecting itself by the sweetness of Quentin's remembered character to condone the crudity of a Jason who did not go under.

For Quentin's story is one of the unforgettable passages in American literature in which a better psychology and a better technique achieve the intention of a Hawthorne in a less Spartan age. Quentin carried to Harvard with him, along with his father's admonitions regarding the futility of effort, his not too distant memories of his sister Caddy. He remembered the day when their bodies came together as they played in the muddy waters of the brook. The evening when she led him chasing her through the woods and she was willing but he was not, and Dalton Ames came up, so that he was saved but not she. The time when she told him she was in trouble, and he was about to use his knife upon them both, when the impulse changed to love and jealousy, and he sought Ames out, but was beaten up himself instead, and he made that strange attempt to save her by advertising his devotion, declaring to his father that he was the one. But he remembered it not as strange, only as though true, as somehow surely it was.

All this paralyzing burden he carries to Harvard with him, and, unable to face the examinations too, he plans secretly to drown himself. He takes a last walk through Cambridge into the string of towns with their foreign population beyond. He buys some buns in a store, and, pitying a little Italian girl, gives her one. Then he falls in with some boys who are going fishing (so real is his own past to him), and the little girl follows, but is surely protected by the crowd of them. Yet, when they return to the streets, he finds a hue and cry from the girl's mother and brother, who have seen her trailing along with him. He is arrested, but some of his wealthy Harvard friends come along in a car, and, though they get him off easily enough and probably don't believe their banter to him of his guilt, he himself cannot forget his sister. The dissoluteness of his family seems in his blood and the weakness of indecision his only virtue. The revelation of his self-knowledge has been completed. Hating himself for the love of which he cannot be rid and which alone gave meaning to his life, caught in the destiny of his own temperament but possessing now the courage of a complete despair, he disappears forever.

The purpose of the book's structure now becomes more evident. It opens with the stream of consciousness of the idiot Benjy. Since he is aware only of the specificity of the image but is unable to distinguish the recollected image from the immediate, the reader is lost in a thicket without a guide. Perhaps it is bad strategy (even in this day of difficult beginnings of great novels) to start with Benjy's succession of clear individual images that do not form a pattern (like some grotesque film montage wilfully planned to obscure the meaning) but resemble certain states of drunkenness in which logical connections have disappeared. The inebriate retains enough normality to feel a certain humor or disgust at this failure of his faculties. Benjy too is sane enough to live in a somewhat parallel state of whining, proof of his irrational fears at this confusion which is all experience means to him. Such a mood, I believe, Faulkner seeks to convey to the reader, at the outset, as not only characteristic of the half-wit, but appropriate to the deterioration of personality in this old Southern family. It is only a distortion (as a painter might say) of the frame of mind of the rest of them. The father's view of life as a confusion of folly and despair is confirmed in Benjy's very inability to achieve the illusion of order which men of normal minds impose upon it.

We are still within the subjectivity of the decadent personality in the second section devoted to Quentin's story. But here, though confusion persists, and Quentin seems like one walking in his sleep, the sense of the past more real to him than the outer scene, relations between images begin to emerge, the conflicts that are the cause of the confusion become definite, outer action grows into a commentary on remembrance of things past, and the two layers of activity work out to a resolution. The emergent conflict of values involved in the theme of love and incest becomes clear enough for a carrying through of the desire for suicide with which the section opened.

Jason's stream of consciousness in the third section, on the contrary, is that common to the extrovert. Since he must bury the past, try to forget Quentin's death, in order to survive, it consists mostly of external happenings. But the reader carries over the mood and the information of the Quentin chapter to clarify Jason's motivation, which must remain obscure to himself. We are thus brought closer to a well-rounded understanding of the family picture, and the drunken blurring lessens with our constantly increasing sense of the richness of new meanings.

The final section, therefore, is somewhat like a slow curtain in the theater. Calming us down, it guarantees that we hold fast the impressions gained. Its reliance upon the conversation of the Negro cook (who plays chorus to the antecedent action here as she returns from church to perform mechanically her household duties): this introduces no new meanings, for these would be disturbing; but only a mood of complete detachment from all meaning and action. Her loyalty to the family is a habit she takes for granted. She has long since given up worrying about them (if she ever did), expecting anything from them but trouble and disturbance. But she refuses to become involved emotionally in their tantrums. Like little Luster, she had the wisdom of the Negro world (as Faulkner sees it) to hold herself apart while she outwardly complies, expecting nothing for her race and anything from the race of whites. She is not a Cassandra, since she has no insight to foresee the future, but takes the day's misery as it comes. She is the voice of the everyday, accurate, indifferent, superficial. But perhaps the implications of her attitude are correct, and we can interpret them to mean that for Jason and his family there will be none of the relief from mental suffering Quentin gained. Their destiny may be only to go on torturing one another. But we at least as readers, through this old Negro's eyes, have at last been completely detached from sharing. When we leave her, we need no transition to the completely objective method of the final episode. Jason, returning from the folly of his trip to force his niece Quentin back home, meets Luster taking Benjy, at the mother's orders, for a ride for the whole town to see. He leaps from his car, strikes the boy, and turns the horse's head about.

> Ben's voice roared and roared. Queenie moved again, her feet began to clop-clop steadily again, and at once Ben hushed. Luster looked quickly back over his shoulder, then he drove on. The broken flower drooped over Benjy's fist and his eyes were empty and blue and serene again as cornice and façade flowed smoothly once more from left to right; post and tree, window and doorway, and signboard, each in its ordered place.*

We too have reached a similar peace of mind. The outer world has proffered the rhythm of this mechanical succession of images which do not have to be analyzed for meaning, for there is no meaning in them. But this peace is of the surface of things. It is the temporary state of an imbecile. If we who can think choose not to put the book down, but to resume thinking, this peace, which looks so normal and objective, we know, is bound to disappear. Benjy will return to the really normal confusion and discontent of the first section. The reality of our inner life is a perpetual contradiction of whatever mechanical order the surface may afford, whether this order be in what we call the objective world or in that area equally detached from our real selves that is called the mind.

If Faulkner had been of a philosophical temper, if he had himself been as conscious of the meaning as of the mood in this ending to *The Sound and the Fury,* he might have found it also a criticism of his own method. Was not, perhaps, his careful planning of the major sections, his arrangement (that looked so spontaneous) of the infinite details of the pattern, like that succession of posts and trees, a tranquilizing order imposed on his material by the author, similarly false to the real drift of life through time and space? If time was as meaningless as this succession of images, to use it to create nothing more than a mood

* Faulkner, William, *The Sound and the Fury,* New York, 1929, by courtesy of Cape and Smith.

of peace might smuggle in the illusion that there was a meaning of peace also. But he was not a philosopher. And so, captivated by the family pattern he had discovered, he sought for new material to apply it to. He found it almost automatically by leaving the decaying gentry and going to the poor whites of the remote hill country. *As I Lay Dying* is his attempt to identify himself with a similar family pattern there.

This time the problem seemed easier, for there was not the complication of literacy and the inheritance of pride. In place of pride there was only duty, the necessity, at this primitive economic level, for somebody responsible for keeping body and soul together. This responsibility he put into the hands of the wife, where probably it usually is among poor whites. As she lay dying, her will, born of necessity and custom, continued to dominate the mature members of the family, and it continues to project itself upon them after her dying, as powerfully as though she were still alive. But this inheritance of a will to duty immediately creates a problem. Her dying request has been to be buried in her family's lot thirty miles away, and a storm impends. They have just got the chance to hire out their horse and wagon for some ready cash they see so seldom. The husband, who has been shiftless since a sunstroke many years ago, on this sole occasion is impetuously for action. But the two sons, Cash and Jewel, who inherit the mother's qualities, and are more sober versions of Jason, decide their mother would have recognized the common sense in delaying. Meanwhile the storm breaks, and causes a longer delay. And accident interferes with a grotesque and horrible maliciousness. The little boy, fearing his mother is suffocating within the home-made coffin, bores holes to let air in, so that they have awkwardly to conceal the damage done to the body. But through the stream-of-consciousness method, we identify ourselves to such an extent with the family that we are hardly more conscious than they of what, from our ordinary level of sophistication, would seem the pathos or even the ludicrousness of the situation: that four men with a horse and wagon have so much difficulty going thirty miles. At the subsistence level, the simplest act requires heroic exertion. Ill luck and accident are taken for granted, and to get a thing done at all, however shabbily, is an achievement. When they find the bridge swept away by the swollen stream so that they have to ford, the action reaches its climax. With an intensity of seriousness we are accustomed to bestow upon the more significant activities of the usual heroes, we follow these men tussling to keep the coffin from swinging off into the treacherous mud, failing when they have almost reached the bank, but getting it somehow back on again. Drenched with water after its days of exposure to the sun, the coffin now draws the vultures. The silent, lazy boy Darl, who was surely modeled on Quentin, notices, senses the larger meanings, grows filled with shame because his mother's body has suffered indignity, because this indignity exposes the abject condition of their common life, that they are poor whites indeed, that night goes raving mad, sets fire to the barn which shelters them, and has to be taken away to the hospital at Jefferson before they can go farther. Charred by the fire and waterlogged, it is a miracle that the body gets buried at last.

The relief then changes to consternation when the father, on the way back home, stops at a house and introduces to his sons the second Mrs. Bundren. The edifice of sympathy Faulkner has so carefully constructed immediately disappears. This final incident reduces the book to the grotesqueness, which had previously been avoided, of *Tobacco Road.* But I find it hard to believe that Faulkner intended this shift of mood. The father's announcement was probably supposed to show that this shiftless old man's tenacity on this single occasion was an appeasement of his conscience. By this act of carrying out his dying wife's injunction, he was freeing himself of guilt for marrying again. By this desperate obedience to the letter of her injunction, he was wiping out past infidelity and guaranteeing the future maintenance of his shiftlessness. But he has not been an active enough character in the book, not enough of his stream of consciousness has previously been given, to justify this interpretation in the light of the text. So what might have been a powerful sinister conclusion is almost reduced to the vaudeville level.

Now the real reason for this failure, I believe, is that Faulkner as a creative author shares the defects of self-control of his characters. For the time being he had secured control against the grain by the most intense cultivation of the stream-of-consciousness technique, which, accepting chaos, submits it to order. But the strain became too great, and the faulty conclusion of *As I Lay Dying* is the first sign that Faulkner is breaking under it. In his next novel he has a plan, but, being no longer under the rigid control of this method, superb material for tragedy turns into melodrama.

Any psychological interpretation of *Sanctuary*, therefore, is baffled from the start. If the book has been the most popular of Faulkner's novels, it is because the sensational material is easy to get at. Using now the traditional method of objective narration, Faulkner produces an atmosphere of fascination with horror, of the same order as that of the tabloid press, only more sustained and intense because more detailed in a book, as the blurbs would say, that is 'packed with action.' Indeed the plot is so repulsive that a synopsis which would necessarily strip it to its essence of sadistic sex perversion would suggest an abnormality in the critic who made it. To describe the scene is forbidding enough: the lonely farmhouse to which the dissolute college boy has brought the judge's daughter for a last drink of moonshine before he passes out; the wife looking on with sullen disapproval as Tommy makes passes at Temple, until the husband, Godwin, bawls him out while Popeye hovers in the background; the woman taking Temple from the house to the corncrib for the protection of distance; both Popeye and Tommy following with the same intent, and Popeye shooting Tommy; then the next morning and thereafter, to our growing surprise, the girl's submission to the man who has mistreated her; her willingness to go with him to a brothel in Memphis, and to submit there, like an ordinary prostitute, to the lusts of other men while Popeye looks on. Gossip spreads the story through the town, but attention publicly shifts to the murder of Tommy, for which Godwin is arrested. Then Temple, brought back to testify, strangely refuses to involve her seducer, and permits an innocent man to die for a crime he did not commit. But when one asks why she did it, the novel gives no answer. Was it fear of Popeye? Or had the judge's daughter been no better than a prostitute all along beneath the respectability of her clothes and her social position? And has this crime of Popeye's against her merely stripped her of her controls and exposed her true self in all its listless worthlessness? The speculation is probable but unproved. In abandoning the stream-of-consciousness method for the objective, in turning from the stress on motive to that of action, Faulkner has gone to an opposite extreme and become negligent of motivation.

Actually, the reason for this vagueness of characterization is more complex than a loss of control over his material because of a change of method. The shift of method itself has been dictated by a change of approach, by a broadening of Faulkner's interests. For if a psychological interpretation of *Sanctuary* is impossible, a sociological one is inevitable. Having found the same decadence in two isolated examples of Southern life, the one from the old gentry, the other from the poor whites, Faulkner appears to have come to the conclusion not only that decadence is characteristic of the region as a whole, but that even more of it is to be found in the more respectable classes. Cash and Jewel resisted a worse environment more successfully than did Jason, and with fewer inner conflicts. *Sanctuary* is proof of a rising interest in social problems, which seems to stem from the very nature of the material he had been working on with a quite different intention.

As the novel progresses, interest turns from the rape to the trial, and the trial, unlike the rape, involves the whole community. Paradoxically, the novel seeks to defy and expose its own sensationalism. To put the action within the framework of Benbow's character and meditation was an attempt to subject it to the control of interpretation. But Benbow himself is not a strong enough person to institute control. He is a more customary version of the Quentins and the Darls, a man of sensitivity who can act. But Benbow has never acted successfully and does not here. His case for the defense is lost. His fit of vomiting is his sudden realization of how much of what he opposes in the community is latent in himself. Yet the book's indictment of the community, though it leave us emotionally in a state of futility, has been convincing to the reason. We recognize in the book a Southern variant of a social interpretation of American life long since established in our fiction. The relation between Popeye and Temple, from this point of view, is only a single symbolic statement that there is no essential difference between the classes. Beneath their contempt for the masses, who are worthy of it, the respectable and wealthy are no better. Fine clothes and a cultivated voice conceal an identical decadence. Benbow's interest in justice for this poor defendant is taken by his social equals as a sign of eccentricity. In fact, almost every rationalization by a character in the book is a fallacious one. Hypocrisy is universal except among the most depraved of the lower classes. If justice is ever done, it is by accident. Godwin is not the only one to be convicted and hang for a crime he did not commit: Popeye, leaving for safety, drifts back to his old home town, where he is tried and hanged for an offense he did not this time commit. It is a crazy world beyond any man's control. Benbow goes to the phone. It is his daughter speaking, explaining her absence from home. Having failed in court, Benbow knows he has to accept a second failure. He knows inside himself that another Temple Drake is breeding and he can do nothing about it. But Temple herself has escaped to Paris, walking in the Luxembourg Gardens with the judge, her father, while the band plays romantic music. In the surface of life there is for the time being the peace of insensitivity.

And, as far as Faulkner's own mood was concerned, he determined to stay there. From now on, he will drift as aimlessly as the surface shifts. He will vacillate in his use of literary forms until it becomes impossible for the critic to recognize a direction. There will be a strenuous attempt to secure form by the use of contrasting panels of narration in *The Wild Palms.* It will lose itself in paradox, but not until it has faltered a statement once more that courage is rather to be found among the criminals of the chain gang than in the ranks of the respectable. Generally speaking, he is content to become a raconteur, a small-town character who has turned out to be a genius at storytelling, like the traveling salesman in *The Hamlet,* who spins one yarn after another to show what crazy fools these mortals be, careless as the whim invites, whether the stories be tall or true, but elaborating them all as though fascinated by every slightest detail and having the infinite time of a country store at his disposal. Sentences twist now like chains of interwoven snakes, lazy in the sun unless stimulated for the time being to a vibrant activity. They are linked by connectives as though, captivated by his own talent for storytelling, he made no attempt to stem or arrange the flow, but only followed it with his consciousness, to polish each detail with fond humor into a jewel-like exaggeration of reality. For the good humor is of the surface, and there is the twist of bitterness in every smile.

Such verbosity stems from a shy fear to expose any longer his ineffectual puzzlement over the meaning of life; just as a similar impulse is behind every storyteller's story. And so, shyly, at the end of these long novels (which are never dull), there emerges the fumbling conclusion Faulkner seems all along to have been stalling to avoid stating. *The Hamlet,* for instance (to belie its title), hazards a definite opinion in regard to the immediate cause for decadence. The competitive demands of a capitalistic culture have corrupted the easy-going feudal ways of the old

South, that made for a certain comfort and security, if not for progress. In the old days, if a poor farmer or tenant owed something at the village store, the owner gave him credit or ignored the bill. It was live and let live with individual property rights respected and comparatively unchanging. Even the poor have security in their poverty; it would not grow much worse. But now with the return to the village of the worst of the Snopes, a transformation begins. Taking advantage of the indolence of the owning class, he worms his way into control, first by managing efficiently for them, and then by gaining ownership through those methods of unscrupulousness on the edge of legal retaliation so habitual to the shrewd entrepreneur. Snopes' machinations in this little Southern community are actually truer as symbolism than realistic writing. They symbolize the monopoly controls that have been set up throughout the nation with disastrous effect upon the ease and security of both the worker and the small owner. From the banter of the story arises a hatred of Snopes of a Puritan intensity. But our almost superstitious dislike and fear of him as an irresistible diabolical personality shows the depth of anxiety in the old South concerning its recent industrialization.

Yet Faulkner, as though hastening to add that he saw no hope from the old either, wrote *Absalom, Absalom,* to show that the old Southern system bore the seeds of its decay within it. A Southern lad at Harvard recounts to a Northern friend the history of one Southern family. Beginning in some unscrupulous acquisition of land and slaves, the family prosperity is corrupted by the very means that made it possible. Slave labor which supported it, facilitated the miscegenation it must, for its own safety, deplore officially as instinct leads to its indulgence. The temptation of the white owner for a Creole woman undermines the security of the family. Two sets of children bred apart come together without recognition, like each other on the basis of natural worth, but the discovery of their relation and the miscegenation involved leads to tragedy. And now the old estate is in the hands by blood right of half breeds. Remote cousins of pure white stock in the town attempt to take over, and the blacks prefer burning it down to its surrender. But one Negro, a half-wit, manages to escape to the North. Perhaps there, ponders this Southerner at Harvard, out of his further miscegenation in a different environment, out of the very ultimate of his degradation of mind and body, will come a strong new race to redeem the country. A fantastic and improbable miracle: this perverse notion that out of the most extreme and abject perversion of human nature its opposite of integrity and strength may dialectically arise. But Faulkner (applying Joyce's phrase in a less rigid and therefore less desperate context) 'will not say it shall not be.'

13

The Promise of Democracy in Richard Wright's *Native Son*

RICHARD WRIGHT is one of the latest and most intransigent representatives of a literary movement among our submerged nationalities that has been developing since the turn of the century as the literary analogy to the extension of our democratic ideals within the sphere of practical life.

The disappearance of the frontier around 1890 is usually accepted as the opening of a new period in our history when we became aware of the presence of minority races and underprivileged workers. From this time until the First World War a movement of 'muckraking' and reformism gathered impetus in the area of politics and business. It was very largely negative in nature, an attack upon graft and corruption, and only incidentally sympathetic to the common man who was their victim. The movement in fiction reflected these characteristics in the work of Frank Norris and Upton Sinclair; except that the nature of fiction demanded and secured a greater emphasis on the human suffering. But it is noteworthy that the literary movement as it gathered momentum in the new century shifted to a positive emphasis. In the work of novelists like Willa Cather, Theodore Dreiser, and Sherwood Anderson, and poets like

Reprinted through the courtesy of *Science and Society*. Originally entitled 'The Promise of Democracy and the Fiction of Richard Wright';

Vachel Lindsay and Carl Sandburg, we no longer see Anglo-Saxon writers bemoaning the misfortunes of the poor and the foreigners, but writers still Anglo-Saxon by birth or thoroughly assimilated to Anglo-Saxon attitudes of temperament beginning to find in the foreign stock qualities superior to their own. Whether these foreigners are workers or farmers, such writers admire their self-reliance, their endurance, their zest for living, in implicit contrast to the lack of these qualities in the dominant Puritan bourgeois stock. Even after the First World War, writers like Ernest Hemingway and Dos Passos carried over this interest in the social and cultural values of common people of other stocks than their own, but infused a new note of conscious envy or sense of inferiority on their own part. The man of foreign birth who had first been commiserated for his unfortunate economic position was now admired for his preservation of the more vital values of personality which the more prosperous native stock had sacrificed. I am here not concerned with the validity of these judgments, but only with their significance as denoting the rise in prestige of the foreign born in the eyes of certain native writers. It would be idle to claim that these writers represented the major tendency in our literature. But they were there to encourage the minorities themselves.

The 'thirties marked the coming of age of these submerged nationalities in the historical development of an independent American culture. When Van Wyck Brooks as a literary critic wrote *America's Coming of Age* in 1917, he was thinking only of Anglo-Saxon America. But no sooner, it would seem, had our Anglo-Saxon writers succeeded in throwing off their deference to English precedents (gaining the strength to do so through their new kinship to non-Anglo-Saxon America), than these other racial elements in American society demanded their share in the new culture. They began to point out their contribution to the national pattern. At first, through autobiography or sociological writing, in the work of Jacob Riis, Mary Antin, and Randolph Bourne, but later on, by the mid-twenties, in literature also, Americans of foreign birth began to make themselves felt, not as converts to the dominant Anglo-Saxon attitudes, but as modifiers of them. These new writers were now insisting upon their contribution to the newly forming pattern of national culture.

Within its limits, which they gladly accepted, they began to express in literary form the idioms they were introducing into the national language and to present with affectionate detail those idiosyncrasies of personality by which some of our Anglo-Saxon writers were already intrigued. Building upon this real but partial acceptance into the literary community, validated as it now was by the holding of political office and the possession of some economic power, these minority peoples could now, for the first time, express their awareness of the meaning of democracy and of the dignity of their share in it. But at the same time they could not fail to be acutely conscious of the partial character of their attainment. What had been achieved only made them the more cognizant of the long road ahead to anything like a real equality of opportunity and prestige. Their confidence in their potentialities as part of the amalgamation of a truly inclusive culture was contaminated by the knowledge that they had been forced to fight every inch of the way and a suspicion that the tolerance of the dominant Anglo-Saxon would lessen the more he found he had to tolerate.

The particular social relationship of the particular people to the Anglo-Saxon control determined the precise blend of suspicion and confidence in the literary expression.

The Negro, who has been treated worst of all despite a Civil War that ended in his specific emancipation, could not fall prey to any delusion of democracy, however personally prosperous. He could not share the optimism of other minorities in our society that their partial acceptance was either a temporary blot upon the escutcheon of our ideals or only part of the neglect of the working class in general. If self-assertion seemed to be winning acceptance for other minority groups, he could only conclude that his traditional policy of trust and co-operation was wrong. He developed a hatred of his old submissive self and a greater hatred for the whites who pretended to love and admire him in proportion as he remained without dignity. The Negro, once given a taste of dignity, drew the lesson that he had only himself to depend upon, and developed an inner core of tenacious resentment as he became aware that he was victim of the most glaring hypocrisy of all.

The new Negro, taught at length by our liberal tradition to trust himself and to expect equality, is alert for any manifestation of its spuriousness and is ready to die in shame or violence rather than submit any longer to the indignities of the past. His intransigence, it must be confessed, can hardly be palatable even to philanthropic whites. We must guard against a retreat into fear when we make the startling discovery that the roles have been reversed. It is no longer we whites who are in the position of granting equality if we please, but the Negroes who are wresting it from us whether we please or not. Such is the first shock that we get from Wright's novels. We are shaken once and for all from our complacency. If we are foolish and reactionary, we shall react by terror. If we are wise, we shall recognize that we have brought this impasse upon ourselves. But, above all, we shall become convinced that the impasse exists, and cannot be conjured away. This is the way the modern Negro feels. He is on the point of rebellion when he is mistreated. He is watchful for hypocrisy, scornful of the insufficiency of the good intention, determined not to sell his birthright for the small change of petty concessions. The Negro today feels that the gulf is absolute between the white skin and the black, save for two exceptions. They will trust those whites who stand shoulder to shoulder with them in a common fight to escape poverty and ignorance. They will trust those whites who risk a similar poverty and suffering to aid them in their own escape.

And so the new Negro literature, at its best when it is least influenced by white modes of feeling, is more bitter than that of any other minority group. This bitterness, turned inward and warped into melancholy during the period of the blues, becomes more and more direct in expression until it reaches an explosive violence, scarcely to be restrained, in Wright's fiction. Though neglected by white readers until the 'thirties, the new movement was actually earlier under way than the expression of other groups. Beginning about the year 1900 (as the *Negro Caravan* suggests), with the stories of Charles W. Chesnutt (whose work was at first taken for that of a white writer), it became a vigorous school early in the 'twenties, when the magazine *Opportunity* was founded and Claude MacKay and Langston Hughes were beginning to attract attention. This later work, especially the poetry, carried into esthetic expression the idioms and cadences of Negro speech, and reflected Negro sentiments in such genuine detail that its Negro origin could never have been mistaken. But though often written in a tone of aggressive resentment, its themes are usually a grim exposure of suffering to which the Negro helplessly submits rather than a narration of his revolt.

Richard Wright, therefore, had the advantage of an already developing tradition of Negro literature of protest. His greatness is to be found in the honesty and the power with which he transfers into fiction these convictions of the new Negro where they presented themselves in their most direct and least sophisticated form, unmodified by bourgeois standards, either Negro or white. In most of Wright's short stories, for instance, the Negro is an uneducated poor farmer or share-cropper of the deep South, living in rigid ostracism apart from the white world. A few stories in which the Negroes have found a common basis of feeling and action with poor whites who know something about Communism are an exception. In most of them, the possibility of equality with whites, or even of any sort of co-operation with them, is beyond the limit of experience. But these men have nevertheless caught the contagious spirit of democracy as it has been sweeping through the masses of the nation generally. All of his Negroes are psychologically convinced that they are men with rights. When his young Negro is caught by a white swimming in a forbidden pond, he talks back, defying the segregation. When the white starts to shoot him, he grabs the pistol and kills. Even though he has to flee north, he carries with him a determined spirit without regret. The Negro who has spent years trying to enlarge his small farm and become prosperous like a white farmer, when he finds his ambition frustrated, discovers his mistake in accepting bourgeois ideals and destroys everything. When such men are put upon, their spontaneous reaction is no longer to cringe, but to fight back; and when the fight proves futile, they prefer to die rather than submit. They are simple persons in the terms of formal education, but circumstances have forced upon them an intensity of emotional conflict which is more like the stuff of classical tragedy than any other quarter of American life can present.

Native Son translates into a metropolitan environment such a temperament where the conflicts become more complex and cause the breakdown of the personality. It is an environment, also, paradoxically, where constructive contact with whites becomes a possibility. The novel treats of the difficulties of such a contact for both parties. For we must remember that, if the short stories were written to reveal the new Negro to whites, *Native Son* endeavors to disclose both to each other.

The first reaction of the white reader is probably an awareness of his own inadequacy in such a situation. It dawns upon him that he is probably only a variant of the Daltons in his good intentions towards the Negroes. If he has taken pride in his practice of equality, in his magnanimous freedom from prejudices, he begins to see how, from the Negro's point of view, he must have appeared as sentimentally patronizing as the informality of Jan and Mary. He begins to recognize that barriers of suspicion and prejudice do not drop on both sides when he wills it. There are two persons concerned in a relationship of equality;

for equality, where individuals are involved, is a form of friendship, and friendship is a reciprocal activity.

Normally, the establishment of friendships is facilitated by the existence of a larger framework of common class or group beliefs and interests. When, in place of this preliminary awareness of common attitudes, the opposite exists, an awareness of hostile ones, the winning of friendship becomes a gradual process. Each side must assure the other that he is an exception to the group to which he would normally belong. It therefore becomes an instance of obtuseness and arrogance, of indifference to the individuality of the other person, when we assume in him an automatic response of delighted receptivity to our advances. Despite Mary's sophistication and Jan's radical beliefs, they have not realized that to Bigger Thomas they are no more individuals than Bigger is to them. When they make advances to him, it is not to him as individual, but to him as Negro, indeed, to him as a Negro of the old school, grateful for whatever charity a white may offer. If they do not see that they are treating him as a type, they cannot be expected to see how inevitably he at the same time is treating them as a different type. Bigger knows nothing of their radical theories. All he knows is that Mary is the sort of girl who is likely to get him into trouble with both whites and blacks, and ultimately with Jan himself, since she is his lover. When they insist upon his eating with them in a Negro café habituated by his friends, they seem to think he ought to appreciate this evidence of their democracy. They do not realize either that to his friends in the café his presence will seem a disloyalty to his race, evidence of his having sold out to the whites, or that his own wishes in the matter have been completely ignored. Their equality therefore becomes an act of racial superiority through the very compulsions they mistakenly think are causing its breakdown. The meaning of social equality has never been as adequately defined in a novel.

Our delusion, however, regarding the nature of equality is but one example of the larger problem of the actual limitation of our horizons. Direct experience is the intensest authentication of abstract statement. There is no financial depression in the effective sense of the phrase, as a determinant of man's immediate relationships with others, if his income and normal associations afford him a way of life bereft of emotional participation in deprivation, lacking any approximation of equality with the deprived, in pain or renunciation or spiritual suffocation. The prosperous, therefore, in all sincerity conclude that the underprivileged who complain are exaggerating, since their own circumstances do not set up a similar compulsion to rebel. Whatever lies beyond the horizon of close personal contacts becomes an abstraction. The poor man who is habitually seen from the window of a limousine is an allegorical man who is defined not in terms that he would himself understand, but those selected by the specific relationship between the two classes, which is to the profit of the person making the judgment. Similarly, the millionaire in his limousine is an abstraction to the man who never meets one in the subway. No amount of education or personal cleverness can overcome these limitations which testify to the authority of direct relationships within the group. Whatever is without the group is distorted, unknown and therefore frightening, or not worth knowing and complacently ignored. Only thus can history explain the psychology of fascists, who are certainly neither stupid nor illiterate.

When one's abstract views are contrary to the movement of history, this distortion is of what is essential in the unexperienced. But where it is precisely the essential or typical which is rightly known, the ignorance of the nonessential tends rather to guarantee the escape from a waste of effort upon the irrelevant. The essential, under such circumstances, is not distorted, but embodied instead in the large simple pattern of allegory. If, in other words, what falls without our immediate experience is always allegory, this allegory may be either a distortion of reality or only a simplified, larger-than-life presentation of it. In the latter case, one will not be in error in the long run, but he will make regrettable mistakes in specific actions. But it remains true, all the same, that even when a theory of society which history is proving to be valid is accepted by the group, whatever passes beyond the horizon of the group will be known only in an abstract way, symbolically, and will remain unknown or distorted in detail. The union worker, we may assume, knows the capitalist more accurately as a type than the employer his worker, because his first hand experience and superior understanding of social conditions affords him a valid insight into his general character. Each, nevertheless, will inflate the specific image of the other to an extent that will make it seem improbable to the other person. The sociological value of fiction is that it provides a partial solution of this dilemma. If it is constructed on the proper abstract basis, it pushes our horizon beyond the limits of our effective experiences, and provides a more authentic understanding of the individual. It is the particular value of *Native Son* that this service, which in most novels is only a by-product of the nature of fiction, becomes the conscious purpose that determines its method.

The conflicts that form the plot of *Native Son* take their particular form from the characters' ignorance of these limitations, just as Wright's firm hand in their delineation is a consequence of his awareness of them. Bigger Thomas, the Negro boy, weighed down by his illiteracy, is no more ignorant of the individuality of the rich philanthropists, the Daltons, than they are of his. They recognize him as a type, the underprivileged adolescent who has been in trouble with the police, and are prepared to treat him according to a formula which seems enlightened to them, rehabilitation through a job as their chauffeur in an atmosphere of kindly intentions. They fail to recognize that their theory is the approach of private charity which the Negro people are no longer willing to accept; and that, despite Bigger's apparent humility, circumstances have fashioned him into its incorrigible opponent. They know Bigger more specifically than he them, but their specific knowledge is worse than useless since it is used to justify an untenable premise. Bigger, on the other hand, who cannot be said to know the Daltons with any specificity, is right in his general view of them. For him they are allegorical figures from another world, millionaires who live sumptuously on rents torn from the poor Negroes of a segregated district. In this fundamental matter his underprivileged station has afforded him a superior insight. He senses their inconsistency and unfairness in attempting to conceal from themselves and the Negro population by the small benefactions of charity the monstrous oppression from which they draw an income, huge by comparison. Despite his illiteracy, then, Bigger's awareness of his relationship to the Daltons is more sound than theirs of him.

But Wright takes the errors of the Daltons for granted. He is concerned, rather, with the fact that Bigger, though his insights are basically more sound than the Daltons', cannot use them constructively. Sensing shame and futility in his mother's consolation from a religion that demands submission to misery and the renunciation of any hope for a better life, what might have been a healthy inner need to act is perverted by the sort of action his environment provides. At the outset, Wright keys his novel to this interpretation. Bigger kills the rat that has been frightening the women folks, and then frightens them the more by flaunting its dead body in their faces. His courage is that overcompensation for fear called bravado. It passes beyond the needs of the situation and defeats its own end here as in later crises in the novel. Its source is his acceptance of the ideals of the white race as they have penetrated his ghetto. Flying an airplane symbolizes the freedom and mastery of the white race he would like to share. Knowing that he cannot, his helplessness creates an inner state of fear which (as it has transformed his healthy impulse of courage into bravado) sets up the direct motivation of hatred, and transforms what might have been a healthy social activity into petty thievery. But, to this uneducated boy, hatred for the whites is too remote and turns inward. It vents itself upon his family with their misguided notion that decency is rewarded, upon his black neighbors from whom his gang steals, upon the gang for the pettiness of its objectives, and upon himself for his inability to attain more grandiose ends. When he accepts the job with the Daltons, it is to escape these pressures which he hates. But they have all the same been furnishing him with the uneasy stability of belonging to some grouping. In his new environment he is alone in a white world, which becomes the more formidable since he cannot treat it with the unalloyed hatred it seems to him to deserve. The apparent kindliness of the Daltons obscures the simplicity of their allegorical meaning and intensifies his inner conflicts by introducing an element of intellectual doubt to add to his fear.

Behind Wright's narrative is the unspoken assumption that Negroes must have some organization for common protest that shall enable them to bring the abstract objective into productive relationship to the specific situation, that will afford understanding and guidance in the specific situations as they arise. In its absence, as riots in the Negro sections of our large cities have shown, an inevitable demand will spend itself in anarchistic violence to the defeat of its profound and laudable intention. For Negroes, *Native Son* is a warning that there is no alternative to right organization except the futility of individual violence into which Bigger is led.

Alone with these whites, whom Bigger fears but is no longer so sure he should hate, his fear and hatred rise into a crescendo as the situation feeds his incompetence with more serious temptations. When it becomes part of his duty to put the drunken daughter of the Daltons to bed, the strain between abstract knowledge and ignorance of the immediate situation reaches the breaking point. His fear that he may be thought by her parents to be planning her rape would have been unjustified had he known the Daltons as individuals. But it is valid both as a generalization of the white world and as a temptation her previous freedom with her lover seemed to be proffering him. In his state of excitement his handling of this difficult situation defeats his intention. He smothers to death the girl he does not wish to be charged with raping. His motives here and elsewhere are quite different from those of Dostoevsky's Roskolnikov, to whom he has been wrongly compared.

His trial of constructive action has been a failure. What follows up to his arrest is the tale of one savage, misguided act after another. But Bigger has become blind to their savagery. His uncertain groping for some valid avenue of self-fulfilment before the murder now gives way to the authority of his excitement. He enters a world of paranoiac fantasy, in which his acts of frenzy seem to him not so much the clever concealment of his initial mistake as the unfolding of a grandiose plan of conquest. He has lost his sense of belonging with anybody, black or white, and his need to belong with anybody. His act of murder seems to him to have released immense potentialities that had lain imprisoned within his personality. While he is actually running away from pursuit in desperation, he conceives himself to be a Tamberlaine capable of reducing the whole world to the prostrate state it had imposed upon him and he has now escaped. He seems now to be flying the forbidden airplane above a remote and impotent world.

But this picture of his immediate reaction to his crime cannot be isolated from his subsequent attitudes. After his arrest he reverts to an apathy of complete worthlessness. His arrest and the white crowds howling for his lynching puncture his fantasy and restore him to the only contact with reality he has ever known. As long as he lacks a fraternal mechanism for its transformation, it is the only contact with reality the underprivileged Negro of our day can ever know: the certainty that there is nobody in our society who is worse treated. Now Bigger no longer possesses the illusion of power in individual hatred. He has reverted to the animal docility of slavehood. His self-respect reawakens when he finds a single man who understands him, and by understanding him enables him at last to bridge the gulf between the abstract and the particular. In the long final section of the novel his Jewish Communist lawyer repeats for him the therapeutic service David performed for the distraught Saul of Browning's poem.

Bigger, it is true, understands very little of the content of these discussions. But the lawyer's patience and kindliness of intention in conducting them are enough to convince him of their central meaning. It is enough that they are taking place in such a milieu. Through this elementary fact Bigger comes to feel that there is one man in the world who understands him better than he understands himself, and can bring to the surface of his consciousness that longing to be of some value to himself and to society which the distortions of his hatred had concealed. So starved and twisted has been his former emotional life, that this simple experience of a single friendship takes on the proportions of a sufficient achievement for a lifetime. He cannot conceive of a further goal to live for. The lawyer embodies that principle of equality which Bigger has been unable to articulate, though he reacted against Mary Dalton's mistaken bohemian notion of it that Jan had shared. Max's willingness to endure criticism for defending him and a social ostracism similar to his own has put them on a common basis of understanding. And from this common basis Bigger is able to see for the first time that he is not alone in his struggle and his torment.

Bigger Thomas is of course not a typical Negro. Some of his actions, like the slaying of the rat, are symbolic presentations of his personal traits. But though Bigger himself is an individual and not a symbolic figure, the reader accepts him as representative of other men unlike him in various respects. As often happens in contemporary fiction, the extreme disorders of personality which he exhibits are only an exaggeration of the latent characteristics of apparently more normal persons. In a world where there is scarcely a man so illiterate as not to be aware of our publicized ideals of democracy and apply them directly to his own circumstances, Bigger's hatred is shared in varying degrees by every Negro and every worker, and indeed by every individual who feels deprived of a chance to fulfill his potentialities. The only differences are in the depth to which the hatred is buried, the adequateness with which it is controlled, or in the extent to which it is diluted by compensations. Other characters besides Bigger turn out to be examples of this common hatred with the variety of qualifications I have just mentioned.

For a time, it is true, we do not get this impression. We follow Bigger's activities so closely that we share his collapse after his arrest. But in place of the apathy into which he falls, we recoil with loathing from a sudden recognition that we have been identifying ourselves too closely with his fantasies. His murders now stand forth in all their gruesome tabloid clarity. At this point, Wright introduces the insincere rhetoric of the district attorney and the white mob's demand for lynching. They reawaken our sympathy for Bigger, and bring home to us the relation between his depravity and the dominant social pressures which constantly verbalize the principles of justice and democracy but deny any adequate application of them. As though to prove that such hypocrisy does not merely produce Biggers in the black race but corrupts our whole social fabric, we become aware that this white mob is only concealing its affinity with what is vicious in Bigger by seeking from his lynching a similar paranoid satisfaction of its own frustration. Our loathing of the mob cancels out our reaction against Bigger, and our disgust turns toward the deplorable social system which is responsible for both of them. Bigger's hatred of the whites is itself a variant of the common insecurity of the common man in our culture.

Fortunately, there are forces at work to avert catastrophe in our national life. The demand for Negro labor in time of war, the growing acceptance of Negroes by the trade unions, the appearance of Negroes in the top ranks of virtually every cultural and intellectual profession, the committees on fair employment practices are but a few of the justifications for optimism.

Wright might have chosen as his theme the conflict between these two groups of forces, and resolved it in an atmosphere of confidence that history cannot reverse itself and progress is inevitable. But if treated generally, with the stress on the social forces, a distortion of the good intention into sentimentality would be likely. If, on the other hand, the stress were on individual relationships, a powerful and beautiful novel might be written. But it would fail to give the right impression of the general state of affairs. Or it would become a novel not of the Negro people but of proletarian life, whites and blacks working together towards a common end, to the neglect, emotionally, of the racial element altogether.

Wright, on the contrary, has preferred to accept the general situation as it is today. He makes his reader intellectually aware of the economic and political forces at work. But he focuses our attention upon their effect on the individual personality. Desirous above all of banishing our complacency, he is not interested in the rosy promise of the future. He knows that this promise will not be valid unless whites are stimulated to action by a sense of guilt and blacks are guided by some better plan than anarchistic individualism. And so he translates the underlying social forces into their specific exhibition in the relationships of individuals. But he does not neglect the case for hope. Just as he depicts the crisis as the immediate consequence of wrong personal relationships, he seeks to show that the promise of the future depends immediately and specifically upon the capacity for making the right ones. Doubtless this capacity itself is contingent upon a plausible philosophical view of the general situation. But the important point Wright is making is that this general view needs to be written into the very structure of the personality as a capacity for friendship. The relation between Bigger and his lawyer, Max, to which the end of the book is devoted, is intended to serve as prototype of the proper constructive relationship between men generally.

Wright's accomplishment, unfortunately, is not as good as his intention. Though he conveys some impression of what he means, he is confused and repetitious in presenting the case for hope. This is in part the result of a change in method. Up to this point in the narrative, he has been following the general plan of Dreiser's *American Tragedy.* Using an objective method to reveal the subjective state of their hero's personality, on the theory of the influence of environment, both authors have tended to pile up an unnecessary quantity of substantiating detail. But Dreiser's trial scene is monotonous rather than confused. He continues to use the same technique. Wright, on the contrary, departs at this point from Dreiser's method and no longer follows the external probabilities of the situation. The character of Max's plea to the court can hardly be justified. His public speeches would never convince a jury, since they are only projections of his private conversations with Bigger in his cell. Even though during the entire novel we have been interested in Bigger's inner life, we have seen it largely through the frank interpretations of the author, without distortion of the probabilities of everyday life either in the action or the dialogue. Both are now distorted. What the lawyer says becomes ambiguous, and where he says it unlikely. The objective method is superseded by a symbolic one. Wright is no longer the detached commentator but allows his personality to merge with that of the lawyer. This change of technique was doubtless dictated by Wright's desire to involve his audience in a direct emotional appeal. He is addressing them symbolically when Max addresses the court symbolically, as though he were still clarifying Bigger's mind. His intention, if successful, would have brought the book to a crescendo of hope for the future, as Max and Bigger, the author, the court, and the readers merge in a common understanding of friendship and equality. But since Wright is unable to put his message in the clear detail of the earlier sections of the book, the effect is not that of the concluding speech in *Waiting for Lefty,* but of a sudden plunge into Dostoievsky. Wright begins to share the confusions and even something of the hysteria, the negative aspects of which he has been elucidating.

The tone of the book changes. What had given *Native Son* its refreshing atmosphere of sanity was the awareness its objective method assured, that the author had been untouched by the maladies he described. The characters, the situations, our whole social fabric, we had realized with consternation, are parallel to the decadence of Russia before the Revolution, which Dostoievsky exposed so thoroughly, and so obviously shared. Wright, like Dreiser, had stood aloof from the terrible deeds of his characters. But when he turns to the case for hope, the ambiguity of its statement is no more convincing than the frank mysticism of Dostoievsky. That social orientation towards the common man, which alone permits a genuine approach to groups beyond our immediate experience, has been clarified. But the clarification is a deduction the reader skims from the restless surface of its vague restatement. One feels that Wright has not understood Max much better than Bigger has done; and Bigger has surely not got the essence of what he was trying to say at all. From Max's fervid proffer of friendship he has drawn no further aid than the recovery of his self-esteem, and no further meaning than the dogged return to his original delusion (though it is now held in a spirit of tranquillity, as though his life had achieved a constructive aim) that his act of murder was an escape from oppression. It was easier, apparently, for Dostoievsky to accept the mystic belief of Christianity, that part of man is innately good and at war with his innately evil impulses, than for Wright to hunt with the aid of psychology for the ray of hope veiled in the depths of social decay. The anxious verbosity of Max's pleas evokes the suspicion that Wright, against his intention, shares that counterpart of the social neurosis he describes, which is the unconscious fear that hope itself is a fantasy.

Perhaps in a world where grounds for hatred are so valid, even so talented an author may be forgiven if he cannot present with equal skill the case for love and understanding. We may expect that among all our national minorities the Negro will be the last to do so, and that he will do so first in those areas of the working class where genuine friendships can be taken for granted. But as the Negro sees the white world yielding before the pressure of his merit as well as his demands, his psychology will change. He will then know that he has won a place of dignity in the American society, and the newest Negro literature is likely to be the story of his positive achievement.

14

The Art of Richard Wright's Short Stories

RICHARD WRIGHT is the first Negro novelist to gain a wide audience of white readers and to be accepted by that audience as one of our distinguished authors. Without feeling any need for a separate category because of his color, we spontaneously mention his name along with Hemingway or Steinbeck or whom you will. At the same time, paradoxically, we cannot fail to be aware that he criticizes his white audience more trenchantly than any other Negro novelist has done. Our acceptance of him under such circumstances does not merely testify to the serious attention problems of racial discrimination today compel; it is a tribute to the quality of his writing. It is evidence that he belongs with those among us who express themselves with distinction.

The choice of a controversial topic, of course, is no guarantee of good writing. On the contrary, it has often distracted both author and reader from a proper attention to it. Unless it is well executed, the popularity of such a novel is likely to be more ephemeral than the issue on which it is built. *Uncle Tom's Cabin,* which was widely read before the Civil War, is said to have intensified the demand for Negro emancipation. But it has survived only as melodrama for children, despite the increasing importance of its general theme. The chief reason, probably, for its failure to hold its public is not the parochialism of the story, but its technical deficiencies. Written in the same decade as some of the best work of Poe and Hawthorne, it shows no sign of kinship in technique. It hardly suggests Mrs. Stowe's better work of a decade later in *Oldtown Folks.* In place of the quiet realism of this latter work, *Uncle Tom's Cabin* utilizes the methodological clichés of the Sunday School tracts of the period. Perhaps its loose narrative structure, its sentimental definition of character, the perils which pursue the innocent Eliza are esthetic proof that its theme was really premature, that, as has often been said, the Civil War was actually fought for the expansion of northern industry and involved the emancipation of the slaves in only a superficial way. If this is true, the superior quality of *Native Son* might be taken as evidence that the question of Negro rights has at last become a central issue for the development of our national society. At all events, unlike its predecessor in theme, *Native Son* is not isolated by its style of writing from the prevalent contemporary techniques.

At the same time, it is not an example of the best of them. Though superior to our ordinary novels, *Native Son* does not possess the characteristics of our most careful craftsmanship. Not only does the author include minute dissection of the motives behind the action and the dialogue, but these explanations are spun out after the manner of one feeling his way into a difficult subject. Grammatically, to take an instance, this means a participial construction left hanging at the end of a sentence where it qualifies a clear statement or leaves a conclusion tentative or ambiguous. It is the method of Dreiser's *American Tragedy.* But since Wright's plot is more complex, the effect is not that of mere padding but of a too conscientious endeavor to get to the bottom against all obstacles. It is at opposite poles from the bright competence of a Proust among the nuances of human motivation. These deficiencies show that Wright, though sensitive to the techniques of the psychological novel, has not yet been able to apply them with a sure hand. Fortunately the short story permits only a limited documentation; and it is upon the quality of his short stories that Wright's reputation as a stylist, at present, rests. *Native Son* widened his audience to include the average reader. But the reader who is sensitive to style will continue to prefer the short stories.

Awareness of the esthetic limitations of Wright as a novelist should not, however, obscure our admiration for the extraordinary qualities of these stories, whether written before or after *Native Son.* If he has not yet conquered the problem of detail in the novel, it is precisely in the handling of detail in his stories that his distinction is to be found. The 'classical' short story was conspicuously lacking in this respect. From the pioneer work of Poe to Maupassant and Stevenson, it might achieve a powerful effect of melodrama or surprise ending. It might be witty and allusive, but it was never characterized by a profoundly moving plot and an abundance of significant detail to assure plausibility. What accumulation of detail there was was generally employed for superficial ends. It either provided a well-knit but flashy plot, as in Maupassant, or merely furnished a background of atmosphere to an even simpler plot, related to it only by the pathetic fallacy, as in Stevenson. There has since then grown up a story of quite the opposite type, in those of Chekhov and Katherine Mansfield and Hemingway, where nothing but nuance falls into some sort of obscure relationship, which could hardly be called a plot with a conclusion. Their themes are smothered and lost sight of out of fear of the crudity of exposure in an open resolution. Such have been the two tendencies in the short story: the one affording the thrill of action without genuine insight into character; the other insight into character which aimlessly evaporates. To the literary historian, Wright's importance is that, by bringing both traditions together, he has moulded a type of story superior to either. When detail becomes significant by being significantly associated, the story not only gains direction and climax, but the flimsiness of a melodramatic climax is transformed into the unforgettable power of tragedy.

From the historical perspective, this, I think, is what Wright has accomplished. But I do not mean to imply that he has worked either directly or consciously with either of these traditions. Unimpeded by the requirements of a formal education, his bent for writing appears to have led him directly to authors of current reputation and the writers of the past who influenced them. He has assimilated from them what his developing talent needed, and taking place as it did without external compulsion, the assimilation has sometimes been so complete as to be fairly unrecognizable. I am told that the most powerful influence upon him has been Hemingway, whose pugnacious, independent temper seems to have appealed to him. From Hemingway doubtless came his objective attitude, his direct, unflinching vision, and the short, firm sentences, with their frequent change of grammatical subject, as the appropriate vehicle of expression. Wright's sentences are stript bare of all but the necessary adjectives and connectives. Each is a vigorous self-sufficient unit, which expels its pent-up meaning and willingly gives way to the next in line. But they all retire before the tense authority of dialogue. The dialogue itself is candid, the sort the character would have used in life, or the sort that aims to give such an effect.

> He saw the mob close in around the fire. Their faces were hard and sharp in the light of the flames. More men and women were coming over the hill. The long dark spot was smudged out.
>
> 'Everybody git back!'
>
> 'Look! Hes gotta finger!' *

If this passage does not remind one of Hemingway, it is because his style has been assimilated into a quite different personality, and used to such different ends that the relationship is disguised. This is partly owing to the fact that Wright is dealing with

* Wright, Richard, *Native Son*, New York, 1940, by courtesy of Harper and Brothers.

Negro dialogue, but mostly because his insights are richer and deeper than Hemingway's. For you will never find the passages of sentimental or sadistic writing in Wright that you will in Hemingway's work. If Wright has emotional conflicts in his short stories, they are dissipated by the act of composition. But Hemingway's emotional blocks are at the basis of his style, which does not resolve them but expresses them, transformed in various ways, as irony, or sentiment, or brutality, or the inconclusive ending; but always controlled by understatement.

> The world was not wheeling any more. It was just very clear and bright, and inclined to blur at the edges. I washed, brushed my hair. I looked strange to myself in the glass, and went downstairs to the dining-room.
>
> 'Here is he!' said Bill. 'Good old Jake! I knew you wouldn't pass out.'
>
> 'Hello, you old drunk,' Mike said.
>
> 'I got hungry and woke up.'
>
> 'Eat some soup,' Bill said.
>
> The three of us sat at the table, and it seemed as though about six people were missing.*

Despite the appearance of directness of statement here, the actual emotional meanings are all transformed and controlled, even negated by the conscious surface of the personality. Both writers begin with objective description of the surface. Hemingway gives us only so much of the depth as the surface reveals, which, with his type of character, is very little. But neither does Wright desire nor are his characters sophisticated enough, to conceal from themselves and others what lies deeper within. So the two styles, technically so similar, are used to opposite ends—in Hemingway to distract attention from the confusions beneath, and in Wright to reveal a process that is going on to eradicate what confusion may exist, and therefore to promote a definite resolution of the action at the end of the story.

* Hemingway, Ernest, *The Sun Also Rises,* New York, 1926, by courtesy of Charles Scribner's Sons.

But Hemingway also did Wright the service of leading him to other authors. Passages, for instance, under the influence of Gertrude Stein are occasionally conspicuous in both writers. They are usually passages, like this from Wright, of interior monologue.

> Never in all her life had she been so much alone as she was now. Days were never so long as these days; and nights were never so empty as these nights.

From such open expression of melancholy Hemingway draws back into his habitual mood of cynical reserve. But Wright proceeds from them further into poetic prose which utilizes contemporary metrical cadences to convey pleasurable emotions, even though they be of hopes as yet unfulfilled. Not from Hemingway but from the Donne-Hopkins' tradition came a later wish of this same girl for 'white bright days and dark black nights' (to which a rare new element has been added since 'dark black' in this context cannot be taken as a sinister but only as a pleasurably mysterious phrase). More generally, such passages are closer to the fiction of Lawrence and Anderson.

> Again she felt his fingers on the tips of her breasts. She backed away, saying nothing this time. She thrust the gourd out from her. Warm fingers met her cold hands. He had the gourd. She heard him drink; it was the faint, soft music of water going down a dry throat, the music of water in a silent night. She sighed and drank again.

Here the mood and the meaning are close to Sherwood Anderson. But there is wanting the slightly neurotic tempo of his cadences and his interrogative appeals to the reader. The description of drinking (like Wright's sentences occasionally) offers the enrichment of insight into aspects of the immediate sensation not indispensable to the plot. In Anderson, such sentences are typical, and their overtones accumulate into a general state of narcissistic revery. But in Wright these impressions, though immediately peripheral to the external action, furnish insight into the character that has them, and so, in the long run, they feed into the course of events, to increase the dramatic power and plausibility of the emerging plot. But the most important stylistic influence hardly needs to be mentioned. For idiom, and cadence, and emotional attitude, Wright was fortunate in being able to use the tradition of Negro folk poetry after it had been given polish and flexibility by two generations of sophisticated Negro poets and prose writers. He could thus combine, without embarrassment of fumbling, white and black traditions of craftsmanship of equal maturity.

His employment of these materials, however, to the attainment of a significant plot must be ascribed to non-literary factors. Fundamental, without question, was the nature of his childhood experiences, which he has described in several autobiographical works. The hardship and cruelty of his childhood set up reactions in him which must be ascribed to the prevalence of a vague awareness of Negro rights in the environment and which led to the personal search for more adequate understanding. He picked his non-literary studies as unacademically as we have seen him choosing his literary. Here again, he had the good fortune never to have had a formal education with its clutter of useful and useless facts, of tenable and fantastic theories. The sociology he chose substantiated his experiential view that our reactions are conditioned by our environments. His study of psychology, especially as illustrated in the psychological novel, gave him a competence in understanding how complex these reactions to environment actually are. His study of Marxist philosophy, in particular, enabled him to understand that these reactions, however complex, are only variants of class attitudes that are fundamentally the same. By its emphasis upon class conflict it gave him the power to sense the existence of plots in life, just as his psychology had enabled him to develop them with lifelike and probable detail.

The theme, then, was at hand for Wright, as it had not been for either Poe or Katherine Mansfield, and Wright was more fortunate than Hemingway in being so circumstanced that he could pick it up without equivocation and efficiently transform it into art without distortion from any personal limitations. I do not wish to derogate the value of the work of these other writers. But it is all the same true that Poe was so circumstanced that he had only the sensational themes of decadence to build into a short story since his personal neuroses led him to the decaying feudal life of the old South. Similarly, Katherine Mansfield's precise but timid vision was too delicate to penetrate beyond the wisps of sentiment floating over the crumbling fabric of the Victorian heritage. Hemingway, on the other hand, tries to conceal from himself by a pugnacious front his identification with the social distemper he despises in the world of the prosperous around him.

Wright's theme, by contrast, is embedded in the structure of our present society, both north and south, and race riots and lynchings have exposed it uncompromisingly to both Negroes and whites. The conditions of his own life afforded him the capacity to sense its significance more sharply than any white man and many Negroes could. His gift for writing was encouraged by his awareness of this material craving representation. And he came at a time when the illiterate folk literature of the Negroes had already been taken over by educated Negro poets and become the dominant tradition of modern Negro literature. Under these circumstances Wright's application to it of the mechanisms of fiction, as established among white writers, was no longer a possible miscegenation, but deepened his penetration of his theme and enabled him to transfer it into the awareness of his readers.

The illuminating contrast here, where the short stories are concerned, is not with Hemingway who becomes the more resentful the further he gets from his normal association with sophisticated people. It is rather with an author like the Irishman Synge who, when he sympathizes with the tragedy in the life of the poor, turns it not into cynicism but pathos. Once more

I cite for the purpose of definition rather than derogation. But, fine as *Riders to the Sea* is as a sad drama of Irish folk life, its sense of gathering doom reminds one more of Maeterlinck than of Wright. The difference that, in the one case, the doom is understood to be imposed by the forces of nature and in the other by men is not a consequence of a difference in intention of sympathy but of insight into the reality of the situation, which was imposed by a difference in the experiential relation to it of the two authors themselves. Synge was a middle-class writer who felt a genuine middle-class sympathy for the poor Irish fisherpeople. He tried to write like one of them, indeed, so genuinely that he lived among them. Though he had assimilated their dialect, he was unable to assimilate the nuance of psychological meanings this dialect was capable of conveying. Furthermore, unlike Wright's Negroes, these back-country Irish were too benighted to understand the real cause of their misery, which surely lay more in their superstitions, their lack of education and machines, than in the implacable cruelty of the sea. Synge seeks to sympathize not only with their misery but with the superstitions they invoke to explain it, which he would never have accepted to explain anything on his own bourgeois level. Thus, instead of clarifying their psychology through presenting a more valid perspective upon the social factors that determined it than they themselves possessed, he actually increased its ambiguity. These people were too foreign to his habitual attitudes, and as a result his diction has more of vague 'atmosphere' than nuance, and his plot becomes dependent upon a mystical naturalism, depicting an ineffectual resistance to obscure irresistible forces, rather than a conflict of recognizable elements which is capable of a solution.

Wright, on the contrary, was born and brought up in the midst of his material. His education, instead of alienating him from his past and its loyalties, was assimilated into already determined attitudes and merely enabled him to express them more adequately than Synge's sincere but external intention of sympathy could do. Nor should it be overlooked that these individual divergences between writers who both shared the same general aim, were magnified by the fact that this aim was interpreted differently by the different milieus of which each was a part. Synge's Ireland was witnessing the rise of the bourgeoisie into self-consciousness with the usual trappings of vague proletarian sympathy, whereas Wright was part of a larger context of the rise of the American proletariat into self-consciousness with overtones of hostility towards the middle class. Synge's spontaneous attitude towards the Irish populace is seen in *The Playboy of the Western World,* where the meanings of idioms and plot are quite clear since he makes no pretense of greater sympathy than is involved in the good-natured exposure of shiftlessness and eccentricity.

The difficulties which Synge encountered in *Riders to the Sea* are analogous to Wright's in *Native Son.* But under the changed circumstances, these latter were not such as to be insoluble this side of mysticism, but were solved, rather, with awkwardness and hesitation to the sacrifice of esthetic quality. In *Native Son,* in other words, where Wright took the larger circumference of black and white, bourgeois and proletarian society, as his milieu, he had to comprehend a comparatively unfamiliar and a predominantly hostile environment. But in the short stories, his locus is the black world of the South where he felt completely at home, and where he had only to articulate the misery and revolt of the black man. Both his plot and his style were implicit in his theme, which naturally sought the direct expression of dialogue in the folk idiom. His knowledge of the white literary tradition was necessary only to enable him to evoke the more perfectly what was latent within. At the same time he knows that his particular subjects are not direct representations of his own experience. He follows Eliot's law of the objective emotional correlative. Because he comprehends it so distinctly and feels its validity so genuinely, he appears dominated by his theme. He seems to forget himself in its expression and follow his own story as breathlessly as any reader. He thus, as a stylist, possesses the assurance that is typical of the writer of distinction, who seems to be merely articulating, by means of his craft and his insight, the significant experiences of his fellow men.

Wherefore Wright can take over the *mot juste* of literary tradition, and can use it with an ease forbidden to the inventor of the term, because he is not expressing an alien and supercilious attitude, but only fulfilling the intention of his people in a refinement of their natural cadence and idiom. His selection of words is that normal to the tradition of good writing, not primarily because he is steeped in that tradition, but because good writing, as Eliot's law suggests, recognizes its fealty to the living situation, and uses 'traditions' only as tools to achieve its clarification. His choice of diction, dictated by the needs of the situation, therefore, follows a middle course between the underprecision of mystic or romantic escapism and the overprecision of the rationalistic. It maintains a balance between the expository and the emotive aspects of words. It meets the demand for the 'right word' because the 'ends,' since they are adequately understood, can determine the 'means.' His words are not chosen so that attention is distracted from the theme (the 'end') and kept centered on the complexity of the immediate sensation or activity (the 'means'). But they are selected, instead, with such judiciousness and economy that suspense is created, and the present scene calls forth its successor until a significant plot has been completely woven. The use of diction in this way is possible only when the social sphere proffers a theme which is not paralyzed by paradox or ambiguity, and which the author's social point of view enables him to recognize.

These comments are applicable to literary forms generally, and their emphasis upon plot does not imply that Wright's stories are virtually one act plays. They do make use of an unusual amount of dialogue, in order to intensify the validity of the action and the degree of emotional response. But they are not open to the usual objection to the one act play, that it does not have space enough for significant accomplishment. Because they are short stories, they can employ other mechanisms besides dialogue, and accomplish more in less space. Though Wright never obtrudes obiter dicta, by employing a certain amount of description and a considerable amount of stream of consciousness, he avoids the limitations of the dramatic form.

How Wright achieves these ends can be illustrated by reference to *Long Black Song.* In this story he builds his climax with extraordinary discretion and subtlety. Beginning with a comparatively simple situation, both action and characterization grow more complex as the narrative unfolds. The characters change as a result of the action. They learn through critical experience. There are therefore two aspects of every situation, since each has an effect both upon the nature of the personality and upon the externalization of its nature in the action. For the most part, of course, it is a new facet of a persistent character structure that the new situation discloses. But at moments of climax the personality is dialectically changed, and its outward expression redirected, although this can happen only to the principal character since he alone is principally engaged in the action. Thus in *Long Black Song,* the wife of the poor Negro farmer is the principal character at the start. Her romantic but entirely legitimate longing for a better life follows the familiar American tradition and affords the story a congenial orientation within which the failure can unfold. Her seduction by a white youth only sets the theme into motion. She then retires, keeping the same character structure and the same accompanying ideals. She becomes a chorus upon the action, through which we remain aware that the dream of a better life is frustrated by the inability of men to co-operate, which to her means, first, the conditions of marriage that led her to seek out a Negro lover, then the war that took her lover away, and now the interracial fighting that proceeds under her own eyes. For, after her husband returns and discovers her seduction by a white man, he takes over the story. The external action, though the tension becomes intense, is easily described. The Negro kills the white salesman when he comes back for the Victrola he had left the night before (symbolic both of the wife's dream and of her downfall). A posse gathers to lynch him. But after killing as many of them as possible, he prefers to die in the flames of his own house rather than surrender to their vengeance.

What gives this story its vitality and its individuality is the fact that its action is associated with an inner revolution in the character of the protagonist. It is this element that distinguishes it from the short story of tradition. The poor farmer had been an exceptional type of Negro. He had been neither easygoing after the old manner nor in conscious revolt like so many of the metropolitan Negroes of the present day. On the contrary, to his wife's discomfiture, he had assimilated the practical version of the American way as completely as any respectable poor white farmer. He had believed that if he worked hard, added to his little property by depriving himself and his wife of casual comforts, above all, if he could acquire a hired man, he would have won all the self-respect and social standing a man requires. Thus, as usual in Wright, although his plot is on the surface sheer race conflict, the deeper implications transcend race, apply equally to whites, and only become the clearer through their more intense representation in Negro material. For here, any reader, black or white, conservative or radical, can agree on the diagnosis: that such a belief, though it looks practical, is actually more fantastic than the wife's romantic dream.

Racial feeling becomes the device through which the Negro farmer rejects a point of view that is not racial at all (but bourgeois), and attains a heroism which transcends its racial stimulus (since it is now shared by all those who have a valid belief in democracy). When Silas learns that his wife has been unfaithful with the salesman, he feels at first that she has been traitorous both to him and to their race, and ruined his lifetime of effort. He soon comes to see that her disloyalty to him is permitted by the white bourgeois code he has accepted in other areas. It is the prototype in personal relationships of his stupidity in the economic. Her error has permitted his discovery of an inconsistency in his philosophy of life. So he reorients his attitudes. His hatred turns away from his wife, whose offense he now sees has been imposed upon her by the social system he had accepted and expected to profit by. But instead of letting his hatred turn inward upon himself for having been misguided, his poverty and his race buttress what had been healthy in his bourgeois attitude. His self-reliance guarantees that his energy continue to be directed outward, but towards a new objective. It gives him the courage to kill the white offender and to fight against the posse as long as he can. On the surface this new aim may look like simple uncontrollable desire for revenge. And part of his motivation also is without doubt a continuation of his old ambition for property. But when he retreats within his own house to die there in the flames, he is doing more than protecting his property to the bitter end. His principal motive, I believe, is to withhold from the posse the satisfaction of their sadism in killing him. When dying must be, he wishes to control his own dying and make it an assertion of his new sense of values. To have fought against the posse until the degrading end of their final overpowering him would have been to have continued on another level the old bourgeois fallacy of free competition. His governance of his own death is his application of a new standard for living. In his final act he is already tasting the freedom of the better life of which his wife had dreamed.

Though Silas' revenge is violent, it is based upon a valid conviction and not a fantasy. The conviction is, of course, that men ought to defend themselves when frustrated of their legitimate expectations from life by continual repression. When this defense, though it benefits the personality, results in outward disaster, this conviction has evoked a tragic theme. It is, in fact, the tragic theme of our time. And as such, should be distinguished from the many themes tangential to it, that have flourished in the recent past, and which are, by contrast, the themes of pathos. Negroes, as they became sophisticated, might conceivably have adopted any number of these bourgeois attitudes, which involve irony or pathos in place of tragedy. In the poetry of Robinson Jeffers, after a life of violent inner and outer conflict, death becomes the desired passage into inert anonymity. For Thomas Mann, sin and suffering, through the violence of war, become therapeutic devices of purgation by means of which we automatically recover our lost perception of the virtuous life. As in Dostoievsky, the act of violence automatically sets up its opposite; a different consciousness is created spontaneously by the mere course of events. In Wright, a learning process is basic. The reciprocity between developing events and the changing personality involves more than the emergence of different orders of intuition. Part of the reciprocity is between the individual's reason and his emotions. The process, thus conceived, assumes the emerging control of the consciousness, both over one's emotions and the external event. In such a process the end is tragedy when the improved personality, though it deserves to be successful, is defeated by the particular order of events concerned. Wright's characters are, strictly speaking, illiterate. Yet they illustrate better than Mann's characters, for all their rumination, this sort of learning from experience, this growth of a more authentic awareness of the individual's relationship to the outer world. Errors in its verbal statement and vacillations of mood are evidence that the awareness is only forming in the consciousness. But it comes through occasionally, and these occasions are reliable clues by means of which we may understand the unuttered internal meanings behind the hero's overt actions. 'Ah'm gonna be hard like they is. So help me, Gawd, Ah'm gonna be hard. When they come fer me Ah'm gonna be here. 'N when they git me outta here theys gonna know Ah'm gone.' The statement is in terms of mere resistance, but it is nevertheless the clue to an inner life, which is expanding on a new basis, with a sense of competence and co-ordination to a valuable end. Silas is turning against his oppressors the principle they pervert but which, all the same they taught him: the principle that a man should stand up for his rights. Justified, unperverted as he accepts it, it becomes for him a new ideal of manhood, and death is taken as only the means to achieve it, when there is no other way.

The nature of the theme and the psychology of the heroic personality are the same everywhere in the modern world. The same need to die rather than suffer the inner degradation of slavery and bitter oppression is the note of anti-fascist literature everywhere. It reappears with only minor changes of emphasis, whether the locus be Spain or China with Malraux, the Soviet Union with Ehrenbourg, occupied France with Pozner, fascist Germany with Anna Seghers, or this account at home of *Long Black Song*. Everywhere, also, in Wright's stories, it is the underlying attitude. Other stories more deliberately than *Long Black Song* define its political implications. There is a community of aim and attitude in the opponents of fascism everywhere, which transcends differences of race and class and nation; so that readers sense this community even when members of their own group seem to be attacked. This distinction Wright makes explicit in *Bright and Morning Star*. In this story he makes you hate the lynch mob with a contempt and ferocity only equalled in Soviet stories of the Nazi invaders or American accounts of Japanese atrocities. He makes you hate the white informer within the sharecropper's union. But he is careful to introduce other white members of the union whom the Negroes trust because of their character and their willingness to suffer. But the protagonist is an old Negro mother, and the emphasis of the plot is upon her expiation of her error, which has betrayed her son to the mob. Under her son's eyes, before they are both beaten to death together, she avenges herself and him by taking the life of the stool-pigeon she had trusted. But this sequence of external events has been accompanied by changes within her personality. Her awareness of betrayal has been the start of a process of inner development. From a passive, old-fashioned Negro, with misgivings about her son's union activities, she has learned from error, and now, instead of wailing and submitting, she turns to action. Her intense identification with her son, no longer merely maternal, becomes the greater since she can now in a measure identify with his values in living. Her view of the world has become more complex because she has learned that people are not always what they seem. Though she is not yet certain of the criteria for trust in other people's actions and ideas, she has at length learned to trust herself. Under these circumstances, revenge is only the negative aspect of an awakening self-respect, and the fact of her own dying is driven out of consciousness by the fact of successful action in behalf of her son and the ideals they now hold in common. She has become capable of the same order of heroism as Silas.

The heroic theme in Wright takes the dramatic form of physical conflict. Through the action, the reader becomes aware of changes within the personality of the hero. But the hero's attention is never centered, as it is in Malraux, introspectively upon himself. At the same time, unlike most of the definitely anti-fascist fiction, unlike *Native Son* as well, the short stories deal with rigidly limited situations. They do not involve any broad picture of social conflict. They are so written that the reader will fit them into the larger frame by himself. Wright's characters are part of that larger frame, but they are too unlettered to be aware of their symbolic roles. They fight generally in isolation, or as a little isolated band, with the intensity and at times the morbidity of those who must fight alone. Somehow, dimly, and quite unverbalized, a faith in democracy animates them so that they seem at times to presage those guerilla fighters so common in Europe during the Second World War. But this isolation of Wright's characters, if it seems politically a proof that the stamina needed to build an organization precedes organization itself, esthetically it permits a plot that, by stressing conflict of individual wills in place of social forces, gains in dramatic intensity.

But this conflict of wills can exist only when there is a valid conflict between reaction and democracy within society. The writer who can believe in the progressive extension of democracy will be able to recognize the conflict and squarely face it. Its recognition, by making possible the construction of a plot, both removes the taint of pathos or sentimentality or melodrama (which are the stylistic evidences of the failure to recognize the conflict or to evaluate it), and restores high seriousness to the tragic action. It must not be forgotten that Aristotle's definition of tragedy was determined by his belief in the dominance of clear-cut moral laws, and that our loss of the capacity to create the tragic plot in the modern world is the result of our pluralism and negation of belief. The difference between plot as defined by Aristotle and as Wright uses it is owing to a difference in the nature of the beliefs the plots subsume. In Aristotle it is an eternal proscription which a superior man unwittingly violates. When he becomes aware of his violation, he accepts outward penalty and physical suffering with inward resignation as justified. But in Wright the belief is one created by man, which unfolds, grows richer in content and greater in extension, by the cumulating pressure of man's exercise of his own potentialities. In tragic action under these conditions, it is not the hero who sins, but his opponent. The hero is a common man who is made to suffer because he has got in touch with reality, because his awakened potentialities have brought him into conflict with the forces of reaction. His suffering, consequently, though it is physical as well as mental, is accompanied by an inner state of feeling which is the opposite to submission, one of active, exalted conviction of self-fulfillment.

In these short stories the tragic action ceases to be a mechanism for preserving the status quo by showing what happens to those who violate it. It becomes the price one may have to pay for the satisfaction of living according to one's ever-expanding convictions, of challenging what one has come to know to be evil, and promoting what is for one's own good because it is for the common good. It becomes the present sacrifice men are willing to make for an awareness of the better life within them. A tragedy, then, as a literary form, consists of a conflict in the objective world, through which a contradiction develops, between the external circumstances of the hero's life, which ends in a death imposed by his opponents, and his internal state of feeling, which becomes a sense of fullest living. This contradiction is promoted by his discovery through action of an error of judgment, and ends, through the right use of that discovery, in what is actually the satisfaction of the better integrated personality, even when unlettered Negroes are only aware of the surge of mother love or the obligation their dignity as human beings has laid upon them.

15

The Lonesome Young Man on the Flying Trapeze

For some months *The Human Comedy*, after its publication, was on the best seller lists and was double checked by the movie reviewers. William Saroyan reached the top of the ladder scarcely ten years after his first steps in learning to please the public. His achievement has not been the triumph of a vulgar opportunism. One can be sure (from reading 'Sweeney in the Trees') that money has meant little to him; and if he has been tempted by fame, as his frequent references to his genius suggest, it is only that fame has seemed the proof of his being a likeable person. Writing has been the decoy by which he has sought to bring people closer to him. It has been the medium through which he could make more people the more intimately aware of his friendly spirit.

The mellowness of success has long since tranquilized his style, which had originally been less confident and more demanding. But it was clear from the start that he was a born writer. His first published pieces were the letters he wrote to the editor of *Story Magazine*, informing him of his genius and his plans as a possible new contributor. Their impulsive mingling of truth and fantasy about himself whetted appetites that had been dulled by a surfeit of sophistication. Their request for recognition was an ingenuous and flattering assumption that the reader possessed both the good nature and the moral integrity to recognize and to further merit. It was obvious that a new comet had appeared on the literary horizon. At the same time it was agreeable to note that this rare personality was not portentous, as Thomas Wolfe had earlier proved, uncastrated and impossible to corral, but a whimsical animal, one eye already cocked on the halter. There were piquant and comforting signs of his not demanding to remain one of the eccentrics of literature. The note of desperation in his appeal was nothing more than a prayer for escape from such an isolation. Saroyan wrote about himself because his competence as a writer was the first problem to be got rid of. Until he had the assurance of being accepted, it hardly paid to bother with any more objective theme.

For the time being he felt very lonely. But because he was absorbed by his own depression, he could hardly realize how typical he was. For it was the era of the great Depression. Other youths felt down and out because they wanted to work and could find no jobs. Saroyan felt friendless because his job was writing and nobody yet knew it, since he had not yet started to publish. Like any other worker without experience, he had only the potentialities of his personality to offer. And he offered them boldly, because he was desperate, hesitantly because he was still unsure of himself, but winsomely because that was the way he was made.

But that was the way the average young American appeared to be reacting in the early 'thirties, when we were for the first time shaken loose from the certainties Americans had taken for granted since the founding of the Republic. The girls might turn to reading *Gone with the Wind* in every leisure hour for at least one winter, and fancy themselves back in the boom of the Reconstruction period. Boys like Saroyan failed to get beyond the title. They were beginning to doubt the promise of American life. Individual initiative, pell-mell for the pot of gold, was useless when the rainbow itself had disappeared. For the first time, they were not sure of anything. Instead of the stable ground of the American way, they found themselves to their consternation on the flying trapeze. And it was revealed to them that that was where most Americans had always been without knowing it, only now it was swinging more wildly than ever. They were very anxious and lonely there, pitched this way and that by the changing course of events, the sudden closing of the banks and the unexpected opening of the WPA. They oscillated between depression and hope, as belief spluttered out like a defective electric bulb. Such was the world of the young Saroyan. He was one of the crowd that had suddenly become aware of the helplessness of individualism and began groping for attachments they had not missed before. But all they found was a common frustration through which they could not break even to reach one another.

Saroyan's best expression of this profound change in the national temper bears the awkward title of '1,2,3,4,5,6,7,8.' A young man is working for the telegraph company. It is a cruel, impersonal corporation, the employees of which are forbidden to use the wires for their personal consolation. Nevertheless, this youth on one dull Sunday does get a 'hello' message from the main office, where it turns out there is a girl as lonely as he. Previously, in the empty hours off duty, he had played Brahms on a squeaky portable Victrola in his rooming house, and escaped into the maternal embrace of art. But he had really enjoyed most a trifling dance hall tune of the day, which was so satisfactory an opium of the senses that he often hummed its theme to himself as '1,2,3,4,5,6,7,8.' Indeed that was the best way to hear it, since his landlady objected to the racket set up by the machine, even though he always turned it off by eleven. Now, fortunately, he need no longer sing his tune. He can go walking in his spare time with this girl. And they fall in love because they are both so lonely working for the telegraph company. They plan the inevitable little house. But they love each other too much to admit they are only singing a new version of '1,2,3,4,5,6,7,8.'

They love each other too much for frankness. And so one Sunday when the telegraph machine fails to spin its usual message, the youth does not fear a breakdown in the efficient equipment of the company, but knows that his girl is no longer there. She has been unable to torment herself any longer with a bliss that can promise no fulfilment. So the youth discards his broken fantasy by giving his portable Victrola to his landlady, and seeks to keep in spiritual communion with his girl's demand for reality by leaving his job also and moving out of town into the certainty of the unknown.

So distraught was this youth that in telling his story he oscillates between the first and the third persons. Clearly he (or his creator who is identical with himself, though the name is Romano) is trying to objectify his own unhappiness. He must project it from him into the third person because he cannot bear to carry it around with him and squarely acknowledge it as his own. The moving style of the story (which is, I think, the best Saroyan has written) is the esthetic reward of this psychological situation. Its nuance in expressing very real emotional conflicts results from the need to give them at least a superficial control. When Romano walks away from his conflicts by leaving the town behind, he also secures their temporary purgation.

For Saroyan the real purgation came with the success of his stories. From now on he writes habitually in the third person. If he uses the first, he is no longer conscious of describing himself, but only of following a customary device to make other people come more alive. In his later stories he is more objective than Hemingway. He feels no need to force inner conflicts to an issue, and project case-hardened words like bullets in a slow-motion film. Saroyan's words were well oiled even in his misery. Now they flow as smoothly as though one of his Greek waiters, off duty, were saying, 'That's life,' over a bottle of beer. He tells his stories as such a waiter would tell them for himself, if he were more articulate, had an ear for the vivid sentence, and knew when to stop repeating himself. Such an artistry charms the respectable white-collar reader. It takes him into that hazardous land beyond the limits of his experience, and shows him he has nothing to be afraid of there. It permits his democratic idealism to resume its innocent play. For these new people of Saroyan's, who are unaware of being inspected, seem quite reconciled to their station, admirably frugal in making the best of anything. The stories of Saroyan, in his middle period, draw apart the curtain on the lower classes and show them to be no menace at all.

A deeper insight might demur that Saroyan's is a superficial view of our underprivileged masses, or that he presents them as they used to be before the CIO, or that he is concerned with only the detritus of the labor movement. But Saroyan has become a success, and the immediate response of his emotions, like a benevolent octopus, colors the world about him. His vision is reversed, and he sees that other people are really as good-natured as he has become. Since there must be some distinction between genius and the commonplace, he doubtless would agree with us that his new people are shallow. But that is a minor matter. They are well-intentioned, though sometimes stupid and generally happy-go-lucky. They may be reckless, but they have little of either money or surplus energy to spend. They are not material for either tragedy or psychoanalysis. With amazement (through one of those unexpected associations the analysts are fond of) one realizes that Saroyan has resurrected a less boisterous, a paler, version of the 'good nigger' of Joel Harris and the old vaudeville stage in his easy-going, unskilled, white-faced workers, from the lower strata of our foreign born, Armenian, Greek, Italian. It turns out (from the point of view of theme as opposed to style) not to have been Wolfe who has been gelded, but Farrell and Maltz and proletarian literature generally. Even the fringe of racketeers is not fearsome, as in Hemingway. They are only a little careless, like the Mexicans in early Steinbeck. Their heart is not in the business, which, after all, is little more than a harmless game, played with the negligible small change of capitalism.

Formerly, Saroyan's characters knew that they were lonely and homeless, and rebelled. Now they no longer know it because they have got used to substitutes for home and friendship in the casual habitual idle hours at the neighborhood bar or the chance acquaintances in the familiar diner. They are the 'rejected children' of our psychologists, who compensate by making acquaintances easily and who come to feel at home in the instability of drift. If they lose one job, they will probably get another. If they fail to get another, they will probably find some similarly jobless girl to commiserate with them. If they squabble or blow off their mouths, the offense is tempered by its being the customary diction of their class and by the certainty that quarrels evaporate as quickly as they form. They take life as it comes, indifferent to our official codes of respectability (by which they seem never to have been infected in their grammar school education), believing tenderly in a romantic love they never see consummated, disciplined indeed by finding it to be another of life's failures, cultivating the simple garden in which they for the time being find themselves, as Voltaire advised. If they have their dreams, they are reconciled to knowing in advance that they will not come true. But they do not understand that what they take for reality (arms around some girl whose last name they do not know) is little more than a dream in relation to the destiny of the country. That greater world of ideals and advancement, caught from Sunday sermons and tabloid newspapers, has left no mark upon their consciousness. They accept it as another world from theirs. But its remoteness has deprived them of ambition and self-confidence. The apathy that cushions their good humor measures their vague awareness of their inability to grasp the traditional ideals of American manhood.

Yet it is this disillusionment on the periphery of consciousness that determines the mood of every one of these stories. It is what makes all the characters so talkative. They talk to keep the truth from themselves. It is what leads one story to spin a design of mock ecstasy out of the clichés of idealism in 'Ah Life, Ah Death, Ah Music, Ah France,' and another to rekindle the flash in the pan of O. Henry's trick conclusions. It is what leaves most of the stories up in the air, concluded by a mere verbalism of hope ('Somehow or other she knew that he would get a piano someday, and everything else too.'), or by a verbalism of pathos ('Go ahead and laugh. What else can you do?'), in a world where everything changes and nothing concludes. Rarely, as in 'The La Salle Hotel in Chicago,' the buried resentments break through the defenses that had become habitual. Saroyan's style then becomes hysterical, his emergent thoughts anarchistic, but the end is the same. The anarchist, like a true Saroyan character, walks away from the difficult situation, and the other men ask, 'What the hell was he shouting about anyway?' If one must think, it is better to forget the future, leave the present, and remember 'The Warm Quiet Valley of Home.' With a little beer and an old Ford, it can sometimes be done. Once there, the irresponsible joy and the unconfirmed dreams of childhood return to wipe out any possibility of mature perception. And one loses there, too, even the dubious perspective of irony when the old folks reconstruct once more their old illusion of the warmer, more distant home in Armenia. Veneration for the dead dim heroes of medieval Armenia distills a peace that passes the feeble compensations of daily life. It is something from which one is not forced to walk away.

The plays of this period, for the most part, are astonishingly different from the stories. In the latter, the presence of the printed page between the author and his audience seems to have imposed the restraint of distance upon Saroyan. But a playwright talks directly to people while his personal identity is concealed behind the protection of a whole series of *dramatis personae*. Saroyan forgot entirely the existence of the proscenium arch, which guarantees so much of critical aloofness on the part of an audience as is implied in their consciousness of being in a public place and listening to persons not themselves talking to one another. Most of his plays have been failures despite the plausibility of his other assumptions. For a spirit of fantasy has hovered over the Broadway stage in recent years. There had been a turn away from the annoyance and the crudity of realism. A delicate sort of banter after the manner of Noel Coward had become the single standard of 'truth to life.' And Saroyan might have become a proletarian Noel Coward, bringing to the stage without gaucherie the 'truth to life' of his short stories. But the temptation was too strong to let himself go, to become the half-dozen personages he could freely imagine himself to be when talking within the walls of a private room, to which he compared the shelter of the apparent objectivity of the dramatic form. Indeed, the theater liked symbolism even better than it liked Noel Coward, respected it as a higher form of art; and it was certainly a more fool-proof protective device. Saroyan let himself go without restraint. Unlike the short story, the stage was all talk, anyway. So much the better if it could be talk to a higher purpose.

But the most careful study of Saroyan's plays fails to trap any coherent meanings. Not even so much of coherent meaning as high-minded theater-goers ride home with, after an evening of Maxwell Anderson, rewards the most acute attention. Whether one searched with the aid of medieval allegory, which demands a logical sequence of ideas, or utilized the more delicate techniques of surrealism, where the coherence is at best an emotional one, the net came up empty. One looked carefully (if of the intelligentsia) for the symptoms of an abnormal personality, hoping for the sake of art that Saroyan might have become our local Kafka, a neurotic personality of great value as symbolic of the interesting decadence of American society. But the incoherence was of no greater moment than the sputterings of someone on a moral holiday, reveling in the childish freedom of saying whatever came into his mind, hoping in an *arrière-pensée* that something brilliant might be turning up, hoping mischievously that whatever turned up might be taken seriously by the amusing people who find allegory significant, and all the time believing in a belated Dadaism that whatever a genius says must somehow be wisdom. But the clue is there for one who listens patiently. 'Come down,' says Miss Eliza to Sweeney, who has jumped up into the tree; 'you fit poorly in a tree.' But Sweeney Saroyan answers: 'Not nearly as poorly as in the world.' For the time being, to play the lunatic anonymously seemed like eating one's cake and keeping it too.

For one cannot say that these plays were Saroyan's recklessly contemptuous conception of what Broadway liked. Otherwise he would not have proffered a change of mood to the same audience. Occasionally, instead of playing the lunatic in a crazy world, where living up a tree is not too conspicuous, Saroyan turns to meditate upon the world as love. *The Beautiful People* runs from his pen, dipped in a more serious color. We look for its meaning, which the accompaniment of music cannot save from the maudlin. To have every character equally sentimental and differing only in the loquacity of their sententiousness may achieve an emotional congruity, but it proves too bland a stew for most tastes. Elsewhere, Saroyan has always managed to catch enough of a hold on the world as it is to afford a degree of plausibility. Here nothing is probable. One of the beautiful people is the stereotype of Saroyan's habitual drunkards, whom one does not entirely reject because he makes no overt pleas to be taken for Christlike. Another is a man who lives, following principles of equity rather than law, by cashing the annuity of a dead man whose house and mail he has taken over. His is perhaps an instance of humanitarian sharing (without the taint of a doctrinaire Communism), and it is perhaps the inspiration of his daughter's compulsion to be nice to the mice in the house. Doubtless the spectacle of these people's mutual admiration should not be corrupted by too much action, and only the most innocent nibbling at its complacency is permitted. Sometimes a mouse gets away, and the girl has to go chasing after. A young man plagues her by placing a mouse-trap in the living room, but there is no cheese for it. The insurance agent, sent to investigate, proves as saintly as the rest, and decides the company can afford to continue paying the annuity to the wrong person. One can conceive of a more mature world, even of make-believe.

This is the world Saroyan is trying to escape to, the tree in which he hopes we shall feel at home. He has entered upon a third period, the most satisfactory record of which is not one of his plays, but his full-length novel, *The Human Comedy.* It is not enough to say that he recovers a sense of form when he returns to fiction. He is writing under the stress of war, when the need for conviction, for some principle to guide one's thinking, becomes imperative, especially for those who stay at home. The situation is too obscure to be treated objectively, and too serious to be passed off with either flippancy or irony. It demands the rallying of whatever has been significant in Saroyan's experience, of everything he has learned from living and writing. Two ideals rise into his consciousness for him to cling to. The telegraph company, once a forbidding impersonal corporation, he now discovers to possess a calm maternal heart. The people who work for it feel they have security in their jobs; and the evidence seems to prove them right, since the two men in the office who are habitual drinkers suffer neither rebuke nor dismissal. But Saroyan's central source of trust is less materialistic. It is the natural affection of human beings for one another. He does not mean anything so mechanical as that the telegraph company is one big family, or even the whole town of Ithaca, California; it is the human race itself. The boys are now delivering sad messages of the death of soldiers, but mutual sorrow only brings people closer together. The soldier dies, but his buddy, who had been an orphan, returns to his home in place of him, and two miseries unite to make one happiness. The Pippa of the narrative is a boy of fourteen, immature and timid for his age; and the book is the dream world he manufactures out of his pre-adolescent need to trust those older and more experienced. He goes about not so much spreading cheer to others as searching constantly for the kindly act and the friendly support at home to compensate for the rumble of guns in distant places.

But *The Human Comedy* cannot be so easily dismissed. To paraphrase its plot would disclose the shallowness of its solution, its sentimentalization of the Christian tradition. It takes war as too many Americans accept it, as a duty to their country, which has called them to die for a cause unknown. One may infer, perhaps, from the single instance of not-nice conduct in the book, the episode of race prejudice when Homer was a schoolboy, that the war is against that sort of thing. But it is the dying that obsesses the author, not the cause worth dying for. The classical names suggest that Saroyan is justifying his indifference to the precise nature of this present war against fascism, by assuming a concern with more universal emotions and more timeless activities. Men will always be leaving for some Trojan War, to return home late and weary, or never. Our human affection is but the compensation for the continuing pathos of human existence. Such a mood brews an apathy in regard to particular justifications in the knowledge that some greater force than the individual is always imposing obedience upon him. The war is only another job that has opened up for these little men of the street corners. The compulsion is new, but their response is the old one of doing what they are not interested in because they have to make a living, even though the living now comes more into question.

Dangerous as this attitude may be from a social point of view, Saroyan has made it insidiously attractive by a flawless execution. One accepts or rejects the book in its totality, according to the attitude toward the war he brings to it. It contains no gross inconsistencies of tone, no errors in the selection of incongruous material, that might warn the unwary. On the contrary, the easy flow of its narration acts as a sedative to troubled spirits, cushions the reality of war for those who cannot squarely face it. *The Human Comedy* provides a refuge from the responsibilities of maturity for the flabby fibered who feel thrust by events back into the helpless trusting period of boyhood's first real job in the wide, wide world. Its success proves how many Americans on the home front, during the war, needed to see the war through the eyes of the faltering inexperience of childhood, how many of us needed to identify ourselves with this overprotected boy of fourteen, for the first time on his own, in his man's job of messenger boy. For this conclusive enlightenment, so perfectly achieved, we should not begrudge Saroyan his embarrassing niche in the fabric of our national history.

16

The Fickle Sensibility of John Steinbeck

The novels of our most distinguished novelist of the 'thirties, John Steinbeck, with one exception treat of farmers, impoverished workers or vagabonds, present life supposedly through their eyes, and create a sympathy for them. They are the most conspicuous examples of a shift of attitude, general to the 'thirties, from the traditional absorption of American fiction with the problems and personages of the middle classes to an intense curiosity about the poor.

This new and magnetic attraction which the lower classes began to exercise upon the American writer induced a variety of responses. Only in a few instances did he see them as they saw themselves. Commonly, the aura of his sympathy was discolored by envy or pity or any number of distortions set up by the outside view. The novelist seemed to bring the hesitancies and confusions of the petty bourgeoisie into the new attachment. The poor appeared at some times possessed of a mysterious strength, which should be admired and imitated, at others victimized by circumstances and therefore to be wept for; but most popularly they seemed caught in a common maelstrom of disaster, against which the best protection was the resignation of mutual pretense that it did not exist. The novelist who presented the widest

Reprinted, with adaptations, through the courtesy of *Science and Society*. Originally entitled 'The Shifting Sensibility of John Steinbeck';

range of these fluctuations was Steinbeck. Although always of a benevolent intention, he swung in his various novels from the extreme of a deep and legitimate admiration for working people to that in which all values are paralyzed in the apathy of the sentimental.

When Steinbeck's novels are taken in the order of publication, these oscillations of attitude form an interesting pattern. His earliest novel, *To a God Unknown,* published in 1933, exhibited as much fascination with the erotic compulsions of farm workers as the writings of D. H. Lawrence or the poetry of his fellow Californian, Robinson Jeffers. The violence of these turbulent passions faded into the mild casual vagabondage of *Tortilla Flat.* But immediately afterwards, with *In Dubious Battle* the stridency returned, only directed outward, from the sexual to the social, in the violence of labor conflict. *Of Mice and Men* represented a compromise between the two. Though the sociological interest had faded into the background, it had determined that the characters be no longer vagabonds or their heightened emotions be of erotic significance. When the national consciousness of the economic depression had reached its height and the country was supporting the New Deal as its remedy, Steinbeck combined elements of both *Of Mice and Men* and of *In Dubious Battle* into a social novel of larger canvas and happier ending, the well-known *Grapes of Wrath.* Later, when the war against fascism demanded a still more comprehensive social awareness, he broke under the strain in *The Moon is Down,* and lapsed into the amiable superficiality of *Tortilla Flat* with *Cannery Row.* These oscillations, furthermore, have been on two different planes. Besides the familiar one between violent and mild emotions in the personal lives of his characters, there has been an oscillation between the decadence represented by an amused tolerance for ignorance, poverty and depravity, and a recovery from decadence in the social novels.

Steinbeck's career, therefore, has been a most unusual one. It has been an exception both to the usual development of the significant novelist and to the mechanical stereotype of the professional craftsmen of popular fiction. Our better writers write what they seem forced to say in the process of their personal maturation; whereas the popular writers repeat the formula the public seems to want. Doubtless in an ideal situation the two approaches would merge. But in a society constituted like our own, the profound approach to fiction has been personal, and those who have sought to meet the needs of the larger public have been aware only of shallow and conventional ones. Steinbeck, belonging in neither group, exhibits the qualities of both, and thus advertises the instability of our society more graphically than any other novelist.

On the whole, one feels that he has been more absorbed in the expert presentation of his theme than in laboring to fathom its hidden potentialities. In a more stable society he might well have been content to write without exception well-made novels like *Cannery Row.* As it is, his efficiency in combining words into stories is of no mean importance. It testifies that we have achieved as high a level of general culture as France, where a sophisticated use of words as tools to secure an emotional effect has long existed in felicitous contrast to the crudity of the amateur spirit in the old Romantic Anglo-Saxon prose tradition. It is proof of how much more the French tradition has contributed to our cultural development than the English. But Steinbeck's sensitiveness has not been limited to such a ready perception of what the public wants and so facile a satisfaction of it. He has shown a capacity to be moved by the deeper urges in the body public when those urges have come to the surface in a time of national crisis and have been molded for the time being into a pattern of national unity. *Cannery Row* should not obscure the fact that *The Grapes of Wrath* reflected such a temporary unity in the acceptance of the New Deal when it became the only novel of the 'thirties which was both a best seller and a darling of the critics.

The parallel between *Tortilla Flat,* at the beginning of his career, and his latest novel, *Cannery Row,* is Steinbeck's evidence of our psychological reconversion after the strain of war. The same types of people do the same sort of thing they did ten years before, and the author smiles upon them with the same sort of indulgence. A pedant might define the mood as the American picaresque, if the emphasis were not less on the sharpness of wit in these vagabonds than on a sentimental admiration for their carefree way of life. Rather, one should say, it is the gentlest *reductio ad absurdum* of the Lawrence ideal. For here are people who have found the correct receipt for living as Lawrence preached. To live for the belly urge alone is most comfortable when the belly is not too urgent; just as living from the belly urge alone by a relentless logic suggests living off somebody else. And so Steinbeck's Mexicans have no inner conflicts. They know that they have turned the laugh on Lawrence by their common sense. They recognize that happiness is more consistent, spreads over a broader area of time, when one does not overstimulate by conscious attention those deep urges from within, but takes them, after Lawrence's bidding, as they come. Indeed they are aware also that in this case there is room also for those many other minor urges for food or sleep or walking slowly or merely sitting in the shade or the sunshine as the day may proffer.

They are quite free from contamination by the evils of modern life since they are immune to that last contamination in Lawrence, the very urgency of his demand. They have the wisdom of an ignorance paradoxically beyond the grasp of Lawrence's genius, like the illiterate Negroes of the Louisiana bayous whom Anderson came at length to celebrate. In Anderson, some echo of appreciation for their folk songs, for the poetry of the imaginative life, remains. But these Mexicans, like Saroyan's Greeks, are also beyond the discipline set up automatically by the orderliness of song. They enjoy in all simplicity, without any lurking melancholy misgivings, the chaotic comfort of their prosaic souls. Content ordinarily to wait, like certain lower organ-isms, for pleasure to come their way in the form of food or chance acquaintance, they break this passivity and avoid monotony by taking the initiative when it is easy, by raiding a near-by chicken coop or dropping in upon some friend who has a job, a larder, and a weak will. Experience has taught them that the world as it is is quite good enough for their purposes, and they do not dilute the purity of their pleasure either, like Saroyan, by an undercurrent of melancholy or, like Lawrence, by the sententiousness of reflection. They have long since learned to avoid situations beyond their control, and to intuit the kindred spirit in those they choose as friends beneath the conventionalism, which, by obligating a job, makes friendship profitable. They seek out those who work from habit rather than conviction; or, shall I say, from a cowardice or a compliance which, in the area of friendship, leaves them the victims of any moderate good-natured pressure.

Within such a compliant milieu, the modesty of their demands and the contagion of their irresponsibility provide them the final luxury of freedom. They achieve a more complete experience of our national ideal than any other citizens; for they are as free from spiritual compulsions as those of ambition or prestige. And they are excellent propagandists for this ideal since, by taking it for granted in their lives, they reduce those they associate with to their own level. A few moments after these rogues have invaded your premises, you forget their tenacious fawning, the insistence of their inertia, the hypocrisy of their friendship, the underhandedness of their methods. The selfishness of their aims is swallowed up by the insignificance of them. And you end by feeling at home in their droll indifference for the conventions.

Decadence could hardly go farther. But its presence is concealed from the reader not merely because of the charm with which Steinbeck invests his vagabonds. We do not recognize it because our Puritan tradition has accustomed us to find it only in the flaunting of sexual abnormality. And I think we also neglect to feel its presence because we secretly envy them. They are not merely like our middle-class selves in our Milquetoast fawning upon our betters, our similar patience in waiting for somewhat larger crumbs to fall our way, the indirection of our boldness behind the boss's back. Our very consciousness of superiority permits us, under the cover of what we take for a literary interest, secretly to envy them. For in them we see these aspects of ourselves, freed from the fetters of duty, and thus capable of being used actively to serve themselves. They use these manners of a servant not to serve but to receive. Their cunning may be as low as their literacy, but it gains their ends; and it captivates us when we are sick of the toiling and the thinking that remain always insufficient for our more comprehensive goals. Peering through the haze of the picturesque, we do not notice that these rogues lack bath tubs and breakfast cereals; we see only that they are living the life of Reilly while we drag behind us the chain of hectic obligations and dull conformities.

This siren call to drifting was succeeded shortly by the shock of its opposite. If the atmosphere of *Tortilla Flat* was that of a lumpen-proletarian Watteau, offering the idyllic domesticity of shacks on a vacant lot or unusually commodious abandoned sewer pipes, the light of *In Dubious Battle* is a battery of kliegs from Hollywood, that cruel photographic clarity of the California sunshine. But this sharp light is appropriate to the new action. It throws into bold outline the conflict between employer and employed when that conflict has reached its most strident crisis, in a strike of unionized workers of the most unskilled category. But the light does not shine with corrosive impartiality upon the just and the unjust alike. Though it emphasizes the sharpness of will on both sides, it etches (like the famous snapshot of the Republic Steel 'massacre') the brutality of the motorized state police as they charge the migrant workers of the California orchards. At the same time, it becomes a challenge to the manhood of the strikers by symbolizing the cruel indifference of nature. It forces them to realize they must depend upon their own energies and join together to utilize them to the utmost. It strips life of the subterfuges of *Tortilla Flat;* by setting the tone of the book, it forces us to face reality without blinking, or not at all. It acclimatizes us to live on a higher level than our usual complacency; so that we do not pity the strikers for their suffering or their defeat, and their courage in defeat leaves us strong with its unspent residue.

In the dreary lot of so-called proletarian novels of the 'thirties, one would go far to find another more lifelike and satisfying than *In Dubious Battle.* The usual charge against such novels is that they oversimplify their characters, especially the union organizer who plays the role of hero. But any forthright physical activity demands a simplification of the personality. It must be freed, if it is to function efficiently, from the scrupulosities and indecisions, the peripheral and personal interests, which form the attraction of the introspective novel. To complain of the imperfection of characterization in the novel of action, therefore, is usually testimony that the action is badly handled; that it has not taken over from the characterization those hesitancies and impetuosities and contradictions which are the necessary preludes to a decision. In the novel of action, it is not the characterization but the action which is too simple. Not only has Steinbeck properly developed his plot; when he puts it in the black-and-white outlines of the California sun, he beguiles the esoteric reader by affording him a completely coherent esthetic experience to compensate for the loss of his customary thrill from introspection. No documentary film, in which the sophisticated observer swallows the document because the photography is so good, could be more successful in winning support for the striking foreign-born workers in the great fruit-growing factories of the California plains.

After this novel, Steinbeck did not revert to the carefree decadence of *Tortilla Flat. Of Mice and Men,* combining elements from all his previous novels, is his most characteristic work. George and Lenny, his new heroes, are ignorant workers of native stock. But their disorders of personality arouse Steinbeck's pity rather than amusement, and they do not form his sole interest in them. These men have modest aspirations for their own welfare, for which he also has respect and attention. Awareness of social issues, though it no longer forms the backbone of the novel as in *In Dubious Battle,* remains to condition both the motivation and the progress of the story. The psychological and the sociological combine (as they do normally in life) to afford a well-rounded characterization. But characterization does not become an end in itself. Achieved through the incisiveness of conversation, it becomes an integral part of the action. Though George and Lenny have their ambitions, they are scarcely in a position to attain them. They are caught between the dual pressures of their own limitations and those imposed by their station in society. The tone of the novel, therefore, is neither the extreme of tension between groups that characterized *In Dubious Battle* nor the opposite extreme of relaxation of tension found in *Tortilla Flat.* The sharpness of tension is dispersed by the fact that in this novel every relation involves it in its own way. The tone of the novel is that precarious equilibrium where various minor tensions for the time being check one another off, where men are uneasy within themselves and in uneasy association with one another, but manage to maintain some sort of control until the storm breaks in the final crisis.

On the sociological side, *Of Mice and Men* assumes that these tensions are set up by the nature of capitalism. The cockiness of Curley, the son of the ranch owner, his willingness to fight at the drop of the hat, is not merely a trait of his individual personality, it is a trait that his position in society encourages; in fact, there is his real strength, it turns out, in his power to fire a worker, for he is, as an individual, a coward, beneath his braggadocio. In a similar way the one skilled worker on the ranch, the mechanic, Carlson, because he is difficult to replace, can assume an arrogance forbidden the others. He is the one employee who might dare to avail himself of the advances of

Curley's wife, and the one who, free also to lord it over his less expendable fellow workers, orders Slim's dog to be put to death.

The other workers are compliant, either because they are old or because they are afraid of losing their jobs. Among the common ranch hands, only Lenny, whose intelligence is too limited to enable him to recognize these realities, stands up against the boss's son, and, when challenged, crushes his hand in his iron grip.

Lenny has the strength to resist. But it is George who has the brains and the ambition. He is the most complex of the characters, because he has not accepted his position, but carries around with him the longing to save money, buy a small farm, work as his own boss in an air of freedom. His ideal has infected his friend Lenny, and, breaking through the barrier of race prejudice because of the need for allies, is taken over by another farm hand and even touches the old Negro, who has lived alone in ostracism from the other employees. But three such as these form an alliance that is pathetically inadequate, and we foresee, implicit in the constellation, its eventual doom.

The pathos of ineffectual struggle toward an ideal, however, is overshadowed by the reader's interest in the difficult relationship between George and Lenny. Their friendship is an obligation imposed upon George by Lenny's aunt, and it frequently irritates George, since Lenny has always got them both into trouble in the past, and George has no patent desire to be ruined. The psychology of the friendship is presented with a deft sufficient outline by Steinbeck. George's generosity of spirit responds to Lenny's need for him, and his self-esteem is increased by the knowledge that Lenny will obey him without question, provided he is around to give the command. What leaves George under constant tension is the knowledge that he cannot always be around, and Lenny is always destroying what he loves, hysterically overexerting his great strength to ward off what he fears, or what George has taught him to fear. The mouse he pets in his pocket (as though the world, even George, would not sanction so much affection if they knew about it), he stifles to death. Under George's injunction to behave himself and not ruin their chances to save money for the farm where he can have unlimited small animals to play with, Lenny's fear of his own clumsiness mounts to a new pitch. And it is not lessened when he senses that all the ranch hands resent the advances the new wife of Curley appears to be making them. When, with that zest for the sexually abnormal which is an irresistible undercurrent of Steinbeck's personality, Curley's wife is especially attracted to Lenny because he seems so grossly masculine, Lenny loses control of himself. He has not been affected by her sexual attraction, merely by the fact that George has told him he must keep from involvement with her. When she asks him to stroke her hair, he finds it as soft as the mouse's head. She draws back in fear at so unusual an interest, and he strangles her out of a strange melange of urges, in which desire to possess utterly so soft an object is intensified by his sense of guilt at doing what he has been told not to do. After such an accident, all plans for a farm become impossible. Knowing that the law of the frontier must overtake Lenny and will hang him, seeing the lynch mob of his own fellow workers gather under the boss's direction, George's last act of friendship is to kill Lenny to save him from the more cruel death at the hands of the mob and to pretend to the mob that he has been one of them in his action. Thus, abjectly the forces of destiny in the novel reduce the struggling manhood of George to impotence. The generosity of his action must parade as a prevarication, and he must appear reduced to the level of brutality from which he had sought escape into the freedom of economic independence.

Thus much of awareness of the uselessness of ambition among men as underprivileged as George, thus much cynical justification for the drifting and vagabondage of the men of *Tortilla Flat,* distills from the course of the narrative. But it is only the appropriate setting for the story of two men. Steinbeck has not yet recovered the social consciousness of *In Dubious Battle.* It would, therefore, be impossible to take the action of these mice and men as symbolic of the working class. Indeed, to find in Lenny a symbol of the power of the proletariat would be to reduce any confidence in the working class to a grotesque absurdity. Nor could anyone but the most cynical opponent of the labor movement find in George the directive intelligence of the organizer, manipulating, however vainly, the brute force of the well-intentioned but uncontrollable laborer.

On the contrary our acceptance of the story will depend upon our attitude toward the two heroes as personalities, and in particular upon our reaction to Lenny. To some readers his strangeness is fascinating. Steinbeck leaves his motivation obscure; he does not make it explicit like that of George. He apparently desires to hold us by the very mysteriousness of Lenny's motives, to arouse a kind of awe for him as we witness this uncanny union of brute strength and childlike affection. But other readers may feel that in Lenny, Steinbeck's tendency toward the sentimental reaches its artistic culmination. And though they recognize the deftness with which he achieves his end, the precision that can create clarity or ambiguity of effect at will, they will nevertheless dislike the end itself. But at least it must be admitted that no character in Steinbeck is more characteristic of his peculiar talent. And the novel becomes a testimonial to the transformation of the picaresque tradition when it comes into contact with the American sensitiveness to the plight of the underprivileged. In more religious countries, such a character would take on mystic proportions, such as Silone gives to his imbecile in *The Blood Beneath the Snow*. It is precisely here, in his capacity to arouse awe without mysticism, that Steinbeck proves how essentially American is his talent. He leaves Lenny somehow entirely natural and human, and yet essentially a mystery, the mystery of the unfit in a practical world. The hopelessness of the petty bourgeoisie and its confusion before the problems of the Depression era are truly symbolized in Steinbeck's attitude of sympathy for Lenny. And we are all, to a certain extent, Georges in the spontaneity of our protective reaction, unless, that is to say, we have a clearer conception of democracy and are ready for *The Grapes of Wrath.* We can scarcely feel much sympathy for Lenny and admire Tom Joad.

What, one suspects, led Steinbeck to acquire this political information when he came to write *The Grapes of Wrath* was not the inclination of his own temperament, but the tremendous pull of the social situation upon him. He seems, like one of his own characters, to have been pulled together by sharing the wholesome reaction of the country under the leadership of President Roosevelt. The novel came at the time when, in reaction to the shock of the Depression, the country united, as never before in our history, in a common recognition of the desperateness of our internal affairs and the need for radical measures to restore order and security to our society. Under these pressures Steinbeck kept his sentimentality in check until the final scene of his novel. Then a meretricious desire to italicize the action got the better of him, and he introduced the only bit of symbolism in the book (save for the dubious turtle on the road at the beginning). The scene of the proffer of the mother's milk to the starving old man, on the practical level, is a useless gesture of aid, and to be acceptable must be taken as pure symbolism. But since there has been no preparation for symbolism in the antecedent action, the reader follows the attitudes the book has set up in him, and rejects the conclusion, instead, as an unpleasant bit of realism.

Otherwise the novel is a fascinating exhibition of Steinbeck's technical versatility. Just as its composition was stimulated by the temporary comradeship between the poor who had nothing and those who saw themselves losing what they had; so too, by the use of diverse literary styles, its appeal was directed to virtually every level of taste in the book-reading public. The reader habituated to the rigid consistency of style characteristic of our best writing (such as is found in Hemingway) may dislike the lush loose style of many passages, the shift into the slick superficial narration of our magazines of national circulation. But it is precisely the presence of the second-rate, the way in which popular techniques are interwoven into the story, which gives this novel, from another point of view, its significance. For the time being we had laid aside our differences of opinion and our practice of acting through the competition of groups. But even though we had thus achieved in a general way an emotional unity, it was impossible to lay aside our ingrained preferences for different kinds of writing. The sophisticated still liked the clipped and sinewy style; the man in the street still preferred the loose sentimentality of old habit. At best, the co-operation tended slightly to bring the two closer: to make the sophisticated more tolerant of the unsophisticated, and to drive the man in the street into a willingness to pull himself together, put his mind to work, bring (for once) to his reading of fiction the act of attention it deserves, change him into a more sophisticated reader. The effect upon the one group was to make it more tolerant of a less esthetic, a broader social conception of the novel; upon the other it was to improve its esthetic insight in the process of satisfying its practical demands. The result was that the novel was more than a best seller. It raised the standard of taste by being the best written of best sellers.

Students of style, therefore, may take pleasure in going through *The Grapes of Wrath* and discovering that hardly any style practiced today is missing from it. The introductory panels, through which Dos Passos sought to present the background against which the story is written, are there. Passages are there in the introspective technique of Joyce; others reminding one of the curt understatement of Hemingway; others which echo the diapason rhetoric of Thomas Wolfe. But at the same time, there are stretches of narrative which might have come out of *Gone with the Wind* or a serial in the *Saturday Evening Post*. Approaching the book in the warm atmosphere of national unity, the sophisticated reader, delighted by such recognitions, was pulled out of his fanatical devotion to a particular style into a more catholic appreciation. Once the unity of the period was lost, doubtless, the old limitations reasserted themselves, and a rereading of the novel today will afford fewer readers so tolerant a reaction. But however one reacts to its style, it will be difficult at any time not to be impressed by the structure of the book. Here again Steinbeck met the social crisis more successfully than any other author, met it within the artistic sphere as successfully as Roosevelt in the political, and thus once more illustrated the dependence of good form upon a valid understanding of objective events. One would be hard put to find in our recent fiction another novel which, judged by purely esthetic standards, had a better achieved plot. Always sensitive to the problems of expression, Steinbeck proves equal to the challenge of his material. And his plot is as dialectic as the events of those disturbing days. It is divided, both vertically and horizontally, into two contrasting yet interacting lines of development.

The first half of the book is a contrast between the attitudes of the Joad family and that of Tom under the guidance of his preacher friend, Casey. Tom has just been released from the Oklahoma State Prison. He had killed a man in self-defense, and Steinbeck sympathizes with his conviction that he has been unjustly treated. He leaves prison in a mood of rebelliousness which may become delinquency (as his mother fears) or may be channeled into a more constructive activity. His good fortune is to meet the preacher Casey, who (in that subtle defiance of popular prejudices so characteristic of Steinbeck) has given up being an evangelist because he found his orgies of pious words ending with the seduction of some woman in his audience. Enough of the impulse which led him to preach has survived to demand that he solve his dilemma in some socially desirable way. By sharing a common problem of social adjustment with Tom, he becomes a force to prevent Tom's false solution of delinquency. In both, therefore, experience has promoted a healthy skepticism, error stimulates an educative process. So Tom returns home to a family which has neither erred nor learned anything, and finds that they are being driven by drought and depression from their small holding. But accepting the traditional belief in the promise of American life, they have concluded that their ruin is a blessing in disguise. They plan to follow the rainbow they have looked at for years to the pot of gold at its end in sunny California. There is always prosperity for the man who will bestir himself to work for it, and nowhere more abundantly than in the golden valleys of the Pacific. Tom, however, with Casey at his elbow, is not so sure, and the opposition of forces in the first half of the novel becomes clear. As the family in its jalopy draws the nearer to California, the more fantastic becomes its delusion of prosperity. But Tom has been using his eyes and ears, and his cynicism has increased in like proportion. Death has taken one member of the family; desertion another. The climactic event is meeting a man who has returned and tells them that the circular they have seen offering jobs is a falsehood. None of them will believe the evidence except Tom. And so, after they have crossed the desert and ascended the hill for their first view of the promised land, they seem to have the testimony of their own eyes, and it is everything they have wished for. The fields stretch for miles in serried rows, succulent with milk and honey; and they descend in a mood for hosannas.

But their optimism proves an error parallel to the erotic one Casey had earlier found in our evangelical tradition. The second half of the story forms the vertical division of the novel, the dialectic complement to the first, now that facts intrude to shatter their dream. The land is already owned and occupied, and there are no jobs on it. They are now forced to accept reality, as Tom has had a growing suspicion they would find it. And the horizontal division also reverses its dialectic contrast. But when Tom takes the ascendency over his family, his growth into a rational optimism has already replaced their fallacious hopes, and comes to dominate the abyss of despair and confusion into which they have suddenly fallen. This new optimism has two justifications. The national government has established a model camp for unemployed transient workers, where they are permitted and encouraged to govern themselves, and thus can recover their self-respect while they hunt for jobs. But since their stay at the camp must be limited to make way for others, it affords only a taste of what a democratic society might be. The enduring factor in the new optimism is that, under Tom's guidance, they begin to trust themselves. Tom has come across Casey again, and learns from him a second and more important lesson. For Casey has at last found himself. He has become a union organizer of the field workers, and in a strike similar to the one of *In Dubious Battle* he is being pursued by the state police. Once more the initial action is repeated, but on a more meaningful level. Under a bridge, Tom sees him killed by the police in the moonlight, and in spontaneous retaliation kills one of the attacking band. Returning to the transient camp that night, Tom realizes that the critical step in his education has been passed. He has learned that one who would co-operate with the proper intention of government, as represented in the existence of the camp, must still fight for his rights against unco-operative forces in the community. Specifically for him, this means his succeeding Casey as a union organizer. When he discovers that the police have identified the license of the family car, he knows that he must act elsewhere with a change of identity. But before he leaves, in a midnight conversation with his mother, he is able to make her feel and understand the authenticity of his newly born conviction. Capable at last of learning from events, she can resume her old direction of the family in a new spirit, since she has always with her this awareness of her son's resolute functioning somewhere for their ultimate salvation. The action of the second half of the book rises into this dialectic contradiction of the first. Immediate events become more desperate. They have outstayed their time at the camp; yet the search for work continues futile, and they drift from place to place. But only the obtuse reader will be deceived by the overt nature of the action. As their material circumstances deteriorate, in their inner selves they are no longer despondent. Tom's shadow hovers over them, from somewhere in the outside world, where his mother is certain he is fighting for the welfare of poor people like themselves. And it would be a strange sort of American who could find this new conviction as spurious as the old fallacy: grounded, as it is, in the belief that a democratic government must respond to the pressure of the people and co-operate to secure their needs.

Indeed, the novel is more than a reflection of the democratic spirit in America. It reflects that spirit, as the principles of the Atlantic Charter have made it, the ideal of a world community, at a time when throughout the world the most backward of peoples are passing through a process of suffering and enlightenment similar to the Joads. The novel mirrors more than the psychology of more than the common people of the United States. It sets the pattern of enlightenment that has instigated the movement for independence in Africa, in Java, in China, in Burma, indeed everywhere that people of good intent are oppressed by poverty. And one may expect that in due time it will be widely translated.

One cannot be quite so certain that its spirit will be repeated in later works by Steinbeck. When the Second World War arose, its gigantic issues proved too heavy a strain upon his talent. *The Moon is Down* is an instance of a new literary phenomenon brought about by the absorption in social issues which the state of the world imposed upon the public mind. A certain order of writers, with the most laudable intention, try to force a response in fiction. It either runs counter to those deeper and already fixed attitudes from which they write, or, in spite of their plan, reveals the reality of the objective situation. For example, the American public says and appears to believe that it is fighting a war against fascism. The writer attempts to compose an anti-fascist novel, but certain emotional qualities seep through and corrupt the plot and characterization as planned; and the total effect of the novel is not anti-fascist. In such a case, either the novelist or the public is trying or pretending to be anti-fascist against the grain of more deep-seated motivations. When the discrepancy is in the public, and not merely a limitation of the author, the novel is bound to be a valuable sociological document. But in either case, it is a poor novel since it will lack artistic unity. *The Moon is Down* is an outstanding example of this tendency. A first-rate novel will remove the contradiction by making us clearly aware of it. The author will present it quite consciously as existing in the objective situation or he will fail to share it because his own orientation of personality is so fortunate as to dictate, from a level below the consciousness, the proper discriminations.

Otherwise, sentimentality is bound to enter when the social point of view becomes obscure, and the author will achieve an effect opposite to what he planned. *The Moon is Down* ends with the triumphant assertion of the native underground, and it is certainly intended to make us hate the Nazi system. Its plan is to contrast Nazism and democracy as two opposed social systems so that we hate the one and love the other. Instead it advocates by inference a third system which is neither Nazism nor democracy but a vague kind of aristocratic government. For it must be remembered that fiction argues not through logic but through the sympathies that are stimulated. We accept the philosophical or political systems implicit in the actions and personalities of the men and women we are drawn to like. And in this novel we sympathize with the Junker general who controls the occupied town, more fully and with fewer reservations than with any other character. He is a kindly cultivated man, well-balanced and efficient, without a trace of the arrogance and brutality we rightly associate with the Prussian Junker officer class. He is Prussian only in the sense that he feels an obligation to do his duty even when it is distasteful to his temperament and contrary to his better judgment. He knows the Nazi way is no way to control a foreign population, but he has no objections to their economic exploitation as a political system. Nor is it part of the Nazi plan to use more force than needed; they prefer the willing obsequious assent; only when this is wanting do they become ruthless. When the Junker turns cruel, it is true, our liking for him disappears. But since we find no one else to like better, he remains in our memory as the ideal governor; only give him the political system appropriate to his personality, only free him from his own serfdom to Nazism and restore the aristocratic formulas traditional to his training, and we should have a happy orderly world. (And it must be admitted that our military occupation of Germany seems to proceed on such premises.) For the only other person we have to choose from is the native mayor of the village, and by contrast his principles are doubtful and his personality contemptible. His principles deny all leadership to the elected official, transform him into a mechanism for carrying out the 'will of the people' as though the perspective of his office had nothing to contribute to good government. Now he is on the awkward spot of having to keep two ears to the ground. With clasped hands and trembling voice, he may occasionally venture an idealistic sentiment. But he requires to be prodded by his people to act, since his functioning ideal is that of the compromiser and he goes to his martyrdom in the best Social Democratic tradition of the leaders of the Weimar Republic: a pitiful example of futility. We do not even sympathize with his final death since it is dictated less by conviction than compliance and is a result, not of any heroic resistance, but only of his being caught between two superior forces which are beyond compromise.

The treatment of minor characters in the novel increases this discrepancy between the ideas the novel purports to serve and the veritable predilections its narration sets up. Several of the German soldiers are also kindly individuals, wishing only to stop fighting and go home, longing for love and pained to find the system which holds them in its grip makes them objects of hatred. One such, indeed, seeks this love from a native girl, who seems to reciprocate and leads him on only to murder him. We recoil with distaste from such duplicity, which can hardly be excused by her secret hatred for the Nazis who have killed her husband. It is instead a perversion of the personality in the literary tradition of the Salomes and the Cencis and those others whose case for revenge is obscured by pathological stimuli which crave the cruel sensation. And this single episode on the side of the resistance seems indeed to lend to the final conflagration of the village something more than the healthful retaliation of the scorched earth. Nazi and underground alike share the same pathology, though to highly varying degrees; just as high principle, whether in German or native ranks, is stained with the same tincture of impotent compliance.

Indeed throughout Steinbeck's work this blood lust of the perverse runs like a thread that now dominates the pattern and then fades into the tranquillity of exhaustion and acceptance. In most of the novels both extremes dissolve in the soft snare of sentimentality. Only in *The Grapes of Wrath* do they merge in such a way as to remove the taint of degeneration and become an altogether praiseworthy demand for self-fulfilment, in which action ceases to be associated with brutality and the ideal with helplessness. It is to be hoped that the course of American life will develop the potentialities that made possible *The Grapes of Wrath.* For Steinbeck, like his own characters, will pursue the weak side of his talent unless the forces that play upon him are imperative to rally the strong.

17

Theodore Dreiser and the Ethics of American Life

DREISER'S place in American literature is secure not because he wrote so well, but because what he wrote cut so deeply to the core of American life. Other novelists of his generation and later were capable of a better style, were more poetic or more brilliant or more subtle. What Sherwood Anderson and Hemingway later said was better said, but it was less worth saying. It was either more superficial or less genuine as a statement in fiction of the American personality and its problems. Dreiser's intention surpassed his accomplishment. But there are men in the arts whose integrity as men distracts attention from their limitations as artists. Their integrity dominates the imperfection of their utterance, draws the reader beyond the verbal statement into the very heart of the intended meaning; so that he is attentive solely to its significance and is willing to co-operate with the author in its elucidation. Dreiser's novels are of this sort. They raise vital problems and invite the aid of the reader for their solution. His novels are evidence from life that compels certain definite conclusions. It is for the evaluation of these conclusions that Dreiser appeals to the reader through the influence of his own unassuming, undogmatic disposition.

His first novel, *Sister Carrie,* published at the turn of the century, illustrates not only the type of problem with which Dreiser was concerned, but the quality of his plea to the reader for recognition of the facts, concurrence in their interpretation, and an awakening to their broader significance. Carrie, coming to live with her married sister in Chicago, is dissatisfied with the pale routine of their lower-middle-class domesticity. Her sister and her husband, cowed by the demands of respectability, possessing neither will nor ambition but only habit, are undisturbed by the pressure of any expanding capacities within. They work and economize and save and fear criticism. Restless under so static and impoverished a conception of the good life, sister Carrie leaves to live with a man who offers her the pleasure of decent clothes and a real interest in her personality. Such nonconformity certainly has its risks, and Carrie shortly finds herself on a train out of Chicago with another man, whose weakness of character has led him to pretend that he is taking her to visit her sick lover. She soon discovers that Hurstwood has run away from his own family with the intention of living with her. Since she already prefers him and is fairly helpless, she yields, and they establish themselves in New York. They become friendly with neighbors, who introduce them to the sophistication of the theater and the glamor of fashionable restaurants. But high living on such a precarious basis is not enough for Carrie. She accepts it not merely as self-indulgence but as an avenue for the release of slowly gathering ambitions. Very soon a contrast develops between her lover and herself, which is that between weakness and strength of character, between a growing consciousness of talents awaiting expression and an increasing self-doubt that shrinks from responsibility. Hurstwood is demoralized by the fact that he came to New York with stolen funds. Under the need to keep his identity secret and his secret from his supposed wife, he loses his grip, sinks into more and more obscure jobs, and finally does the shopping for the house while Carrie, turning frivolity into opportunity, tries out for the stage. She becomes a successful actress in comedy on her own merits, and is at length freed from dependence upon men. Though she continues generously to support Hurstwood for some time, he recognizes that she no longer loves or respects him, and they eventually drift apart. Hurstwood degenerates into a derelict, while Carrie stabilizes her success.

Obviously the story has the simplicity of a formula. If, as you read it, the unpleasant awareness of a formula is wanting, it is not that the shocking nature of the one he has chosen distracts attention from its presence, but that the inductive method Dreiser follows does away with the sense of formula altogether. For Dreiser seems intent only to discover through his observations the ethical principles by which men and women actually live, and is not at all concerned to impose a preconceived ethical rule upon them by a preconceived selection of material. More empirical than Zola's *Nana, Sister Carrie* is free from the taint of special pleading through the accumulation of sensational detail. Its proof appears limited to the essential, and the essential appears valid because it is clearly the very stuff of daily life in the colloquial diction men actually use. Dreiser's conclusions, therefore, seem, like those of the scientist, to arise solely from an honest examination of the material. It was probably the unassailable nature of his evidence that caused the contemporary reactions of hostility. Dreiser faced his public with conclusions, incapable of rebuttal, which exposed the hypocrisy of official standards. After his story had been thus simply and directly told, however, he did not hesitate to drive the lesson home in the now quaint diction, blended of the ages of enlightenment and evangelicalism, which came naturally to him when he generalized. 'Not evil, but longing for that which is better, more often directs the steps of the erring. Not evil, but goodness more often allures the feeling mind unused to reason.' *

Now what is intriguing in the present day about this concep-

* Dreiser, Theodore, *Sister Carrie*, New York, 1917, by courtesy of the Modern Library.

tion of goodness is that it is, as theory, no more than an honest extension into the field of ethics of the philosophy of practical life dominant in America during the period of industrialization. It has been clarified for us, as far as business is concerned, in Gustavus Meyer's *History of the Great American Fortunes*. This work not only proves that these fortunes were assembled by means of a ruthless breaking of the statute laws for which the average man was penalized; it suggests that the average man, when he admired the millionaire for breaking the very laws he dared not break himself, was accepting a double standard. Our popular pragmatism in practice turned up rudiments of Nietzsche's belief in the two moralities, the one of conformity applicable to the common man, and the other permitting the superior man the right to make his own rules. In both instances a distinction of quality of personality was taken for granted. The man who got ahead by breaking laws thus proved his possession of superior qualities of purposiveness, integration, self-confidence, whereas the ordinary man, unsupported by these admirable internal qualities and therefore incapable of breaking the laws without making a mess of things, by his inner weakness recognized his need of these outer controls. Dreiser did no more than extend these assumptions of business ethics into the sphere where the mores of the day refused to recognize they could also apply, but here he found them equally valid. He had been enabled to do so because his insight as a novelist into personality enabled him to pass from the ethical into the psychological aspect of the situation. And in psychological terms he saw that the private life of Carrie's sister was qualitatively similar to this dependence upon the law by the average man; whereas a woman like Carrie herself clearly obeyed inner pressures whose legitimacy her later success pragmatically announced. Her breaking of the ordinary precepts of personal ethics in twice becoming a man's mistress was in obedience to a higher law of her own personality. Dreiser recognized that she suffered no more penalization by so doing than did the elder Morgan or Vanderbilt in their public careers. The strong individual imposes his will upon society and is accepted at his own evaluation.

Such was the way of the world in the United States as Dreiser found it. But though he was quite willing to accept this prevalent idealization of success and to extend its application thus boldly to every area of human interest, though he himself shared the ambitious man's contempt for failure when he thought in general terms, he was troubled because success did not bring happiness. By becoming better than the average, one alienated himself from human contacts. Sister Carrie, 'since the world goes its way past all who will not partake of its folly . . . now found herself alone.' Love and friendship are somehow associated with the weak and commonplace, and by demanding to be superior, Carrie has missed them. 'Know, then, that for you is neither surfeit nor content. In your rocking chair, by your window dreaming, shall you long, alone.' At the end of his novel Dreiser left this dilemma for his reader to meditate upon.

But in his next novel he was ready with a partial clarification of his own. In *Jennie Gerhardt,* parting company with the ethic of the marketplace, he finds a higher law than success. That emotional loyalty we call love he now understands better than he did in *Sister Carrie.* It is no longer merely a natural yielding to sensations of pleasure and almost casual companionship. An emotion that is constant, co-operative, and self-sacrificing, it now seems the opposite to the will to success, which is self-centered and competitive, ruthless and disloyal. Dreiser turns in something like disgust against the code he had been expounding.

> Virtue is that quality of generosity which offers itself willingly for another's service, and, being this, it is held by society to be nearly worthless. Sell yourself cheaply and you shall be used lightly and trampled under foot. Hold yourself dearly, however unworthily, and you will be respected. Society, in the mass, lacks woefully in the

matter of discrimination. Its one criterion is the opinion of others. Its one test that of self-preservation.*

Clearly from this passage the direct influence upon his thinking has not been Nietzsche but social Darwinism. His social views at this time were a projection upon his observation of our competitive life of his desultory reading about Darwin's survival of the fittest. He recognizes the accuracy of the description. In *Sister Carrie* he sought to explore its potentialities for good, and had found them limited. The system now began to offend his moral sense. But though his pity deepened for every individual caught either by its cruelty or its limitations, he began to identify it with 'society, in the mass.' And he developed a Nietzschean contempt for 'society, in the mass' just at the time when he began to reject those justifications of the superman he had found in the pragmatic American worship of success. He still puts the superior individual against society. But his new definition has responded to his better understanding of moral values. The superior individual is no longer the tycoon who seeks the material security and shallow satisfaction of success, but a woman whose understanding of love is deeper than sensuality.

The shift of attitude, however, has not eradicated the dilemma of human happiness. Though Jennie Gerhardt's ideal of life is better, though she has a richer personality than sister Carrie, she is perhaps even more unhappy. For she enjoys neither worldly success nor any requital of her love. Jennie remains poor and miserable not because she has sinned with a lover, not because she is a weak person, but because her lover, bowing to the pressure of his wealthy family, is himself too weak to carry out his desire to marry her. His acceptance of conventional morality is a hypocrisy which he uses to yield to an even more shallow convention of social status against the promptings of his better nature. Strength, now dissociated from a vulgar success, becomes constancy in love in defiance of external circumstances. When

* Dreiser, Theodore, *Jennie Gerhardt,* New York, 1926, by courtesy of Horace Liveright.

Jennie's lover, long since estranged and married in a distant city, falls critically ill, he sends for her; and for this moment of crisis love renews itself in spiritual support. But convention once more resumes control and Jennie is left more desolate than Carrie.

In *Jennie Gerhardt,* however, one must dissociate the meanings of the narrative from Dreiser's own interpretations of these meanings. Actually, 'society, in the mass' is not to blame. The action points the sharpest contrast between ways of life in the proletariat and in the upper classes. Bourgeois standards, not working-class ones, are responsible. Jennie's old father, the night watchman, has qualities of fidelity and humanity which are reflected in the daughter. His freedom from meretricious conceptions of status, which have also been an influence upon Jennie, cannot fail to be contrasted with the shallowness of aims, whether of morals or manners, in upperclass circles. Jennie's lover is weakened in moral character by his social milieu in which the 'ambition' of poor sister Carrie to keep her head above water has been only too lavishly rewarded. Dreiser is still consciously thinking rather in terms of purely personal relations, of relations between individual 'wills,' than in the terms of environmental influences. But the nature of the plot shows the direction in which he is tending.

Not until almost fifteen years later, when *An American Tragedy* appeared, did the new direction emerge into Dreiser's conscious thinking. During the long interval he mulled over the same problems in the same terms, as though, hypnotized by their significance, he could solve them by repetition. The story of Cowperwood in *The Financier* and *The Titan* does not clear up the ambiguities, only buries them in the garrulities of social history. It presents the environment instead of using it; and one who would like to know what life resembled in the financial circles of Philadelphia before the Civil War and in the sprawling young Chicago afterwards will read them with interest. The relation between graft in politics and success in business is laid bare.

But the ethical problems involved remain in suspension: the problems of separating the good from the bad in sex and ambition, of discovering what strength of character means, of relating strength and weakness to the mores of society. The appearance of *The Genius* only increased the confusion. Perhaps, when these problems were made applicable to the artist, they struck too close to home. Whatever is laudable in ambition, in fulfilling one's talents, is now corrupted by a weakness for women, to whom the artist is drawn with a monotony of 'biological urge,' and from each of whom he parts in rebellious disillusionment. Only his wife, Angela, remains constant as a shallow version, almost a parody, of the faithful Jennie Gerhardt.

When he did reach a conclusion, he chose to state it negatively. *An American Tragedy* accepts the principle that the environment is responsible for the individual personality. But the novel presents a warning rather than an ideal. A society that operates upon the wrong principles will train individuals who do wrong. *An American Tragedy* is not, like the early novels, the story of a woman of strong character, but of a weak boy who finds himself convicted of murder. With sedulous care Dreiser traces the environmental influences which assembled so pitiable a specimen of American manhood. No longer contrasting the individual to his society, he continues nevertheless to indict our society for its low standards and hypocrisy. He has grown out of his previous social cynicism, just at the time when the other novelists of the 'twenties were plunging into it. Finding the individual now inextricably bound to his society, he now extends the large-minded pity he had always felt for the individual to the society that produced him. And his novel becomes an appeal to that society to understand itself, to understand that Clyde Griffiths' tragedy is not an individual one, but typically 'an American tragedy' in the present generation. What gives the novel its significance is not so much the convincing accumulation of proof, but that what is proved about Clyde Griffiths typifies the combination of good intention and ineffectuality in the American youth of the respectable deferential lower middle class.

Trained with the aid of an evangelical religion into an unrealistic ideal of virtue, over-protected by their struggling parents from the vulgarity of the workaday world into which they must enter, our lower-middle-class youths too often grow up with meretricious aims and no strength of character to achieve them. The code of virtue they have been taught to follow has filled them with shame for their biological urges, so that, when these break forth, they are unable to control them. So Clyde Griffiths lives on two levels, both in love and ambition. Working in his rich uncle's factory, he will not admit to himself that he is a worker among other workers, but assumes that he is slated to rise into an economic position comparable to his uncle's. In these circumstances, which compel him to meet the world on its own terms without the protective coddling of his family, he becomes involved in an affair with a factory girl at the same time that his relation to his uncle has enabled him to meet the country-club set and choose the girl he hopes to marry. When Roberta becomes pregnant, therefore, he is incapable of reaching any sort of decision. He cannot make the vulgar decision to throw her off; nor, seeing his dream of social advancement through marriage fall through, can he bring himself to marry her. He is caught in that hopeless contradiction between respectability and virtue, which is our worst American inheritance. Incapable of the firmness to do right by the girl or himself, as he conceives it, he grows hysterical. He takes Roberta boating, and by one of those accidents which are clearly planned by unconscious impulse, he knocks her out of the boat so that she drowns. And his spurious ambitions crash in his conviction for murder. The attrition of the ruthlessness of the Cowperwoods and the sister Carries has left only its demoralization of the steadfastness and sincerity of Jennie Gerhardt's proletarian character.

Dreiser's novels are the most accurate account in our literature of life as it was actually lived during the period of capitalist expansion and its apparent stabilization in monopoly. And since his understanding of American life was thus accurate, he was able the more soundly and profoundly to fathom its baffling effect upon the American character. He was aware of the good effect of capitalism. He recognized the value of self-reliance and initiative. But at the same time he was troubled by the limited conception of these virtues. He saw that they had never been properly adjusted to those demands for love and co-operation which are certainly of greater ethical import. Recoiling from the spurious conceptions of virtue in our tradition, to which the better placed in life seemed especially addicted, he found, beneath the commonplaceness and uncouthness they found in the working class, the survival there of a more admirable ethical code. Not since Hawthorne and Melville, not in James or Howells or Mark Twain, have we had a novelist more concerned with moral problems. Working virtually alone against a rising tide of cynicism from which there was to be no escape until the 'thirties, he not only restored to our novel this sense of the moral dignity of man; he was in the end less baffled by its definition. He saw that it demanded more than material success, more than that slavery to respectability into which our conception of virtue had sunk. He saw that it must become free from hypocrisy by being grounded in the facts of daily life. It must recover those simple virtues of personal conduct which democracy had once stimulated but which appeared to survive at present only under the harsh conditions in which the working class lived. He would have a nation in which the Jennie Gerhardts no longer suffer and the Griffiths are no longer bred.

18

Thomas Wolfe's Discovery of America

THE career of Thomas Wolfe is the spectacle of a novelist who began with the sole concern to transfer to others his fascination with his own family as material for fiction, who turned thereafter in the same simplicity of intention to his own relations with persons outside his family, but who found pouring into these relationships all the disorders of the contemporary world until at the end he was forced to attempt their solution in a letter to his editor on his social views, in which his work as a writer culminated and, it may be said, his life concluded.

The bridge between the personal and the social was Wolfe's discovery that his own personality was a microcosm of the state of society. It was not quite a conscious discovery. He was not only the least intellectual of novelists; he was altogether incapable of writing well unless deeply moved by the personal contact. The transformation in his case was, therefore, a gradual and an almost automatic broadening of his interests until he had passed from one of the most subjective of novelists at the beginning, to one of the most objective at the end. Having exhausted his relationship with his family (which was virtually a part of himself), and then his relationships with friends and lovers, as he groped in his isolation for new ties he discovered

Reprinted, with adaptations, through the courtesy of *The Virginia Quarterly Review;* copyright 1946 by E. B. Burgum.

his fellow men. Through the projection of sympathy alone, and not any actual awareness of the parallel, his imagination turned to the social scene. But his new attitude of sympathy for human misery in general took the form of his break with his one remaining friend.

Perhaps also, for his readers as well as himself, consciousness of these facts has been clouded by the spirit of gusto that seemed to dominate his first book, *Look Homeward, Angel.* We have gained a mind set from first contact with that book which we have carried over into his later books. Different readers have reached this state of mind in different ways. But we have all made some extravagant emotional response to some extravagant emotional assault this book has made upon us. Those who dislike extravagant emotion altogether have escaped into a distaste for the unevenness of its style, the lifeless prose of passages in which Wolfe's emotions were not involved, the adolescent rhetoric into which his emotion too often evaporated, the overwritten formlessness of the whole. Others, younger or less sophisticated, intoxicated by the gusto, accepted it at its face value. They found something epic in its exaggeration, something tonic and awesome about their participation in its emotional excess. And so they called it the transfer into fiction of the spirit of Paul Bunyan, forgetful of the careless ease, the robust self-assurance with which Bunyan acted; whereas in Wolfe the utterance is explosive, the strength illusory, the action destructive, as the individual seeks in vain to free his tortured spirit, madly to break through the inner conflicts that reduce him to impotence. Or they were reminded by his style of the Teutonic humor of Carlyle, its earthy vulgarity transfigured by the lightning flash of the Valkyries, though they then forgot that there is no humor in *Look Homeward, Angel,* only a hypnotic identification with the violence of despair. Or they thought of Whitman, sensing some small cry for warmth and understanding, lost in the impulsive clamor of Wolfe's egotism. But they then forgot that he was a Whitman disillusioned, a Prometheus forced back into his chains.

More accurate certainly, since the imitation of his style betrayed Wolfe's awareness of the parallel, was the echo of what has been called the Rabelaisian spirit in James Joyce. But since almost everyone misinterpreted Joyce on this point, failing to sense the pessimism beneath the burly façade of humor, the comparison only strengthened the delusion about Wolfe. Nevertheless, those who liked this novel were more sound in their reactions (if not in their reasons) than those who rejected him on grounds that missed his main intention. Better than Hemingway (who represented the minority of the sophisticated), better than Dos Passos (who could only describe the appearance of things), Wolfe was the novelist of the average American youth of the postwar period, the small-town boy who confused his restlessness with ambition, who thought himself a profound optimist when actually inhibited by inner doubt, and who was sustained chiefly by an illusory identification with the grandiose.

What is taken for gusto in *Look Homeward, Angel,* then, is actually a grandiose illusion expressing itself in random and futile violence of word and action. And this dubious gusto belongs to the father rather than the son. It is under the spell of his father's spirit that the young Gant falls, until it seems to become his own and the reader's. Later on, in the false and doubtful maturity of the son in later volumes, this imaginative identification will become real, and the son will succeed his father. For the time being, the father's spirit, once identification has been exhausted, is sublimated by the inexperience of youth into the justifiable inevitable dreams of adolescence, which reach out for the life that lies ahead in an ecstasy of escape and self-fulfilment. But even vision cannot be kept steady and uncorrupted. The youth recoils from it, looking homeward, until his leap into the future for a security he has never known degenerates into an ambiguous nostalgia. 'Oh lost, and by the wind grieved, ghost, come back again.' Specifically, the ghost is the spirit of his dead brother Ben. But since only through his friendship with this brother had he known love and the security of home, the ghost symbolizes these qualities, and the plea for his return becomes a restatement of the title of the novel, a demand at one and the same time for the satisfaction of his dream in terms of his subjective needs, and its satisfaction in the objective form of a decent family life. 'Come back' means not only 'come back to me as a person,' but 'come back to secure for me what should be mine, the sense of being at home in my family and in that larger family which is Altamont.' But such a homecoming of the spirit is impossible on the level of reality. Though almost drowned out by the theme of identification with the father, a second theme finds its origin in this dilemma. Eugene's helplessness takes refuge in the substitute paternity of friendship with this older brother, though this tenuous intermittent substitution is soon broken by Ben's death. In the strong somber elegy of Ben's dying, the identification changes, and the second melody succeeds in dominating the book. Ben having died, what made home endurable has been withdrawn. But in the moving hallucination of the return of his spirit as Eugene stands in front of his father's shop at midnight, Ben counsels his younger brother more fully and more intimately than ever in life, leaving Eugene 'like a man who stands upon a hill above the town he has left, yet does not say "The town is near," but turns his eyes upon the distant soaring ranges.' For the time being the dilemma has been resolved by the restoration of adolescent optimism, and the possibility of a home is the hope of a future elsewhere.

Life there, when he gets to know it, will only repeat the same patterns. Indeed, they are already emerging in equivocal form in *Look Homeward, Angel.* The tenderness of Ben and Eugene for each other, born out of their mutual loneliness, must seep through an appearance of gruff detachment on the part of the older son and a timid inarticulate assent on the part of the younger. Their great need for each other makes this surface unimportant to them. But in other relations, the negative emotion is not a façade, easily ignored, but an active ingredient corrupting the superficial optimism in which Eugene takes confidence. He is scarcely aware of how much contamination from the family pattern is already present in his dreams of the future. The town he has left is nearer than he thinks.

> Ah [he says in the easy assertion of reverie after he has left Altamont], I'll tell you why you laugh; you are afraid of me because I am not like the others. You hate me because I do not belong. You see that I am finer and greater than any one you know; you cannot reach me and you hate me. That's it. The ethereal (yet manly) beauty of my features, my boyish charm (for I am Just a Boy) blended with the tragic wisdom of my eyes (as old as life and filled with the brooding tragedy of the ages), the sensitive and delicate flicker of my mouth, and my marvellous dark face blooming inward of strange loveliness like a flower—all this you want to kill because you cannot touch it. . . Ah, but she will know. . . Proudly with misty eyes, he saw her standing beside him against the rabble; the small elegant head, wound with a bracelet of bright hair, against his shoulder, and with two splendid pearls in her ears. Dearest! dearest! We stand here on a star! We are beyond them now. Behold! They shrink, they fade, they pass—victorious, enduring, marvellous love, my dearest, we remain.*

This is the essence of his youthful vision, and his vision expresses the subjective state of his most enthusiastic audience, the youth of the early Depression years. Wolfe could no more have spoken thus frankly in actual life than the youth he represents. But this is the way they both felt, with an intensity that varied only with the differing pressures of their individual potentialities. Most of them, having less promise than Wolfe, doubtless experienced a less intense conflict, and it was easy for the observer to recognize the inertia, the lassitude, and hopelessness in which the conflict ended. But the youth himself, no more than Eugene Gant, recognized the stalemate; instead he festered in his inner

* Wolfe, Thomas, *Look Homeward, Angel,* New York, 1929, p. 523. By permission of Charles Scribner's Sons.

rebelliousness, supported by its justification in lack of opportunity, and willed the happy ending in fantasy when he could not in fact. His was as false an affirmation as that with which Joyce's *Ulysses* ends.

In another mood, toward the end of the book, Wolfe expressed more frankly the typical American characteristics of his hero.

> He had no greater need for rebellion than have most Americans, which is none at all. He was quite content with any system which might give him comfort, security, enough money to do as he liked, and freedom to think, eat, drink, love, read, and write what he chose. . . He did not want to reform the world, or to make it a better place to live in; his whole conviction was that the world was full of pleasant places, enchanted places, if he could only go and find them. The life around him was beginning to fetter and annoy him; he wanted to escape from it. He felt sure things would be better elsewhere. He always felt sure things would be better elsewhere.*

This passage is typical even in the unconscious hypocrisy of its denial of rebelliousness. An interesting confirmation of it, at a much later date, may be found in Ralph Ingersoll's *The Battle is the Payoff,* in which he describes the American soldier in North Africa during the Second World War in almost the same terms, as always restlessly expecting happiness not where he is, but somewhere he has left behind or hopes to go to.

But I must not press too far this comparison between Wolfe and the average American boy. The differences of potentialities in them produced a difference in the degree of assertiveness. But assertiveness there was in both cases, ranging from mere querulousness or disorderly conduct to active participation in radical or reformatory measures. Where Wolfe's rebelliousness, as an example of the most active type, differed from the ordinary (where it proved perhaps that he was a production of the postwar generation rather than the Depression) was that it remained

* Ibid. pp. 588-9.

purely personal at first, and uninterested in politics. As we read this first volume, if we are not intoxicated by its rhetoric, we recognize how much need to compensate for frustration and wounded feeling by an attempt at domination of other individuals lurks behind the affirmation of mutual loves just quoted. His egoism buoyantly reasserts itself, whatever the obstacles, and always in a demand for the individual contact. And it is, I believe, in this reaction of buoyancy that his unique, his specifically American contribution to the contemporary novel is to be found. The inability to make friendships, the predominance of rejection, the sense of everybody's being hostile or indifferent, I have elsewhere described as the theme of Joyce's *Ulysses* and much of our other good fiction. Most authors have been resigned to the situation they depict. The characteristic contribution of Wolfe is both that he presents characters in rebellion against their isolation and shares the optimism implied in the new positiveness of their demand.

In the portrait of his father (whom I do not pretend to be typical of an older generation), the rebellion is certainly a futile one, and the warmth of spirit which might attract a response has all but died within. His is the failure the son must avoid, obscured by the excess of the moment, substituting a grotesque and desperate sadism for the love that has passed beyond reach. Actually this parent, who has so bound his sons to himself, has very little to do with them. He proffers usually the hostility of his explosive moods, whether he is rousing them from bed in the morning with the same familiar imprecations hurled from the bottom of the stairs, or making himself in the only way he can the center of a distraught family by coming home drunk, needing eventually to be subdued and put to bed. Such conduct forms a precedent as dangerous as tempting to the son, for it is altogether without promise.

But in later novels, in which the focus shifts from father to son, and in which I have said the son takes over his father's personality, an important modification appears. The father's personality in the son proffers a constructive aspect. When the young novelist turns to explore his own difficult attempts at friendship, if attachments are eventually broken, it is not from perversity alone. The valid evidence of optimism in Wolfe, the justification for thinking of him as a belated successor to Whitman rather than an American version of Proust's or Joyce's despair, is that his breaking of a relationship is always bound up with an obscure kind of growth. He reacts from a friendship partly because he has discovered an imperfection in it he can no longer tolerate. He learns something from every new experience, as he passes from a provincial boyhood where a lust for money has corrupted the quality of the folk inheritance, through the social contacts of a college education in which only the voracious reading of literature counted, into restless travelling that gave him a cosmopolitan knowledge of the world. Under these circumstances, each new friendship starts on a higher level than the last, and has stimulated a superior sense of human values.

Thus, I imagine, the cold precepts of his mother, which she never practiced, got written the more indelibly into his unconscious, precisely because (in contrast to his father's expletives) they carried so shy an emotive content. After a bitter quarrel, instigated by the father, in which for all her stubborn self-assurance she played as usual a passive role, when left alone with her son, 'Poor child! Poor child!' the mother whispered faintly. 'We must try to love one another.' Such remarks must have become convictions buried deeper than thought, buried so deep that they may seem scarcely to influence conduct at all, yet hibernating within to rise into authority once the process of living gave them any verification. Never systematized into a philosophy, set in the context of American history, they brought him against the grain of the surface into the tradition of Whitman, causing him to scorn the cant of our Puritanism and our democracy. These ideals were too precious for lip service. They remained a deeper order of compulsions than his apparent belligerency, at the very basis of his personality where they could order his experiences the more and more openly as life allowed. When once we escape the irrelevant details of the particular novel and see the series together as his life's tale, we become aware of the grandeur of the forming pattern. A modern Prometheus, because he recognized he was in chains, and sought with a terrible sense of isolation to wrest himself free of them, he discovered that toward the end of his short life he was not alone. The distortions of his personality turn out to be his challenge to the forces in contemporary life opposed to the tradition of Whitman. When the shock of the Depression reveals to him that his problem is common to Americans generally, the distortions disappear; for he has gained allies in deprivation, and the mere reality of this sympathy of kinship reawakens a confidence in the principle of kinship as the fundamental and persistent directive of American life.

When we read Wolfe with a sense of the cumulative power of this unfolding pattern, the important passages are those in which the tensions of intimate relations are conveyed with all the vividness of an actual experience in Wolfe's life. The shifts he made in the details of his experience appear unimportant. What arouses the impression of distortion differs on different occasions, but it is always instigated by the quality of his subjective response. When it verges on the magnification of the grotesque in the portrait of his father, its blending of terror, awe, and helplessness is characteristic of the traumatic events of childhood. And the reaction of outrage at his helplessness fixes upon the traditional victims; he becomes surly with hatred for Jews and Negroes and foreigners and the vast masses of the underprivileged like himself. If later passages appear less distorted, it is that maturity enables the youth to cope with a situation on terms of approximate equality with the other participants, and the irrelevant compensation of race hatred, becoming less necessary, loses its intensity. The final style is altogether lacking in distortion, is as evenly sustained objective writing as one could wish, in which the actions can carry their meanings by themselves because the author has attained the serenity of perspective to recognize their presence; and it is in this work that race hatred changes to contempt for the overprivileged. That Wolfe had some awareness of what was taking place within him seems denoted by his shift of hero in midstream. Eugene Gant, who is associated with the events most illustrative of distortion, gives way to George ('Monk') Webber in the two posthumous novels of his later transformation. But the development was actually a gradual one, and may be represented by five episodes in the novels, each of which denotes a new stage by its change of tone.

The first influence upon him was his English teacher at Pine Rock College, who later came to New York and was his colleague at the School for Utility Cultures. He is a Southern version of that phenomenon of American college life, the popular instructor who is recollected in after years with enthusiasm by those of his students who do not major in English, but whom those with a serious interest soon outgrow. Doubtless such teachers are desirable members of faculties. They take the naive student at his own level of appreciation, and, without frightening him by a violation of his own predilections, lead him on to make the best of them through their own intoxication by the superficial values of great literature or the self-evident pleasures of minor. The rock upon which our hero's discipleship foundered was Dostoievsky, who, to this Southerner of the slow drawl, the portly figure and sloppy garb, was unknown, foreign, and, the more Wolfe said about him, immoral. But Wolfe, remembering his father, sensed the affinity, and discovered his greatness. Such a victory was easy, even in adolescence; and the tone of the telling is a tranquil drollery of exposure.

More complex was the friendship with Starwick, whom Wolfe describes his hero as meeting in the interim before he went to New York and with whom he traveled later in Europe. To Starwick, Wolfe, a little awed by Harvard besides, was attracted by a veritable superiority of knowledge and sophistication. Impressed by the fact that some of Professor Baker's students got their plays produced on Broadway, and that Starwick reflected the better taste in the theater, Wolfe learned only through the failure of his own play, which was never accepted for production, of the meretriciousness of the contemporary theater. He continued to accept Starwick's guidance because it seemed to give him as a provincial boy the benefits of a cosmopolitan experience. But he soon found that his innocence had involved him in a situation that had other aspects than the purely cultural. Even this situation is typical of the American college, where the youth of literary promise, attracted to a personality finer than his own at the moment, sometimes discovers to his amazement a homosexual element. Wolfe's case forms an interesting variant. For Starwick and he traveled with two protective maiden ladies from Boston, who arranged everything, drove the automobile, often paid the bills, but with whom Starwick was always quarreling, so that the youth would have remained entirely the passive observer had he not fallen in love with one of them. Since this lady thought she was in love with Starwick, Wolfe became directly involved in this odd situation. Everyone, therefore, became jealous when Starwick forced into their snug little party a French youth whom he had picked up at a bar. The situation then became clear to Wolfe, if not to the ladies; and his friendship with all of them ended when he found the ladies critical of him for picking a fight with Starwick out of disgust at his discovered homosexuality.

Because Wolfe writes with power only when his own emotions are deeply and directly affected, the tone of this long episode is hardly more moving than the narrative of Jerry Allsop. But the quiet banter of the first episode loses its complacency. In its place is an uneasy tension, in which a mild alarm merges with curiosity. The suspense with which we await the next delightful revelation of eccentricity in others is somewhat tinctured by the fear that it may suddenly veer to affect ourselves. A kind of amazement distills from the simple graphic description of these people's stalemate of bickering, which is broken by a sudden decision of do something, go somewhere, until it explodes to demolish the association.

Perhaps the affair with Mrs. Jack, the scenic designer, is not so different as would appear on the surface. It is essentially the same kind of relation, but infinitely more intense, since it is clandestine and consummated, and more acceptable since it is not entangled with homosexuality. Indeed, since Wolfe as usual forces the reader to share its intensity, we may forget that it is only an American version of a well-known Romantic literary tradition. It traces not to Dostoievsky this time, for the women of the Russian author inhabit a world in which the dominance of men is taken for granted, but to the episode of Julien and Mathilda in Stendahl's *The Red and the Black*. Our awareness of the tradition is further weakened by the greater urgency of its contemporaneousness. For it defines what is probably the prevalent abnormality in relations of love in our own country at the present time. The man who needs the support of affection and the steadying influence of a mother's care must hate himself for wanting it and project his hatred upon the one who gives it; while the woman who must serve advice as well as meals gets a sense of indispensable superiority, which demands constant satisfaction and will endure any rebuff to secure it. The competence of the writing is shown by the fact that, though these quarrels and reconciliations follow the same pattern, the vividness of the conversation prevents an impression of repetition and each scene becomes more violent than the last. Feeling suffocated by her constant attention and self-sacrifice, George Webber turns upon Mrs. Jack with completely irrational, unjustifiable abuse, projecting his sense of blame upon his jealousy of her affairs with imaginary lovers, who for some curious reason must be younger than himself and less rugged. But it is all useless; either he seeks her out or she returns to haunt him. He can break away only by leaving for Europe. But associated with the cruelty of his attacks upon her, which would be fairly unendurable to the reader if he were not forced into an identification with the hero, is the learning process once more. Mrs. Jack had introduced the young author to the fashionable literary society of New York. He found there another version of the fraudulence he had discovered in Starwick, and when he becomes aware how completely Mrs. Jack accepts its praise and its standards, his rebellion against her love gains a plausible justification. He rejects Mrs. Jack because his conception of art cannot be limited to the tastes and interests of the Broadway audience of the well-to-do.

The next episode, like all the others, involves his response to the advances of another person whom he values as superior. By this time he has become famous himself, partly through the enthusiasm of the famous American novelist, Mr. Lloyd McHarg. So, when McHarg insists upon his accompanying him on a week-end visit in England, he accepts, only to discover that the state of the great man's personality is worse than his own. That strident, virile attack upon life, which had made McHarg so magnetic as a novelist, now turns out to have its unpublicized obverse side of drunken prostration. The parallel was probably as reassuring to his own troubled spirit as the dominating immediate contact was dangerous to his ego; and Wolfe withdrew too quickly for a quarrel to develop. But the incident had its larger aspect also. Through it he learned the limitations of fame; and the lesson was possible since he had already become famous himself.

Meanwhile, Wolfe had been learning from the countless observations he made everywhere. Following the American practice of Sinclair Lewis and the later Dreiser (in defiance of the sophisticated or European demand for the well-tailored novel), Wolfe crowds his novels with excessive detail. But before dismissing him with contempt for his garrulity, one ought to recognize that there is a highly personal respect for form behind it. Wolfe's interest in detail is always subject to the authority of his own inner needs. In a general sense, his styles of writing represent the mood of the moment bruising the facts of observation in the violence of its embrace. He sublimates his torment in various ways, which almost run the gamut of possible emotive reactions and their analogues in the great literary styles of the past. And the sublimation is the uneasy one which tends to repeated shifts in the type of equilibrium. When the equilibrium is more stable, the whole episode gains a unity of tone and style. When it is less, the changes of mood may appear even within the individual sentence with the fickle charm of stormy summer days. And these moods pass not only from an irony directed now against himself, now against the outer world, into a bitter cynicism poured consistently outward, but indeed into a state of exhaustion in which he seems to continue to write automatically, repeating platitudes of fact or reflection to an extent rarely found in an author of similar talent. For the shifts are not confined to mood or style. There are also the changes from observation, however colored, to commentary. Like the great divines of that other troubled period, the seventeenth century in England, Wolfe takes refuge in the poetic homily upon the nature of life. Indeed the measure of his rebellion against the predominant tendencies of his own time is best measured by his finding the most congenial style (where action does not dominate the narrative) in this reversal of the whole modern trend in prose style, back, even beyond Shelley, to the periodic sentences and the consolation of abstract statement in Jeremy Taylor and Thomas Browne. In such passages indubitably Wolfe becomes one of the great stylists in the English language, submitting the undisciplined cadences of Whitman to the control of an ear and a mind working in complete harmony to achieve a subtle unity of tone and idea.

And yet he thought that no Spring ever came more sweetly or more gloriously to any man than that one came to him. The sense of ruin, the conviction that he was lost, the horrible fear that all the power and music in his life, like the flying remnants of a routed army, had been blown apart into the fragments of a ghastly dissolution so that they would never come back to him, never again the good times, the golden times, the nights his spirit prowled with the vast stealth and joy of a tiger across the fields of sleep, and the days when his power leaped on from strength to strength, from dream to dream, to the inevitable and sustained accomplishment of a great, exultant labor—the sense of having lost all this forever, so far from making him hate the Spring and the life he saw around him, made him love it more dearly and more passionately than he had ever done before.*

Now it is worth noting that these fine passages are found most often in the later books as commentaries upon his most objective writing in the episodes of action I have been stressing. His growth of mastery of style accompanied his growing perception of the world outside himself. The writing in the first is the most uneven; out of reaction to its favorable reception, *Of Time and the River* takes on a monotony of Biblical unction with sentences of similar construction strung together by initial connectives. It is in the two latest volumes that he hits his stride. In these, though the same variations of style persist, they are better disciplined by a matured talent.

At the same time, it should be noted that, amid all these variations, two opposite tendencies persist. The one is familiar to all readers, and the source of a great deal of his popularity, his escape into the consolation of ambiguity.

O death in life that turns our men to stone! O change that levels down our gods! If only one lives yet, above the cinders of the consuming years, shall not this dust awaken, shall not dead faith revive, shall we not see God again, as once in morning, on the mountain?

Hope here oscillates with despair. But the second tendency is for observations of the miseries of the poor, quite specific in content to accumulate in the later volumes into political enlightenment. They reappear in the midst of the narrative like faint

* Wolfe, Thomas, *The Web and the Rock*, New York, 1940, p. 540. By permission of Harper and Brothers.

sounds which gather power as they draw nearer. These observations, which seem cursory, perhaps irrelevant, when they first appear, flash forth symbolic meanings of what is to come. When he rides all night in the subway and finds himself on the surface in a poverty-stricken section of Brooklyn, his own inner misery becomes one with that he observes around him. A more indelible impression than this one must have been made upon him by two casual images of the Depression because they are repeated at least once in the course of the story. He stumbles over men sleeping wrapped in newspapers on the steps of the urinal at the City Hall in New York, and he finds the subway platform at 33rd Street crowded with sleeping vagrants, who have sought to escape there the bombing of the Depression.

Such images sank deep within him, where with the aid of those slumbering aphorisms from his mother's lips they made contact with his deep sense of himself always having been an outcast. Community with the unloved brought love into his world, took him out of himself, afforded his ego the legitimate stimulus of sympathy. At length, these free floating impressions coalesce into a positive conviction in the description of the marionette show at Mrs. Jack's apartment in the final volume, *You Can't Go Home Again.* Here at last the facts are allowed to carry themselves. There is no distortion set up by the author's inability to adjust to the outward circumstances. He is no longer tempted to do so. In complete philosophical and emotional control of the situation, he can use the method of contrasting panels of narrative familiar in contemporary objective prose. As this absurd exhibition of polite society's sensational pursuit of any new artistic experiment draws to a close, the guests are thrilled by the unexpected climactic sensation of a fire in the huge Park Avenue apartment house. Descending by the novel inconvenience of the staircases, on the street they mingle in a mock democracy, meet neighbors for the first time in the geniality of temporary deprivation. Later they return to their apartments, neither knowing nor in a mood to care that two elevator boys have lost their lives. For Wolfe this was the final lesson in human values and their proper relation to art; and it forced his reluctant final break with the man who had been editor and foster father to him.

The long letter with which the series of novels ends is not fiction. It is the credo to which Wolfe attained through the method of fiction. What it has to say of democracy and the common man is commonplace today. What counts is the process of utilizing experience, that has brought it into the awareness of expression. For we forget that all functioning truth is ideationally platitude, and that what is important is that the platitude be true and functioning. The 'proof' in fiction, as it is essentially in life, is not to be found in logic but in the perception of order in the sum total of a man's experience. It is in default, at best in clarification, of this order that argument needs to enter. But for Wolfe the clarification had come already in his last trip to Germany under Hitler. He had gone there with his aroused human sympathy still uncrystallized into political conviction. Always an admirer of things German, he accepts the immediate surface impression as usual. But the more he sees of his friends, the more he comes to know that the surface is a façade, beneath which their real emotional state is one of agony at the fate of relatives, and a paralyzing terror as they face their own. A similar affectation of gaiety, he sees now, concealed in his Park Avenue friends, an indifference to the larger social issues, such as had promoted the advent of fascism in Germany. His political lesson, as usual, is knit up with a literary one. Never having permitted the sham of the façade in his own personality, he refuses to rest in appearances when he becomes absorbed in the world about him. He returned home not only convinced that fascism was possible in his own country, but realizing also that a novelist could not be content with the narrowly personal concerns of men and women. He must go deeper into their emotional life, and when he does he finds them indissolubly mingled with social and political issues. The only doubt remaining is that his new conviction is not shared in his most stable and profitable friendship. He is left with the dilemma that his editor's stability of character, so admirable in his family life and personal contacts, seemed purchased for the price of a stoic retreat from these larger problems, from which, Wolfe now sees, retreat is in the long view impossible. His friend will not act in any public capacity. He sticks to his last, living within the framework of each day as it passes. More serious still, he advises Wolfe to do the same, to continue writing within the subjective perspective of his earlier novels. Wolfe does not expect that his letter will enlighten his friend; but its tone of tact and clarity betrays his desire to part without a rupture of his respect. The side of him that will always require a father surrogate cannot be crippled too openly; and yet it is the side of him that has faced life with a resolute and desperate demand to fathom its secret that has now the upper hand.

The vision is there. But the competence to pursue it friendless and alone is wanting. Wolfe's dilemma cannot be broken so easily by either word or action. It still exists as a cleavage of his personality between the opposite needs for a very personal dependence and a rebellion against it. The clarity of his recent experience has freed him from the ambiguity of constant querulousness, translated it into an analogous definiteness of absolute contradiction. Such a dilemma cannot be broken within the area of life. But in Wolfe's case, it was temporarily assuaged by transference into an imagined future.

Dear Fox, old friend [he ends his letter], thus we have come to the end of the road that we were to go together. My tale is finished—and so farewell.

But before I go, I have just one more thing to tell you: Something has spoken to me in the night, burning the tapers of the waning year; something has spoken in the night, and told me I shall die, I know not where. Saying:

'To lose the earth you know, for greater knowing; to lose the life you have, for greater life; to leave the friends you loved, for greater loving; to find a land more kind than home, more large than earth—

'Whereon the pillars of this earth are founded, towards which the conscience of the world is tending—a wind is rising, and the rivers flow.' *

With the aid of the mysticism of Christ and Shelley and Whitman, Wolfe sought finally to will a fantasy in defiance of the actual world about him, just as he had earlier imagined his lover and himself together against its hostility. Only now his lover is justice and the rights of man; and he turns his eyes from the hostility of the world, impatient to leap from present difficulties with which he cannot cope into the ideal of a better world to come. For he was so constituted that he must fight alone. Beneath the show of optimism, beneath the apparent ecstasy with which he called upon the great styles of past literature to aid his present purpose, there remained a sense of personal inadequacy. In his floundering between an awareness of the tragic choice facing his country and his own incompetence as an isolated individual to promote the right choice, he differed from the ordinary American only in his violent will to reach a decision, and his capacity as a man of letters to draw a dubious and temporary comfort from the long literary tradition of reconciliation with despair.

In the backyard of the old brick house in which he lived, one of those small, fenced backyards of a New York house, a minute part in the checkered pattern of a block, there was, out of the old and worn earth, a patch of tender grass, and a single tree was growing there. That April, day by day, he watched the swift coming of that tree into its glory of young green leaf again. And then one day he looked into its heart of sudden and magical green and saw the trembling lights that came and went in it . . . and it was so real, so vivid, so intense that it made a magic and a mystery, evoking the whole poignant dream of time and of man's life upon the earth, and

* Wolfe, Thomas, *You Can't Go Home Again*, New York, 1942, p. 743. By permission of Harper and Brothers.

instantly it seemed to Monk, the tree became coherent with his destiny, and his life was one with all its brevity from birth to death.*

But what by contrast was not so fleeting a revelation of changing beauty leading but to death, he had since come to learn, was the spectacle of man's ever more successful pursuit of the security of friendship, even though he found himself cut off from sharing.

* Wolfe, Thomas, *The Web and the Rock*, New York, 1940, p. 540. By permission of Harper and Brothers.

19

The Novels of André Malraux and the Dignity of Man

ALL of the fiction of André Malraux has sought the answer to the question: what leads men to risk violence and death? In early works, such as *The Royal Way,* the query presented itself to his imagination in purely subjective terms which imposed a morbid emphasis upon suffering and an obsession with the idea of death. But in his best known novels, although his approach has still been through the subjectivity of the individual, he has rejected so pathological and decadent an attitude. His widening observation had led him to believe that men typically risk their lives for more noble ends than the perverse enjoyment of pain, for ends which are in some way larger than themselves. And so he turned to study the motives prompting the individual to engage in assault or resistance in situations of social crisis or civil war which arouse the maximum of tension, make the most extreme demands upon his capacities, afford him the sense of fullest living. He found, in his novel of the Chinese Civil War, *Man's Fate* (*La Condition humaine*), that there is only one motive which adequately fulfils man's human nature by securing for him his own respect and that of his fellows. It is the motive that leads him to spurn humiliation at the hands of other men, and, through action for the common good, to reach that state of individual dignity which he calls 'la condition humaine.'

It testifies to the subjectivity of art in our time that the culmination of Malraux's search, when defined in general terms, has been the initial assumption of art from the earliest periods. The tradition of the arts has taken for granted that the deed of violence is only the sensory and materialistic means for securing an end which, whether rightly or wrongly conceived, possesses a value transcending the pain and the effort. Only in our own period of western culture, with its often masochistic attitude toward life, has the pain attendant upon an action become the focus of analysis, to the neglect of what has traditionally been held either its spiritual justification or its violation of ethical principle. Nevertheless, violence and death have formed the materialistic matrix of great art, and Malraux's work may be considered a modern version of the age-old concern with tragedy as the most venerated of literary forms.

But if the tradition of tragedy saw more clearly than did Malraux at the beginning that the purpose behind the pain was more important than the pain itself, if it started from a point which Malraux reached only after painstaking inquiry, it was never conscious of so noble a definition of purpose as was the reward of his effort in *Man's Fate.*

From the modern point of view the deficiency of the literary tradition has been its limited conception of the noble end, which has been confined to problems of personal ethics and has neglected all direct concern for the good of society. Epic, of course, with its emphasis upon the hero's service to his tribe or racial group, has been an exception. But in tragedy, with which we are concerned, and which forms a more continuous tradition through the ages, only at the Renaissance, with the birth of individualism, does the emphasis upon the individual cease and a social consciousness arise.

Classical tragedy takes place within a framework of tranquillity precisely because the social consequences of the tragic act are taken for granted. The authority of eternal law dominates the action and guarantees to the individual in the audience a certain measure of security with which to face the suffering observed. The modicum of fear to which Aristotle refers should not be exaggerated. The audience, which has not made the fatal mistake and is not likely to, since it is composed of average men, will fear accident. But it is sustained by the probability that the taller trees are the more liable to be struck by the lightning. Provided the average man remains docile and obedient to the law, he has little cause for anxiety. Classical tragedy may be a warning to the individual regarding how he should himself act. But it is not a warning that the actions of others may be disastrous to himself, however correct his own conduct.

Elizabethan tragedy, on the contrary, since it is beginning to become aware of the complications in the relationship between the individual and society, offers its audience no similar basis of security. It emphasizes the inevitability of mistakes where the law cannot be known because of differences of opinion about its nature. And at the same time it underscores the results of such mistakes by showing them to produce disasters far more extensive than the downfall of a single hero. Whether Thebes suffered as a result of Oedipus' conduct is of little moment, since Sophocles was not concerned with the social ramifications of his theme. But the problem whether England suffers when Lear acts unwisely is so interwoven with the theme of Shakespeare's tragedy that it remains on the threshold of consciousness throughout the play. Similarly anyone who sees the whole of *Hamlet* acted cannot fail to realize how the disorders in the state of Denmark are knit up with Hamlet's uncertainty where his duty lies, and how many persons, good and bad, he carries with him in his downfall. *Hamlet* has remained throughout the long history of Shakespearean productions in England and America, in Germany, and perhaps universally, the most popular and fascinating of Shakespeare's plays, precisely because it holds in solution so many of the problems of tragedy to which the minds of the Greeks were closed, but those of the Elizabethans, as modern men, were gradually opening.

However obscure its ideological acceptance of violence, on the whole Elizabethan literature gave it emotional assent. It was certainly not afraid of it. Sometimes a decadent attitude is anticipated in such plays as *The Duchess of Malfi*, the most Italianate of Elizabethan tragedies, in which there is a kind of exultant participation in passions that are intellectually recognized to be deplorable. Generally speaking, violence is accepted as a risk any man of spirit and ambition must take. Throughout the tragedy of the period there lurks in a confused way somewhat of the same spirit which condoned buccaneering and thought bloodshed worth while if for the glory of an England, not yet conceived as old, but on the youthful brink of power. The courage that forms the emotive tone of Drayton's poetry takes for granted in a manly way the possibility of constructive national and individual consequences from war and aggression.

In our period, this confusion regarding the ingredients of the deed of violence has only been clarified into a dichotomy. As we have grown more averse to violence both in theory and practice, violence as practice has become more frequent. Never was a more dreadful war fought than the First World War, save for the Second, and never have men been more concerned with the mechanisms of peace. The ending of the First World War left western Europe in a reaction of depression. The horror and the waste of the war and the social disorders that followed it created in men of letters a profound pessimism that was tacitly pacifistic. They recoiled from the threat of pain and death as evils in themselves so unendurable to the individual that they became detached from any possible association with the larger and more noble issue. Generally speaking, they shared the decadence of Malraux's early work. Only with the appearance of fascism did they become capable once more of the more healthy and realistic view that fire must sometimes be fought with fire. When the individual good was thus glaringly, by the very course of events, revealed as inextricably associated with the social good, men once more became capable of the belief that the act of violence, under the proper circumstances, with the proper social objectives, might become the instrument for good. But even so, its cost to the individual could not be thrown out of mind by so subjective an era. Even those who recognized the need to oppose fascism by war generally assumed that the price of war was the deterioration of the human character.

The significance of the fiction of Malraux, therefore, is that he has been so acutely aware of this basic human problem of our time. Other writers of anti-fascist novels, especially the German refugees like Anna Seghers and Bodo Uhse, have dealt with themes of violence and have portrayed its various effects for good or bad upon the individual character. But very few have elaborated its philosophical implications. Even Thomas Mann, who does elaborate a philosophy to justify war, chose one of so mystical a naturalism that it is of no aid at all in clarifying its psychological or social effects. Malraux's approach has been the more empirical one, which reaches general conclusions only from a detailed examination of the activities of individuals.

In his approach to the problem, the range of Malraux's mind is observable in the contrast between two of his early novels. He did not see its ramifications at once and the earlier of the two is little more than the presentation of material he did not yet understand. *Les Conquérants* is scarcely more than a journal of his experiences in China during the Kuomingtang uprising of the mid 'twenties. But while he was meditating its significance, he was able to write another novel on a more limited aspect of the theme. As a man maturing in the 'twenties it was easier to assimilate first its decadent aspects.

The Royal Way is a study of the motives which led a Frenchman named Perken to seek a lifetime of hazardous adventure in the wilds of tropical Siam. What such a man did resulted in the extension of French imperialism, and in a pinch he was rescued by it. Like the American frontiersman, he could count on the support of French troops, though generally too little and too late. But in his own consciousness, it is equally clear that he was not acting as its agent, any more than the American pioneer looked upon himself as the advance guard of an expanding industrialism. Each rather followed a personal motive, only indirectly inspired by the larger economic pressures. He wished to be his own imperialist, to act as an individual without the immediate aid of the social system which ultimately supported him. He sought to secure through his own initiative and for his personal satisfaction the control characteristic of imperialism. But the control the American pioneer sought was over nature rather than men. Indians he regarded as nuisances standing in the way of the better life he hoped to wrest from nature for himself. Perken's motives are more complicated. He is more interested in his personal power over the native population than in the accumulation of property.

But the essence of his conduct lies elsewhere. It is more even than power that such men as Perken demand from life. What they really desire is to act successfully in the most critical of situations. Not the end of authority obsesses them, but the process of gaining it. They delight in situations where the risks to themselves are at a premium since danger arouses their energies to their highest pitch, makes the greatest demands upon their ingenuity, brings their whole personality into exercise in the most subtle flexible tense responses to the most touchy of situations. Their rewards are thus neither power nor fame nor self-indulgence. Such a man cares nothing for his reputation among other Frenchmen nor does he ever think of retiring to enjoy the profits of his risks. It is the risk itself that fascinates him.

A man like Perken is only a variant of the decadent personality in the culture from which he comes. His aim is not to escape from his cultural environment, but only to transfer its potentialities to a locus where they may be afforded a superior gratification. He only seems to elude the evils of decadence because he has shifted his activities into an area where their pursuit is no longer a conspicuous folly of passive yielding or self-indulgence or retreat into eccentricity, but affords the illusion of self-fulfilment. The appeal of the tropics remains essentially a decadent one. Its strangeness becomes his substitute for absinthe. Its risks are as nerve-racking as some perversion of the senses, but perhaps of a different quality because exercised in a world whose elusive savage mores and loathesome tropical diseases seem themselves, from the norm of civilization, perversions that must be recognized and resisted. The danger of violating a taboo thus resembles the temptation of a drug, and yielding to it may cause a similar mental and physical torture. The oppressive climate abounds in the gaudy insidious flowers of evil, overwhelming odors, abnormal sounds, which become minor sensations of the same order. When a man like Perken talks of sex, he discloses the same pattern of personality. It is a sinister attraction. He faces a woman in the same mood in which he takes a trip into an unknown jungle. She is something to be resisted in the very act of seduction, and she can afford no challenge unless she is of an unknown type.

Such a man, accepting the isolation of the individual in the modern world, becomes the most detached of personalities. He is so self-centered that the problems of loyalty and friendship have ceased to exist, and an act is humanitarian only in appearance. If he undergoes extraordinary hardships to rescue a fellow countryman enslaved by a jungle tribe, it is for the subjective satisfaction of a new accomplishment. Satiated by the familiar, craving an ever new and more exotic risk, the ultimate, the most tantalizing adventure becomes the probability of his own death. In the paradox of defying its inevitability he will receive the greatest sense of achievement. The climax of the novel comes when, wounded in the knee, Perken cannot receive adequate medical attention and faces his slow death by gangrene as the consummate experience.

Il éprouvait si furieusement l'exaltation de jouer plus que sa mort, elle devenait a tel point sa revanche contre l'universe, sa liberation de l'etat humain, qu'il se sentit lutter contre une folie fascinante, une sort d'illumination.*

Victory over the jungle and its savages is supplanted by a sense of victory over nature as a whole in this final rejection of the importance of his own life. Perken's courage in the face of his own death proceeds from a hatred so unqualified that it has ceased to be hatred and become a principle of cold narrow integration of personality. It proceeds from a selfishness so 'pure' in the terms of esthetics that it seems to be selfless, as it severs mind from body, freeing the sense of self from the pain which overwhelms the body and will eventually overwhelm the consciousness also. For Perken at bottom, life is not a gamble. It is an attempt to achieve Gide's 'l'acte gratuite' in the most fissionable of material. Only Malraux's emphasis is upon the subjective gratification rather than the objective detachment. In Perken's dying, pure will, indifferent to the utility even of his own survival, by the mere act of rejection of his own body, appears to reach an independent emotionless existence. Decadence here ends in a psychological state of detachment analogous to the mystic definition of the freeing of the individual soul. But a paradox (as Gide discovered) is not true because for the time being it appears so; and Perken dies.

Early in *The Royal Way* Claude (who represents Malraux) had recognized the morbidity which lay behind Perken's conscious motivation. Despite the intensity of his living, he was more interested in death than life. And Claude also realized that what drew him to Perken was his sharing the same curiosity. Claude 'decouvrait se qui le liait a cet homme qui l'avait accepte sans qu'il comprit bien pourquoi: l'obsession de la morte.' But Malraux's obsession was a temporary one, perhaps purged away by his analysis of it in this novel. He returned to the preference for life over death, that feeling of obligation to the objective world of the living which had led him already to write *Les*

* Malraux, André, *La Voie Royale*, Paris, 1930, by courtesy of Grasset.

Conquérants. The problem had then been beyond solution; and with characteristic honesty Malraux was content to let *Les Conquérants* remain (like so many of Gide's books) material for fiction, the frank journal of his first impressions of men and events. The difference between his journal and Gide's was that his intention to report objectively was not distorted by the intrusion of an idiosyncratic principle of selection. His selection of facts and his attitude toward them was not warped by atypical elements in his own personality; so that he could view events more closely in the terms of those participating in them.

A comparison between *Les Conquérants* and *Man's Fate* is therefore imperative for those who desire to distinguish between a realistic novel (one not based on mere fantasy) and the reporting of actual events. The chief difference is to be found in the emergence of theme. Reporting is not only limited to the fact; its principle of integration is the temporal sequence and the spatial relationships: a kind of unity of time and space. But in proportion as value is discovered in these events, theme crystallizes, not to negate the reality of time and space, but to substitute, through a now directed choice of detail, a less mechanical relationship. What has been at best a loose hypothesis not integrally related to the facts changes into a theme closely interwoven with them. Of the many things that have happened, the significant are chosen; or, since the significance that lies within the events now directs the creative activity, it may at times be exposed the more vividly by a shift to fictive detail. The novelist transforms the actual facts into new combinations which, precisely because they have never actually existed, clarify with superior verisimilitude the nature of the discovered theme. In this sense the surface of life is of no more importance to the novelist than to the sociologist or the philosopher. All alike are seeking to discover the forces at work beneath its obvious fluctuations, among its obvious contradictions. But since by definition, unlike these other specialists, the novelist must use the surface to expose what is beneath it, a fictive surface, or one very radically reconstructed from the actual, becomes a superior vehicle for the vivid presentation of the theme. No matter how detailed a novel is by definition (in contrast to a poem), it is always a simplification of life. And the only difference between the old 'slice of life' school and good fiction is not that the one insisted upon objectivity and the other did not, but that the one secured a useless objectivity through its random choice of detail, whereas the other waited until it has secured a theme to govern the narration. Time and space alone are unable to conjure up a theme, since they condition values without being themselves values. The values come from what man has done with his living and thinking within their limits. And it is with the presentation of these values in all the verisimilitude of their practice in living that fiction is concerned.

Nevertheless, *Les Conquérants* remains material for the use of a novelist rather than a historian or a politician. The novelist is interested in the whole personality of the individual acting in a society, and his definition of a society is the interrelation of such whole personalities. However important, therefore, to the individual politics may be, to a novelist politics is as a means to a more important end, men's sense of full and happy functioning. And likewise for his society, it is not the mere political platform of the moment (however invaluable in actual life it may appear) that concerns him, but the consequence of such platforms and similar activities for his picture of the nature and direction of the social life as a whole. For such reasons as these Malraux does not make it his main problem either in *Les Conquérants* or *Man's Fate* to decide whether the tactics of the Communist Party of China during the Civil War with the Kuomingtang were correct or not. To do so, according to his view, would have demanded the sort of analysis a historian or a military expert might be expected to make of military and political campaigns. Malraux actually has certain doubts concerning the feasibility of the Communist tactics, but he presents them tentatively as though beyond both his competence to decide and his need as a creative writer. Whether correct or incorrect they stand in no important relation to the structure of his novel. The outcome of the Chinese Civil War, he believes, was determined by larger factors than the political program of one left party. His view of the struggle from the top in *Les Conquérants* had rewarded him with this perspective.

It was with the analysis of this perspective that he was working when he wrote the earlier novel. But at that time he did not know what these determining factors were. When he had discovered them, he had discovered his theme both as history and as philosophy, and he was ready to write *Man's Fate.* In specific terms, events came to seem to him best understood by the aid of Marxism as a philosophy of history, which explained upheavals in society as the climactic moments of a dialectic development ultimately determined by economic processes. He saw that the dialectic movement of history remains whether the Communist Party of China made mistakes or not, and that its nature was more involved than these mistakes. Philosophy of life was broader than philosophy of politics. It included it as only one factor, since philosophy of life took into account the whole personality of the individual, not merely his political aspect; the whole movement of society and not its political activity alone. Furthermore, whether there had been political mistakes or not, the results were there in the fact of the defeat of the left wing; and what he wished to study and to present was the entire picture of the dialectic movement of events, not colored by some hypothesis of what it ought to have been, but as it was.

As far as the political aspect of events was concerned, Malraux's judgment seems to have been that the dominant factor was not the activity of Chinese Communists but of foreign imperialisms. The political inference one draws from the general structure of the book is that with any tactics the left would probably have gone down in defeat because of the strength of the imperialist pressures upon China. From this point of view, the novel is an admirable and subtle delineation of how these pressures are exercised, through the manipulation of Chinese bankers most dependent upon foreign funds for their own prosperity. And the manner in which this political thesis is presented furnishes an example of how a political theory of imperialistic influence must be translated into the flesh and blood of specific human relations. But such a problem, though central to the external action of the novel, is only a subordinate aspect of the more significant theme that dominates the action. This is concerned with the relation to events of different philosophies that are presented as the ideological summations of the more than political motivations behind these individual activities. Above all, Malraux had to furnish a narrative that reflected the complexity of actual life, where there may be a dozen different motives for the same act, where into the political motive there may also enter (if only as interference) those of love, friendship, past training, income, the temporary loss of perspective or integration under an intense immediate stimulus, in short, the many influences that determine the personality of the individual and the definition of his type.

But to clarify the theme in such a way necessitated a shift from the perspective of *Les Conquérants.* When Malraux first came to China, as an archeologist of liberal political sympathies, he naturally associated with leaders, and saw events through their eyes. Some of the men he met were conservative Frenchmen, some conservative members of the Kuomingtang, but mostly they were leaders of the various left-wing factions. To see the civil war through the eyes of such men would have facilitated writing a political novel. The view from the top tends to sink the individuality of men into the forces that seem to use them as puppets. It overemphasizes those aspects of personality involved in the particular view from the top, whether it be the economic one of the business man or the military one of the general. To remain the sort of novelist he desired to be, Malraux had to go down into the marketplace, get in touch with common types rather than leaders. Only thus could he give a picture of the struggle with the verisimilitude of a living situation, through the use of men directly involved in its intense human conflicts.

Only thus, furthermore, could he answer adequately the question that remains uppermost in his mind, why men are willing to suffer the pain and take the risk of dying. But the old inquiry arises now in a new and more valuable locus. It is now concerned with men who posit a social end, who are, in other words, revolutionaries in their use of violence. But he puts it as closely as possible in the old form. His first inquiry is, how does the individualist like Perken act when his motive has a social rather than an individualistic goal, when he is not presumably a decadent personality.

What happens to the Perkens when they remain decadent was a simple preliminary investigation. When the foreigner of Perken's tastes lacks the quality which integrated them in him, his thoroughgoing detachment and hatred, he becomes his opposite, a parasite, eventually victimized by those who have tolerated him. Clappique is a familiar type in the literature of imperialism, amoral, dissolute, acting as agent in any shady deal which will reward him with a rake-off. But associated with these weaknesses there survives a shred of friendly feeling which Perken certainly lacked. He does have a genuine sympathy for his friends among the revolutionists for whom he has arranged an illicit sale of arms. When the plot is discovered he makes efforts to contact them, but irresolution of character prevents his good intention from succeeding. His impulse perhaps has been paralyzed by fear of exposure, and he lingers so long at a café that he arrives too late.

When, on the contrary, Perken's individualism is associated with a personality of less exotic tastes and a social objective, it becomes, according to *Man's Fate,* the anarchistic type. Since Ch'en's advocacy of assassination has the avowed objective of the good of society, Malraux's attitude changes from his nervous speculation about Perken to a tolerant and more objective sympathy. Malraux has sought to bolster his intention to make *Man's Fate* an objective study by omitting any character who might be taken for himself. But a certain feeling of affinity for the individualist persists, perhaps, in the fact that the novel opens with Ch'en, and Ch'en's philosophy is the first that must be disposed of, almost as though a temptation in Malraux himself had thus to be faced and eradicated. Since anarchism posits a social aim, he judges it in terms of its social consequences. The answer is simple. The good such a deed of violence does is nil. The first bomb Ch'en throws at Chiang Kai-shek's car finds it empty. But when he decides to follow his philosophy rigorously and to act completely alone so that there may be no mistakes, to come close where he can use his own eyes alone, to throw himself under the car with the bomb so that there may be no question of failure of aim, from the social point of view the result is one of bitter irony. Chiang is not in the car this time either, but as Ch'en dies in agony, no one answers his inquiry, and he is beyond caring whether he has been successful or not. 'The general's car was five meters away, enormous. He ran towards it with an ecstatic joy, threw himself upon it, with his eyes shut.' Clearly the essence of his satisfaction is subjective. The social ideal seems only to enhance the value of the act to his personal esteem, to increase his ecstasy, expand the afflatus of what is no longer, as with Perken, the intense compression of resistance until it seems infinite power, but its opposite, the outgoing activity of an infinitely expanding egoism. In contrast to these preliminary emotions is what, from the outside, appears an ignoble anti-climax in the interference of pain; for death is not sudden, as it ought to have been to prevent disturbance to this mystic ecstacy of self-fulfilment.

With a violent kick in the ribs, the policeman turned Ch'en over. He shrieked, fired straight ahead, at random, and the rebound rendered the pain, which he believed limitless, even more intense . . . He made the most terrific effort of his life, managed to get the revolver into his mouth . . . A furious kick from another officer caused all his muscles to contract; he fired without being aware of it.*

In short, although the evidence must remain doubtful, it is likely that Ch'en did not get the sense of personal fulfilment which was his real motive behind the screen of his social idealism. Neither subjectively nor objectively has his act been successful. He has only managed to avoid further agony by committing suicide. His death is not only without social utility. It is ignominious and leaves him stripped of human dignity.

Meanwhile the activities compelled by his philosophy have set the tempo of the novel from the start at a pitch rarely adopted in fiction. The book opens with Ch'en stealing into a moonlit room in order to plunge a knife into a sleeping man. Since we do not know the man, since his fat nude figure is repulsive and we see the action through Ch'en's emotions, we are caught up in its intensity and accept it without aversion. Through succeeding passages, which are all in various ways concerned with sudden death, in street fighting, third-degree examinations, and so on, this initial tension is maintained until it becomes the tone of the book. Without this background of strident tension the climactic scene in which action sinks to a minimum would have fallen flat. But its intensity impregnates the simplest of acts with a suffocating suspense.

As the prisoners, charged by the right wing with Communism, await death by torture in the courtyard of the prison, an event that appears trifling in itself symbolizes the theme of the novel. Katov splits the cyanide tablet he had reserved for himself and passes the fragments to two fellow prisoners. One drops to the ground in the gathering darkness, and the fumbling to regain it sets up a suspense such as Henry James could not achieve through his less vital themes. The pill is found and the reader's attention returns to the personality of the giver. On the surface

* Malraux, André, *Man's Fate,* trans. by H. M. Chevalier, New York, 1936, by courtesy of Random House, Inc.

Katov's act appears similar to the final scene with Perken. In each instance a man trusts to his capacity for self-control, demands that will become complete master of body. But the quality of the two acts is entirely different because of the social purpose that animates Katov. His self-control is possible because his act has been the final seal of a long and desperate pursuit of common goals by all these prisoners. 'Impossible to see anything; Katov was making this gift of something that was more precious than his life not even to bodies, not even to voices, but to the warm hand resting upon him.' To aid the weaker brethren becomes an act not of superiority to the whole external world, but one of equalization. Fraternity becomes equality when he thus shares his courage with his comrades. By this act of generosity Katov brings the two up to his own level. Through their use of the poison they can now maintain that dignity which is 'la condition humaine,' the psychological goal of their common cause. Katov's act of friendship not only lends them his own courage; at the same time it deprives him of his own last excuse for weakness. He can now in a finer way fulfil himself, by different methods reach the end the anarchist vainly sought. 'As soon as I'm outside,' he says to himself, 'I'm going to try to strangle one of [the guards], and to hold my hands tightened to his throat long enough so they will be forced to kill me.' And again we have an example how the right action successfully secures a multitude of objectives, all of which the wrong action, like Ch'en's, misses. For thus Katov will, through aiding his friends, gain for himself the satisfaction of fighting to the very end and avoid the passive suffering of slow torture. 'They will burn me, but dead,' he says. Katov's deed is an answer to Perken as well as to Ch'en. Both the anarchist and the adventurer, despite differences in their avowed objectives, share the same qualitative deficiency inherent in individualism. Lacking the bond of mutuality in a common cause, neither could find in death the ultimate satisfaction of his dignity as a man. Ch'en did not even secure the appearance of it. But Perken's lonely act was only an appearance. For a valid dignity must be shared. We have no awareness of a full-valued integration of personality apart from relationship with others. It is this awareness that his own dignity flows from his comradeship with other men in a cause he rationally justifies which frees Katov from any temptation to retreat into the vagueness of mysticism and affords him his consummate sense of self in this final act of friendship.

The question raised in *Les Conquérants* has been answered. The act of violence achieves dignity only when it possesses an ethical integrity, and that integrity, as a quality of the personality, is dependent upon a right analysis of the objective situation. Integration of personality implies ethical integrity. Hypocrisy, as a subjective trait, is inevitably associated with a wrong diagnosis of the social malady. The hypocrisy in Ch'en's motivation is dependent upon his delusion regarding the value of the isolated act of violence. Already in *Les Conquérants* Malraux had considered this aspect of his theme. Common planning among anarchists can get no further than a mendacious theatrical gesture. Contrary to their theory, it means no more than an attempt to submit the masses to the will of a single individual who believes that his personal and isolated activity is for the common good, but who has not in advance shared either his affection or his planning. An anarchist kills himself in such a way as to make it appear that he has been murdered by the Kuomingtang, leaving a letter to that effect. The only act of co-operation his anarchist associates are capable of is to spread the rumor of whose validity they are uncertain in the hope that it will arouse the populace to indiscriminate violence against the right wing. A vast procession, disruptive of the common effort needed at the moment, weakens the resistance to the foreign enemy. The lie, based upon the wrong analysis of the objective situation, defeats itself. But what impresses Malraux in such a situation is its lack of dignity. Not right reasons alone, not the mere fact of self-sacrifice, but an integrity of personality such as Katov revealed, less through speech than in action, is needed if the deed done is to bind men together and further the social aim. Success is not intrinsically in the objective victory or defeat, but in the state of the human personality.

For, just as Ch'en's deed was either socially useless or deleterious, so Katov's and the many deeds of others like him was what left the radicals in China potentially strong despite their immediate failure. Men like Katov create a tradition which is more authentic, and hence more useful, than myth or legend. Each act of theirs may be obscure, witnessed by only a few survivors. But it existed, and proves their heroism to the emotions as well as the intellect, and less by documents than the known impact of their character. The memory of an act of such quality becomes a legacy of courage welding men the more firmly together, the more capable of understanding its integrity they have become through the effect of similar experiences upon their own personalities. Unlike the delusory myth of the fascist, such integrity, constantly tested in action, grows stronger of its own impetus, and does not disclose a basis in hypocrisy and lack of insight by a sudden collapse at the critical moment.

Malraux seeks to drive his point home by a second illustration. Always the philosopher who is not content with action alone but must also meditate upon its motives, he introduces another character who is inspired by Katov's personality and speculates upon his actions, to his own self-education. To retain the objective tone of the novel, Malraux gives Kyo a different personal history from his own, but he is still at heart the rather shy observer. And to clarify his meditations, Malraux puts him between the revolutionary like Katov, who acts without hesitation according to his belief, and his father, Gisors, who has spent a lifetime of speculation troubled by an inability to act at all. Kyo's father, an old-fashioned liberal university professor, has retreated from attack into retirement and a discreet use of opium. Influenced perhaps by his father's personality, Kyo's courage, in contrast to Katov's, is more of the mind than the body. Although he is tortured like the rest of the prisoners, we do not expect him to die as heroically as Katov. But when challenged on his own ground, he will be capable of an equally stout resistance. When the German chief of Chang Kai-shek's staff, counting upon Kyo's superior social position, tries to win him over, Kyo defies him, borrowing, as though by recollection, Katov's courage, as he seeks to convey to this brutal German his own conviction of the nobility of the Communist cause and personality.

> 'I've been told that you are a Communist through dignity. Is that true?' . . .
>
> There was a menace in the tone, if not in the words themselves. Kyo answered:
>
> 'I think that Communism will make dignity possible for those with whom I am fighting. What is against it, at any rate, forces them to have none, unless they possess a wisdom as rare among them as among the others—more perhaps, for the very reason that they are poor and that their work separates them from their lives. Why do you ask me this question, since you aren't even listening to my answer?'
>
> 'What do you call dignity? It doesn't mean anything.' . . .
>
> 'The opposite of humiliation,' said Kyo. 'When one comes from where I come, that means something.' *

Sustained by this theoretical defense of his position, Kyo refuses to disclose the source of the Communist arms.

But there is another reason for Kyo's presence in the book. Through his relationships we learn the limitations of love as a binding element among men. The comradeship of love, to be sure, is needed. And to define its nature, I think, Malraux introduces the otherwise unnecessary and ambiguous episode of Kyo's discovery of his wife's impulsive infidelity. She confesses to him that she took pity on a soldier she was nursing and yielded to his desire. At first his jealousy forbids his allowing her to accompany him on a dangerous mission. But a second thought restores his awareness of their bond of common purpose and of a love

* Malraux, André, *Man's Fate*, New York, 1934, p. 306. By permission of the Modern Library.

that is beyond sensuality, and he returns to get her. But love alone is ineffectual. In his sorrow at his son's death, Gisors feels closer than ever to his son's wife, who also loved him. Grief, taking courage from May's living presence, leads him to identify himself with his dead son in the one way that now seems left. Through empathy, he feels for the time being an identity with Kyo's beliefs and personality, and determines to go to Moscow with May, and continue his son's work there. But, never having acted before, he is powerless now to act through love alone. At the last moment he leaves May to go by herself. Thus again it becomes evident that emotion, intellect, action, all three, are needed to secure that integration of personality which is Malraux's definition of human dignity and which sets up the tradition of courage and heroic action. Then grief can be assuaged by a compulsion to carry on the work to which persons one has loved and respected have dedicated themselves. Out of the multitude of such associations mankind gets the will to survive disaster, and the cause that appears hopeless renews itself like the phoenix. In this sense the love implied in comradeship among Communists, as Malraux sees it, is a revival of the emotional aspect of primitive Christianity. But this revival, coming under the circumstances of a later period in history, Malraux shows to differ from the earlier precedent in an opposite attitude toward the objective world, which must now be as clearly understood to be a valid process of social forces as it was earlier to be rejected as the abode of sin and error.

As though he had ended his investigation and needed no further exploration of it, almost as though he had exhausted his theme, Malraux turned to *Man's Hope,* where virtually the same theme of the risk of death that secures dignity to man is elaborated in the new material of the Spanish Civil War. The comparatively simple structure of *Man's Fate* is abandoned, through which, by keeping his characters few in number, Malraux had been able the more vividly to explore his problem. But in *Man's Hope* the supererogation of more investigation leads to the piling up of characters and incidents until the thread of the story disappears, and the characters, many of whom spend more time talking than acting, become hard to identify. Separate scenes are unforgettable: the quarrels of the foreign aviators in their quarters; the recovery of his sight by an aviator who has been blinded; the rescue by hospitable peasants of the airmen who had crashed in the mountains; the retreat of soldiers and civilians along the coastal road sprayed with death from Italian fascist planes; the music Manuel plays on the organ of the ruined church where Ximenes has come alone to pray. And one is impressed also by the originality of the plan of the book. *Man's Fate* had contrasted different philosophies by contrasting their results in the lives of different men. This novel, in addition, presents the education of a single young man through action that brings him into contact with many types of men. A sportsman, named Manuel, who is interested only in what the joy of his youth can get out of life, begins by grudgingly loaning his new racing car to friends who need it for a government mission after the unexpected rising of the fascists. But as he is drawn into the struggle for the people's freedom, his personality matures, and he becomes aware of the world beyond his own self-indulgence, until the victory of Guadalajara seems his personal victory and he seems to comprehend the exultation of all Republican Spain. His own spirit, like Whitman's, seems at last to contain within itself the entire society of which he is a part. But this significant design conflicts with the carry-over of the plan of *Man's Fate* into numerous subordinate characters with whom Manuel has little or nothing to do, and gets lost in the elaborate detail of its exposition.

Not only the amount of detail, but its quality weakens the authority of the plot. For the most part, the dialogue is abstract speculation which offers nothing that has not already been presented in *Man's Fate*, except perhaps a change of stress. The siege of the Alcazar continues the inquiry into the nature of anarchism, which still fascinates Malraux, but who this time criticizes its sentimentality. A curious blind trust in the abstract goodness of man is set up by the anarchist's individualistic detachment from the warm personal contacts of comradeship, from his scorn for co-operation. An anarchist who offers to mail a letter from a fascist within the besieged fortress to his wife believes that by this act he is softening the hearts of his opponents and making them aware of the universal brotherhood of man. But it only impresses the fascists with the weakness, the instability, the lack of common sense of the anarchist personality, with its oscillation from the hatred implicit in the desperate act of violence into an impotent sentimentality that idealizes its implacable foes. At the same time the general theme of the novel in the story of Manuel may be taken as a reply to Hemingway's *For Whom the Bell Tolls,* in that it shows how men with the same general purpose of the social good, through the obligations of common action, discover the impracticability of anarchism, and in due time learn through action to implement their common purpose with abstract conceptions more in accordance with the facts of life.

But the obscurity of the novel has another explanation than this conflict between the survival in it of the design of *Man's Fate* and the new aim to make the experiences of a single hero transcend the entire action. Certain of the subordinate philosophical discussions raise an entirely new order of problems. In passages of *Man's Hope,* Malraux seems on the verge of questioning the central thesis of the Chinese novel. He seems to begin to doubt the interdependence of the spiritual and the material, the principle that each is the necessary qualification of the other, that there is a reciprocity between right thinking and right acting. As far as action itself goes, Hernandez says in *Man's Hope,* Communism is the only possible philosophy. 'The Communists, you see,' he says to Garcia, '*want to get things done*. Whereas you and the anarchists, for different reasons, want to *be* something.' In a revolution, as in a war, certainly, being has to be postponed in favor of doing or the enemy will do away with being altogether. In *Man's Fate,* 'doing' in a critical situation had proffered the finest crystallization of 'being.' But from a later passage in *Man's Hope* one cannot be sure that 'doing,' even under the guidance of the most impeccable philosophy, can ever lead to a proper 'being.' Garcia is speaking now of the difference between the philosopher and the man of action, of the difference, shall we say, between a man of action like Katov and the sense of separateness from the proletariat of an intellectual like Kyo, which seeps through the strong convictions of his I have just quoted.

The great intellectual is a man of subtleties, of fine shades, of evaluations; he's interested in absolute truth and in the complexity of things. He is—how shall I put it?—'antimanichean' by definition, by nature. But all forms of action are manichean, because all action pays a tribute to the devil; that manichean element is most intense where the masses are involved. Every true revolutionary is a born manichean. The same is true of politics, all politics.*

But Garcia, though expressing a point of view Gisors would have understood more instantly than his son, does not reach the Chinese sage's conclusion to retreat. At the same time he believes that one can make the best of his life only by 'converting as wide a range of experience as possible into conscious thought.' The obligation to act remains upon the individual, and the social consequences of right action are still beneficial. But for the intellectual the dilemma is insurmountable. For him the crisis of revolution only makes glaring the inherent deficiency of human life itself. 'For a thinker the revolution's a tragedy,' Garcia continues. 'For such a man, life, too, is tragic. And if he is counting on the revolution to abolish his private tragedy, he's making a mistake.' To the thinker, then, life is inevitably tragic because, action being inescapable, he sees that every action, whether predominantly right or wrong, has its modicum of

* Malraux, André, *Man's Hope,* trans. by Stuart Gilbert and Alastair MacDonald, New York, 1938, Random House, Inc.

wrong. Basically the intellectual must be a pessimist. Unable to accept the unalterable conditions of living, he is always aware that the purity of goodness is beyond the immediacy of experience.

Such are Garcia's conclusions; and there are other episodes in *Man's Hope* that suggest that they have become tempting to Malraux. In them Malraux revives certain aspects of the personalities of Ch'en and Perken, and, by relating them in a new way to the problem of action, reaches an idealistic position in philosophy. As Claude has formerly been drawn to Perken, Manuel has become friendly with the former chief of police in Barcelona, who used to arrest radicals and now is fighting by their side. Ximenes' duty to the government he serves has not changed, only its application. His personality remains tranquil because he, too, accepts the defect inherent in all action. He regrets his cruelty as chief of police as little as his present cruelty in leading his men against the fascists. He retains the same shy and kindly detachment, whatever his action. His personality has been neither contaminated by his deeds as chief of police when he was hated by the radicals nor improved by any difference in the moral quality of his new employment against fascism. In both instances he has been sustained by a belief in a higher law than action, of which his sense of duty is only an overt sign. The essence of this higher law he finds embodied in religion, not in the hierarchy he accepts but does not respect, but in the spiritual solace of prayer and contemplation. In him, acting and being are qualitatively distinct. But he is not a philosopher, and passes with greater ease than Garcia from the impurity of the act into the higher level of religious consolation. Obviously his way out is beyond Malraux the intellectual. But in the same manner in which the decadent side of Malraux was drawn to Perken, what he now takes for a more spiritual side draws him to Ximenes. Since, in contrast to the individualistic Perken, the Spaniard accepts a social objective when he acts through his sense of obligation to authority, his detachment seems to Malraux transformed into a positive good. But his capacity to retreat into pure being, however admirable Manuel finds it, is a mystery beyond Malraux's power of analysis.

Nevertheless, Malraux's closest emotional identification is with Manuel himself. And Manuel, who resembles Ximenes only in also not being an intellectual, also in the end reaches a parallel detachment on a higher level than action. His road has been different. It has not been a religious compensation for action, but an escape through action itself. To an intellectual it is similarly beyond analysis, but it can be understood and contemplated with a similar admiration. This much about it is clear. It is the reward of growth of personality through action. It is based upon a feeling of comprehensiveness of all the men and deeds he has experienced, which is like Whitman's conviction that he contained within himself the totality of democratic America, of democratic impulse everywhere. But Manuel's euphoria has set up a dialectic shift of emphasis. Whereas Whitman's remained on the same level with the human experience it comprehended; Manuel's has subtly shifted away from experience altogether. His comprehensiveness has become a detachment from what he has comprehended. In a kind of parody of Marxism that transforms it into a religion of mystical naturalism, Manuel has made a dialectic leap beyond the actuality of things experienced into the area of the suppositious future. 'For the time being Manuel was hearing the voice of that which is more awe-inspiring even than the blood of men, more enigmatic even than their presence on the earth—the infinite possibilities of their destiny.' Doubtless such an extravagant euphoria is explicable in a man who has fought well and feels his imagination bounding beyond the exultation of the actual present victory into Shelleyan vistas of an absolute perfection. And Malraux admits that his state is temporary. One would not subject it to so rigid an inquiry if it were not so consonant with the new criticisms of action which are arising in *Man's Hope*. From this point of view it seems a groping for a way different from Ximenes, this time through action itself, to escape from the Manichaean imperfection of all action. Incapable of the finesse of the intellectual, Manuel had been able to use action to leave action far behind, to free it from the error of the actual, by the invocation of a future that has never been, and is so distant from the present that it seems free from its modicum of error.

Manuel's final state is, therefore, one of pure spirituality, following upon action and qualitatively its opposite; like the pure form the symbolist poet distills out of experience to transcend it, or the fantasy of the natural goodness of man the anarchist conjures up as the supplement to his arrogant individualism. Psychologically, it is the inevitable consequence of an individual's failure to accept the Manichaean quality of the act. When an act, or life conceived as a totality of acts, is taken to be either all good or all bad, it sets up this oscillation to the opposite pole. Manuel's naive but delusive belief in the goodness of action turns out to be not so different from the conscious but equally delusive philosophy of the anarchist, which leads him to extol the act of violence as a good in itself. Both, to the perception of the intellectual, compel a similar fling to an opposite position in which the infinite possibilities of the human destiny become synonymous with the universal brotherhood of man. Both are emotional states of absolute and blissful tranquillity, entirely free from the struggling and the suffering involved in action.

Perhaps by giving to Manuel the concluding scene in his novel, Malraux sought to conceal the paradox of his own position. With his emotions he follows Manuel, but his intellect is with Garcia, and he has not reached the solution of Ximenes. Through action Manuel has become a better man, but neither Garcia nor Ximenes seems to have felt any need to. Malraux likes Manuel, but, as an intellectual, he finds his ingenuous acceptance of action impossible. Herein, to another order of intellectuals, is the fallacy by which Malraux is tempted. For only the idealist in philosophy will be alarmed to discover that all action is Manichaean. The common-sense view has granted the fact to begin with; it has never demanded an absolute purity of goodness. It has been content that the good in an act outweighs the evil, and, in recent centuries, that human history seems to contain a law of progress according to which human life becomes qualitatively better for more men, the better men understand themselves and their universe. The philosophical fallacy that demands pure goodness parallels the psychological, which would ask for pure optimism. When Malraux implies that one cannot think and remain an optimist, action becomes no more than an escape from pessimism, which, for the intellectual, must be temporary.

Malraux's dilemma is essentially the same as Kafka's, that any real interpenetration of the spiritual and the material is impossible, that the good and the actual, though associated with each other by the initial conditions of life, remain qualitatively separate. Kafka, too, found experience unavoidable and yet unavoidably sullied with evil. If Manuel may be 'K' at the beginning of his quest for the castle, when it seems gleaming in the distance with 'the infinite possibilities of man's destiny,' Garcia has not yet been tormented by the 'trial' the inevitability of which he recognizes intellectually to be the destiny of the intellectual, the eternal tragedy of the human spirit which, trapped in this imperfect world, has no infinite possibilities save confusion and suffering. Malraux's latest novel, *La Lutte avec l'ange,* when it is finished and available, may show whether the mirage of the castle in Manuel's final vision is giving way to the conflict of the 'trial' which has gone no deeper than intellectual perception in Garcia.

But men reconciled to living with error, so long as it does not predominate over the good, whose conflict is not with the angel but with that very error whose presence they accept as the inevitable limitation of human existence, will return to *Man's Fate.* They will not divorce the possibility of man's dignity from the necessary conditions of his being. They will not be driven into the indignity of pessimism by demands for a quixotic perfection. Continuing to associate human worth with right action, they will desire to stay at the side of those they love and respect in a world that is to be also loved and respected because we are all together in it, and prefer its possibilities of warm contact and immediate activity to however pure a state of personal ecstasy that is bought at the price of isolation.

Index